INVENTING THE
THE ONTARIO LOYALIST TRADITION AND
THE CREATION OF USABLE PASTS

The Loyalists have often been credited with planting a coherent and uni-fied tradition that has been passed on virtually unchanged to subsequent generations and that continues to define Ontario's political culture. Challenging past scholarship, Norman Knowles argues that there never has been consensus on the defining characteristics of the Loyalist tradi-tion. He suggests that, in fact, the very concept of tradition has constantly been subject to appropriation by various constituencies who wish to legit-imize their point of view and their claim to status by creating a usable past. The picture of the Loyalist tradition that emerges from this study is not of an inherited artefact but of a contested and dynamic phenomenon that has undergone continuous change.

Inventing the Loyalists traces the evolution of the Loyalist tradition from the Loyalists' arrival in Upper Canada in 1784 until the present. It explores how the Loyalist tradition was produced, established, and main-tained, delineates the roles particular social groups and localities played in constructing differing versions of the Loyalist past, and examines the reception of these efforts by the larger community. Rejecting both con-sensual and hegemonic models, Knowles presents a pluralistic under-standing of the invention of tradition as a complex process of social and cultural negotiation by which different groups, interests, and generations compete with each other over the content, meaning, and uses of the past. He demonstrates that in Ontario, many groups, including filiopietistic descendants, political propagandists, status-conscious professionals, reform-minded women, and Native peoples, invested in the creation of the Loyalist tradition.

By exploring the ways in which the Loyalist past was, and still is, being negotiated, *Inventing the Loyalists* revises our understanding of the Loyalist tradition and provides insight into the politics of commemoration.

NORMAN KNOWLES teaches in the Department of History at the University of Calgary and has written for *Canadian Ethnic Studies* and *Ontario History*, among other journals.

NORMAN KNOWLES

Inventing the Loyalists: The Ontario Loyalist Tradition and the Creation of Usable Pasts

UNIVERSITY OF TORONTO PRESS
Toronto Buffalo London

© University of Toronto Press Incorporated 1997
Toronto Buffalo London
Printed in Canada

ISBN 0-8020-0950-6 (cloth)
ISBN 0-8020-7913-X (paper)

Printed on acid-free paper

Canadian Cataloguing in Publication Data

Knowles, Norman James, 1963 –
Inventing the Loyalists : the Ontario Loyalist tradition and
the creation of usable pasts

Includes bibliographical references and index.
ISBN 0-8020-0950-6 (bound)   ISBN 0-8020-7913-X (pbk.)

1. United Empire loyalists – Ontario – Historiography.
2. Ontario – Social life and customs.   3. Ontario –
Historiography.   I. Title.

FC3070.L6K58 1997   971.3   C97-930412-1
F1058.K58 1997

University of Toronto Press acknowledges the financial assistance to its
publishing program of the Canada Council for the Arts and the Ontario
Arts Council.

This book has been published with the help of a grant from the Humanities
and Social Sciences Federation of Canada, using funds provided by the Social
Sciences and Humanities Research Council of Canada

TO MY PARENTS

Contents

Illustrations follow page 66.

Acknowledgments

This book would not have been possible without the assistance and encouragement of many individuals and institutions. Financial support for my original research was provided by a Social Sciences and Humanities Research Council of Canada doctoral fellowship and an Ontario graduate scholarship. The staffs of the Archives of Ontario, the Diocese of Ontario Archives, the Hamilton Public Library, the Hastings County Historical Society, the Lennox and Addington County Museum, the Adolphustown Loyalist Museum, the Metropolitan Toronto Reference Library, the National Archives of Canada, the United Church of Canada Archives, and the Archives of the Toronto Branch of the United Empire Loyalist Association of Canada were very generous with their time and help. Professor Ramsay Cook supervised the doctoral dissertation from which this book originated. His high standards and unfailing encouragement have been most appreciated. Professors Jean Barman, David Bell, Douglas Francis, Susan Houston, David Marshall, H.V. Nelles, George Rawlyk, and Donald Smith offered wise advice and cogent criticism at various stages of my research and writing, as did the anonymous referees who appraised the manuscript for the University of Toronto Press and the Social Science Federation of Canada. The book has benefited greatly from the guidance and editorial advice of Gerald Hallowell, Catherine Frost, and Robert Ferguson at the University of Toronto Press. I owe a great deal to Richard Anderson, Jeffrey Keshen, and Jonathan Vance, who assisted in retrieving materials when time and distance precluded a visit to the archives, and to Monika Rieger, who produced the map on Loyalist settlement found in the first chapter. My greatest debt is to my wife, Margaret Anne, whose advice, patience, confidence, and companionship have sustained me throughout this project.

INVENTING THE LOYALISTS:
THE ONTARIO LOYALIST TRADITION AND
THE CREATION OF USABLE PASTS

Introduction

Throughout the summer of 1884 celebrations were held across Ontario to commemorate the centennial of the settlement of the province by the United Empire Loyalists. During these celebrations the Loyalists were remembered variously as the province's first settlers, hard-working pioneers, principled defenders of the British Empire and constitution, persecuted refugees, and members of an educated and cultured elite. Twelve years later, Loyalist descendants founded the United Empire Loyalist Association to preserve the history and to defend the traditions of their ancestors. The years between the 1884 celebrations and the First World War witnessed the publication of an extensive body of Loyalist historical and genealogical works and the erection of monuments honouring individual Loyalists and their exploits. The 1884 celebrations, the formation of the United Empire Loyalist Association, the erection of Loyalist monuments, and the popularity of Loyalist publications were public manifestations of a pervasive phenomenon historians have labelled the *Loyalist tradition*.

The Loyalist tradition is usually identified with a cluster of related ideas: unfailing devotion to the British Crown and Empire, a strong and pervasive anti-Americanism, suffering and sacrifice endured for the sake of principle, elite social origins, and a conservative social vision. This tradition occupies an important place in Canadian historiography. Several generations of scholars have identified the Loyalist tradition as one of the defining elements of the English-Canadian identity. In his classic survey of Canadian history, *Colony to Nation*, Arthur R.M. Lower asserted that the Loyalist migration 'gave to English Canada a body of sentiments and traditions, an outlook, and a certain social tang, which cause it to differ from the United States.' 'The anti-Republican animus of all the Loyalists, great and small,' Lower insisted, 'made it certain that there would be a second group of English communities in North America and supplied for them a common bond, the primary expression of which was anti-Americanism and the secondary, strong sentiments of loyalty to the conception "British."'[1] Similarly, in *Canada: A Story of Challenge* J.M.S. Careless maintained that the Loyalists 'brought to Canada a conservative outlook, a quick distrust of any new idea that might be called republican, and a readiness to make loyalty the test for almost everything.' According to Careless, the Loyalists 'represented a declaration of independence against the United States, a determination to live apart from that country in North America. As a result, they helped to create not only a new province, but a new nation.'[2]

The Loyalist tradition became the subject of considerable interest and debate during the 1960s as Canadians became increasingly concerned about the economic and cultural influence of the United States. Influenced by the work of Louis Hartz and Seymour Martin Lipset, Canadian scholars began to look for the ideological 'fragments' and 'formative events' that had shaped the Canadian nation.[3] A vigorous exchange occurred between political scientists Kenneth McRae, Gad Horowitz, and David V.J. Bell over the precise nature of Loyalist ideology and the degree to which it contributed to the creation of a distinctive social and political culture in English Canada.[4] Among historians, the impact of the Loyalist tradition has been most thoroughly analysed by S.F. Wise, Carl Berger, and David Mills. In a series of important articles Wise credited the Loyalists with establishing a conservative 'counter-revolutionary society.' According to Wise, the Loyalists' conservatism consisted of 'an emotional compound of loyalty to King and Empire, antagonism to the United States, and an acute if partisan sense of recent history.' However, 'Loyalty did not simply mean adherence to the Crown and Empire'; 'it meant as well adherence to those beliefs and institutions the conservative considered essential in the preservation of a form of life different from, and superior to, the manners, politics and social arrangements of the United States.'[5] In his influential study of imperialist thought, *The Sense of Power*, Berger concluded that the union of the Loyalist tradition and imperial sentiment produced an almost 'indescribable sense of mission and destiny' at the end of the nineteenth century that constituted one variety of Canadian nationalism.[6] Most recently, David Mills finds loyalty and the Loyalist tradition at the centre of Upper Canadian political discourse and suggests that it continued as a vital influence long after Confederation.[7]

In all of these studies the Loyalists are credited with planting a coherent and unified tradition that has been passed on to subsequent generations and constitutes one of the defining elements of Ontario's, and indeed English Canada's, identity. Preoccupied with questions of national identity and political culture, authors of previous studies of the Loyalist tradition have not adequately acknowledged the ways in which the Loyalist tradition has changed and evolved over the decades; nor have they addressed the ways in which the tradition has been shaped by the 'limited identities' of place, class, gender, and ethnicity.[8] In viewing the Loyalist legacy primarily through the lens of nationalism, scholars have imposed a unity and coherence that obscure the diverse set of interests and motivations that have shaped the Loyalist tradition over the decades.

This study traces the evolution of the Loyalist tradition from the time of the Loyalists' arrival in Upper Canada to the present. In the process it explores how the Loyalist tradition was produced, legitimized, and maintained, the roles particular social groups and localities played in constructing differing versions of the Loyalist past, and the reception of these efforts by the larger community. The picture of the Loyalist tradition that emerges is one not of an inherited artefact but of a contested and dynamic phenomenon that has undergone continuous change as successive generations and interest groups have assigned different meanings to the Loyalist past. The process has been both selective and controversial. Only certain elements of the Loyalist past have been deemed 'traditional,' while other aspects have been ignored or forgotten.

Ontario's Loyalist settlers were in fact a diverse group that lacked a clear and unified identity. Over the years, however, they became identified with certain traits and characteristics that changed according to the needs and circumstances of the times. A theme of suffering and sacrifice on behalf of the Crown was dominant in the years immediately following settlement, when the Loyalists presented the British government with claims for compensation. As Upper Canadian politics became divided between conservative and reform factions, the Tory establishment emphasized the Loyalists' devotion to the British constitution, anti-Americanism, and distaste for republican government. At mid-century, economic growth, expansionist ambitions, and sectional tensions resulted in the rise of nationalist sentiment in Upper Canada and the transformation of the Loyalists into a heroic set of founding fathers. By the end of the nineteenth century, filiopietistic descendants and status-conscious members of the middle class recast the Loyalists into a principled and cultured elite. Imperialists stressed the Loyalists' commitment to the Empire and attributed to them a divinely inspired sense of mission.

Nationalist politicians and educators looked to the Loyalists' example to inculcate patriotism and proper values. Such official Loyalist history was frequently challenged, however, by popular and locally based alternative traditions and by subordinate groups such as women and Natives seeking to create their own pasts. On a popular level, the Loyalists were often remembered as hard-working pioneers who cleared the wilderness and laid the basis for Ontario's progress and prosperity. More recently, the Loyalists have been portrayed as Ontario's first refugees and the founders of multiculturalism.

The idea that traditions change and evolve and are continually invented and re-invented challenges the concept of tradition presented by many social theorists. Edward Shils, for example, defines tradition as 'a consensus through time.' Although Shils acknowledges that traditions do change, especially in crisis situations, he insists that all traditions are characterized by an unchanging and consistent core of meaning.[9] This study presents a different understanding of tradition. Tradition is treated not as a unified, static, and independent body of inherited ideas, values, and behaviours, but as a product of social and cultural negotiation continually shaped and reshaped by contemporary conditions and concerns. To say that traditions are invented is meant to imply not a simple and straightforward case of fabrication, but rather a process of selection that is both conscious and unconscious and arises from a wide range of motivations and circumstances.

Traditions do not exist in a vacuum independent of changing social, economic, and political realities; it is thus imperative to examine the contexts in which they are constructed. The Loyalist tradition has meant different things to different people at different times and places. Constructed by a variety of groups intent on the creation of usable pasts that spoke to contemporary concerns, anxieties, interests, and realities, the Loyalist tradition underwent continual change. Filiopietistic descendants, political propagandists, status-conscious, middle-class professionals, textbook writers, local promoters, reform-minded women and activists from the Six Nations all sought to establish continuity with the Loyalist past to legitimize and perpetuate particular political points of view, to inculcate social values, and to promote claims to status and recognition. The changes in the purpose and meaning of the Loyalist tradition can be understood only by placing those changes within their historical and social contexts, by carefully looking at the participants in the process of invention, and by assessing the response of the wider audience to such innovations.

The invention of the Ontario Loyalist tradition is part of a larger international story. Celebrations of great persons and events in the past, the erection of public monuments dedicated to historical figures, and the creation of historical and patriotic associations were distinctive features of European and North American society during the late nineteenth and early twentieth centuries. In France, the annual Bastille Day celebration was inaugurated in 1880, and in 1889 the nation observed the centenary of the Revolution with much pomp and pageantry. In Germany, the number of local and national commemorations of historical events and figures increased so dramatically that in 1897 a national festival society was established to promote and organize such public celebrations. Similar developments occurred in the United States. In 1876 the centennial of the Declaration of Independence ushered in a host of observances, including the centennials of the Evacuation of New York in 1883 and Washington's inauguration in 1889 and culminating in the 400th anniversary of the discovery of America in 1893 at the World's Columbian Exhibition in Chicago.[10] The successive anniversaries were accompanied by the appearance of a multitude of patriotic and historical societies, beginning with the creation of the Sons of the Revolution in 1883. By 1900 there were over seventy similar associations in the United States.[11] Many communities in Europe and North America witnessed the erection of monuments and memorials that gave concrete expression to the proclivity to look to the past for guidance and inspiration.[12]

The politics of commemoration have recently become the subject of considerable historical interest and debate. In his introduction to *The Invention of Tradition*, the British historian Eric Hobsbawm explores the hegemonic uses of the past by the state. Hobsbawm asserts that the commemorative impulse was essentially a product of the social, economic, and political changes that transformed Europe and North America into mass industrial societies. In societies experiencing rapid social and economic change the state develops a vast range of practices that allow citizens to identify with an earlier, more heroic age. In so doing, the state provides a sense of permanence and continuity in the face of constant innovation. According to Hobsbawm, 'invented traditions' attempt to 'establish continuity with a suitable historic past' in order to reassert a threatened social cohesion, to legitimize institutions or status, or to inculcate beliefs, value systems, and conventions of behaviour. Tradition thus becomes a tool used to assert a set of ideas, practices, and social relations that reflect the power and influence of the dominant groups in society that control the state.[13]

A different view of the function of tradition is presented by David Lowenthal and Michael Kammen. Both scholars stress the multiple uses that can be made of the past and the complexity and ambiguity that often surround our relationship to traditions. In *The Past Is a Foreign Country*, Lowenthal draws upon a wide array of British and American examples to illustrate how that past is essentially 'an artifact of the present,' continually made and remade by changing concerns and habits of perception. According to Lowenthal, traditions are essentially expressions of popular culture and imagination rather than manifestations of material interests.[14] In *Mystic Chords of Memory: The Transformation of Tradition in American Culture*, Kammen describes how contests of meaning and value produced changing versions of the past in American public and everyday life. According to Kammen, different class, ethnic, racial, and sectional groups have all looked to the past to contain feelings of anxiety and displacement that accompanied unsettling social and economic change. In sharp contrast to Hobsbawm's approach, Kammen argues that the state played a relatively 'modest role' in shaping American traditions and that the process has been 'decentralized, ad hoc, diffuse, and relatively non-coercive.'[15]

John Bodnar attempts to reconcile these two approaches to tradition in *Remaking America: Public Memory, Commemoration and Patriotism in the Twentieth Century*. Bodnar maintains that the process of commemoration has been shaped by a struggle between a nationally oriented 'official' past aimed at promoting unity, cohesion, and political consensus and a locally based 'vernacular' past rooted in immediate memory and personal experience. The politics of commemoration are thus both hegemonic and 'multi-vocal' and involve the complex interaction between a nationalistic official emphasis and a more heterodox vernacular outlook. Bodnar acknowledges, however, that the struggle between official and vernacular interests over the content, meaning, and purpose of the past is increasingly an uneven one as the memories of 'ordinary people' are appropriated and recast by agents of the 'official culture.'[16]

Although each of these interpretations touches upon aspects of the emergence and evolution of the Ontario Loyalist tradition, none of the models fits entirely. While Hobsbawm provides considerable insight into the ways in which the state used the past to respond to the disruptive effects of industrial capitalism, he presents an overly mechanistic view of hegemony that leaves little room for the role of public discourse and exchange in shaping the past. Hegemony is more effectively understood as an uneven process that involves both accommodation and resistance.

Nor is the process limited to the hegemonic efforts of national political and economic elites. Other groups, acting independently of the state and national interests, also look to the past in their efforts to come to terms with social change. One of the most striking characteristics of the Ontario Loyalist tradition is the relatively small role played by governments in its invention. While the state was initially responsible for identifying the Loyalists as a distinct group, supported the first efforts to collect and preserve Loyalist records, and actively participated in shaping the Loyalist tradition through its control of school textbooks, many of the commemorative exercises associated with the Loyalists resulted from the efforts of individuals, local communities, and private groups and enjoyed only limited government sponsorship or support. Hobsbawm's model provides little insight into these parochial manifestations of tradition building, but it was at this level that the Ontario Loyalist tradition aroused the greatest interest and had its most immediate impact. In their efforts to portray the 'conflict and complexity' that surrounds the 'politics of culture,' Lowenthal and Kammen avoid the dangers inherent in overly deterministic and functionalist interpretations of the construction of the past.[17] Both authors, however, are primarily concerned with text rather than context. Preoccupied with understanding the evolution of the ideological and cultural content of traditions, Lowenthal and Kammen give relatively little attention to the social forces and processes that shape the creation and use of the past. Although Bodnar attempts to integrate both approaches, there is a danger in his official/vernacular paradigm of creating a false dichotomy, which obscures divisions within groups and oversimplifies the process by which the past is shaped and constructed.

In attempting to understand the significance of the commemorative events that give expression to historical traditions, we must give careful attention to both the broad historical context in which such occasions occur as well as the immediate social context occupied by the individuals and interests actively involved in the process of cultural construction. Such an approach necessitates a good deal of 'thick description.' As Clifford Geertz has shown, it is only through an in-depth and detailed consideration of particular contexts and conditions that the complex forces at work in shaping a culture are revealed.[18] In order to comprehend the meaning of such events, we must go beyond the events themselves and ask how, when, and by whom they become articulated. The result is a recovery of the varied and nuanced meanings and motivations often concealed by the apparent consensus that surrounds acts of commemoration. A close examination of participants, conditions, and contexts reveals that the meaning of the past is a product of cultural negotiation that frequently involves a struggle between champions of varying ideologies, sentiments, and interests.

To focus simply on the tradition builders provides a very incomplete sense of the social meaning and significance of any tradition. Attention must also be given to the intended audience. It should be remembered that commemorative acts may be interpreted differently by various social groups and that it is only by examining the responses of the larger community that we can assess the degree to which efforts to articulate a particular version of the past finds acceptance. Historians must be careful not to confuse objectives with end results. A case in point is Carl Berger's treatment of the Loyalist tradition in *The Sense of Power*. Berger describes how a select group of English-Canadian imperialists appropriated the image of the Loyalists as a noble band of fearless patriots who sacrificed all to remain true to the principles of the British constitution and preserve the unity of the Empire in order to legitimize the imperialist position.

For Berger, the union between the Loyalist tradition and imperial sentiment was symbolically expressed in the 1884 Toronto celebrations of the centennial of the landing of the Loyalists. 'The literature of the centennial,' Berger concluded, 'contained the quintessence of the Loyalist tradition' and confirmed the existence of 'an indigenous variety of Canadian imperialism.'[19] Berger explores the backgrounds of the Toronto organizers and discusses the events and rhetoric surrounding the centennial. He makes no effort, however, to analyse in detail either the process through which the celebrations were conceived and implemented or the manner in which they were received by the public. One cannot simply assume that the beliefs of prominent individuals reflected popular opinion and concerns or that elite views trickled down to the masses. Recent studies of the Loyalist tradition in New Brunswick and Nova Scotia have convincingly demonstrated the dangers of presenting the views of Berger's Toronto-centred clique of Loyalist imperialists as indicative of a national sentiment or mood.[20] Nor can the Toronto celebrations be assumed to be indicative of a distinctive Ontario tradition. Berger is far too quick to dismiss as aberrant remarks made during other celebrations in Adolphustown and Niagara that fail to fit into his Loyalist-imperialist matrix. A complete understanding of the significance of the Loyalist tradition must go beyond the rhetoric of individuals, events, and organizations and examine both the process by which the past is constructed in the present and the public reception that greets such efforts.

In the chapters that follow I examine how the Loyalist past has been used, interpreted, and understood over time. Chapter 1 examines the Loyalist reality. A survey of recent Loyalist scholarship challenges the notion that the original Loyalists possessed a coherent identity and ideology to pass on to their descendants. The portrait of the Loyalist as a member of a superior, cultured, and elevated group that endured untold sufferings and privations for the sake of principle bears little relationship to the historical record. Such idealized images emerged gradually and haphazardly during the course of debates over government land and immigration policy. With the resolution of these issues by the 1830s the Loyalists faded to the periphery of Upper Canadian political discourse.

In chapter 2 the tension that emerged between official and vernacular pasts at the middle of the nineteenth century is explored. A steadily rising population, economic growth, expansionist desires, and sectional rivalry contributed to the emergence of nationalist sentiment and expansionist ambitions in Canada West. Convinced that all nations needed heroes and that founding moments were vitally important in shaping a people's identity, Upper Canada's political leaders began to sponsor official efforts to recover the records of the province's Loyalist founders. These efforts received added impetus as the last living links with the province's Loyalist origins passed away and Loyalist descendants anxiously set about collecting the papers and reminiscences of the surviving Loyalists. The reminiscences gave expression to a nostalgic vernacular past that did not provide the basis for the heroic history of origins that politicians hoped to create; they did, however, produce a sense of filial obligation among Loyalist descendants, who set about writing an embellished history of their forebears that drew heavily on the work of contemporary American historians and the conventions of romance.

Chapters 3 and 4 provide a detailed analysis of the 1884 Loyalist centennial celebrations in Adolphustown, Toronto, Niagara, and the Six Nations reserves at Grand River and Tyendinaga. Historians have often looked to commemorative celebrations for insight into the mind-set of a period or people. In their examination of events of this type, however, historians have often failed to go beyond the rhetoric uttered on such occasions and investigate the relationship between such public enactments and their social context. Careful examination of the conception, organization, and reception of the 1884 celebrations reveals a complex range of ideas and motivations. Although the Adolphustown, Toronto, and Niagara celebrations commemorated persons and events of the previous century, each celebration was a distinct product of local conditions and contemporary political and social concerns. The celebrations were surrounded by controversy as organizers and the public debated the meaning and significance of the Loyalist past.

The period between 1884 and the First World War witnessed a tremendous proliferation of publications dealing with the Loyalists, and the erection of several monuments honouring individual Loyalists. In chapter 5 I examine the treatment of the Loyalists in the political pamphlets, textbooks, local histories, and genealogical works of the period and how different aspects of the Loyalist tradition were employed to legitimize and perpetuate political points of view, to inculcate social values, and to promote claims to status and recognition. The movement to erect monuments commemorating Loyalist heroes such as Joseph Brant, Laura Secord, and Barbara Heck is the subject of chapter 6. All three of these figures became the subject of monuments less for their own intrinsic accomplishments than for their ability to carry the political or social aspirations of their promoters.

Chapter 7 examines the origins, membership, and initiatives of the United Empire Loyalist Association of Ontario. The association was a product of the middle-class anxieties that accompanied industrialization and urbanization. Confused about their identity and position in society and concerned about the future, the middle-class professionals who joined the association sought a means of affirming their status and defending their social and political values. The tensions that surrounded the founding of the association and the various strategies pursued by its members to secure public recognition of their claim to genealogical and patriotic superiority are discussed in detail.

Inventing the Loyalists provides a comprehensive analysis of the creation, evolution, content, and uses of the Ontario Loyalist tradition. The study challenges many of the assumptions that have come to be associated with the Loyalist tradition. The Loyalist tradition was not inherited, but was continually re-invented by groups seeking to create usable pasts that spoke to contemporary circumstances and concerns. The invention of tradition is not just a means by which people identify themselves; it is also an expression of the stresses and strains within society. The Loyalist tradition was often surrounded by controversy as different interests debated the meaning of the Loyalist past and competed to control its use. As a case study in the invention of tradition, this examination of the Loyalist tradition broadens our understanding of the ways in which the past is written into present social reality. Traditions are not a fixed set of immutable ideas and actions handed down directly, and often unthinkingly, from the past. Nor are they simply tools of hegemony or social control manufactured by political or economic elites. The invention of tradition is a complex process shaped by the concerns and conditions of the present and involving a wide array of groups and interests from all levels of society. It is only by placing traditions in their social and historical contexts and by examining their evolution over time that a complete understanding of their significance can be attained.

1

'Chiefly landholders, farmers, and others':
The Loyalist Reality

In his 1861 work *The History of the Settlement of Upper Canada*, the Belleville physician and amateur historian William Canniff described the United Empire Loyalist as 'one who advocated, or wished to have maintained, the unity of the British Empire' and 'who felt as much a Briton in the colony of America, as if he were in old England.' Guided by 'higher motives,' Canniff proclaimed, many of 'this noble class relinquished comfortable homes, rather than live under an alien flag' and 'preferred, above all measure, to enter a wilderness and hew out a new home.' 'They would live anywhere, endure any toil, undergo any privation,' he insisted, 'so long as they were in the King's dominion, and the good old flag waved over their head, and their families.' Finding themselves in a threatening landscape with few resources, these 'honest, devoted, loyal, truthful, law abiding' refugees overcame repeated hardships and setbacks and transformed the Upper Canadian wilderness into a fruitful field through collective cooperation and hospitality. Ever vigilant in their guard against American aggression, Canniff concluded, the 'U.E. Loyalists have been as a barrier of rock, against which the waves of Republicanism have dashed in vain.'[1] Canniff's portrayal of the Loyalists as an elite group of anti-American Anglophiles and aristocratic imperialists is a classic statement of what historians have labelled the *Loyalist tradition*. Canniff's description of the Loyalists, however, bears little relationship to the historical reality.

Surprisingly little is known about the approximately 7,500 Loyalists who by 1785 had settled in what would become Upper Canada. The Loyalist settlers fell into three distinct categories. The largest group encompassed the 3,500 soldiers and dependants of the provincial regiments. These

Regimental Loyalists were supplemented by a much smaller group of unincorporated civilian Loyalists who had migrated to the province over-land and by two companies of Associated Loyalists who had sailed from New York City under the leadership of Captain Michael Grass and Major Peter Van Alstine.[2] These groups of Loyalists were joined in Upper Canada by over 2,000 of Britain's Native allies among the Six Nations and the tribes of the Ohio country. One group, under the leadership of John Deseronto, settled at Tyendinaga on the Bay of Quinte in 1784. The following year a second, larger group settled with Joseph Brant along the Grand River on lands purchased for them by the British government from the indigenous Mississauguas of the region.[3]

While some Loyalists were undoubtedly ideologically dedicated to the preservation of the Empire, the motives of many were decidedly mixed.[4] Patronage and commercial ties dictated the position of many Loyalists; others were merely opportunists who pledged allegiance to whichever side appeared to be on the ascendancy locally; still others were reluctant Loyalists, who took sides only when forced out of a preferred state of neutrality by Patriot harassment or Loyalist intimidation.[5] The motives of the Loyalist refugees did not impress Major Robert Mathews, the secretary to the governor of Quebec, Frederick Haldimand. Most of the refugees, Mathews asserted, were 'in fact only Mechanics ... removed from one situation to practice their Trades in another.'[6] Natives had their own reasons for allying themselves with Britain during the American Revolution. The tribes that sided with the British did so as allies, not as subjects of the Crown, and they fought largely to preserve the integrity of their tribal lands against the rising tide of white settlement.[7]

In a report to the Loyalist Claims Commission in January of 1786, the administrator of Quebec Lieutenant-Governor Henry Hope, observed that the Loyalists were 'chiefly landholders, farmers, and others from the inland part of the continent' and that there were few 'persons of great property or consequence' among them.[8] Although no comprehensive analysis exists of the backgrounds and occupations of the Upper Canadian Loyalists, two studies shed considerable light on the nature of the Loyalist migration. Bruce Wilson drew a rough portrait of Upper Canadian Loyalists from the 488 compensation claims filed between 1783 and 1789 with the commission established by the British government to investigate the losses and services of the American Loyalists. Wilson discovered that 90 per cent of the claimants were pioneer farmers of modest means. Almost half of those seeking compensation indicated that they had cleared less than ten acres of land. The remaining 10 per cent of the

LOYALIST SETTLEMENT IN UPPER CANADA

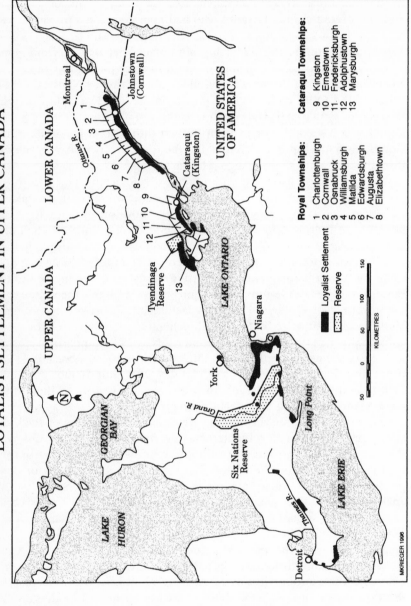

Royal Townships:
1 Charlottenburgh
2 Cornwall
3 Osnabruck
4 Williamsburgh
5 Matilda
6 Edwardsburgh
7 Augusta
8 Elizabethtown

Cataraqui Townships:
9 Kingston
10 Ernestown
11 Fredericksburgh
12 Adolphustown
13 Marysburgh

Loyalist Settlement
Reserve

KILOMETRES
50 0 50 100 150

MKRIEGER 1996

claimants included five public office holders, a teacher, a physician, two surgeons, and a handful of merchants and tavern-keepers. Just over half of those applying for compensation were foreign born and only 8 per cent were English by birth.[9] A similar picture emerges in Larry Turner's study of the Associated Loyalists of Adolphustown. Of the 240 Associated Loyalists who settled at Adolphustown in 1784, Turner found that only five of the families had accumulated any significant degree of wealth before the revolutionary war. The majority were drawn from the middle and lower strata of society. Farmers were by far the largest occupational group, although there were a number of skilled craftsmen. The Associated Loyalists of Adolphustown were also an ethnically and religiously diverse lot. Turner estimated that about 37 per cent were of Dutch ethnicity, 28 per cent British, 20 per cent French, and 15 per cent German. The overwhelming majority appear to have been Methodists, although there were a significant number of Quakers and only a few Anglicans.[10]

The Loyalists who settled in Upper Canada were not members of a 'noble class' representing gentle birth, wealth, and learning. While a small officer class did exist, the Loyalist rank and file consisted primarily of farmers and artisans of modest means. Most Upper Canadian Loyalists were in fact recent immigrants to the American colonies who had yet to establish themselves. Not yet fully assimilated into American society and feeling themselves threatened by more powerful elements within the colonies, many immigrants chose loyalty as an alternative to economic and political subjugation. Loyalists also tended to be members of ethnic and religious minorities who feared domination by their more numerous neighbours. A culturally diverse group, the typical Upper Canadian Loyalist would not, as Canniff asserted, have 'felt as much a Briton in the colony of America as if he were in old England.'

Discontent, disappointment, and division characterized the resettlement process. Rumours that all the best land had been granted to Native peoples or that the settlements would be of a military nature and the settlers obligated to serve at any time produced unrest and unease among the anxious refugees. Loyalists encamped in Quebec during the winter of 1783 constantly complained about their primitive accommodations and besieged government officials with petitions for supplies and assistance. One particularly 'extravagant' petition demanded that each family be equipped with a complete set of tools, building supplies, arms and ammunition, one year's clothing, a supply of seed, two horses, two cows, and six sheep.[11] At one point, an exasperated Haldimand curtly advised the Loyalist refugees that he would find passage for them at the earliest date for

Nova Scotia. Disenchanted with conditions, many left the camps, not for Nova Scotia, but to return to their former homes in the new republic to salvage what they could.

Matters did not improve once the Loyalists arrived at the site of their new homes. Incomplete surveys, inadequate supplies, and disputes over location tickets produced widespread bitterness and resentment. In July of 1784, for example, Robert Mathews informed Sir John Johnson that 'the settlers at Cataraqui are in great disorder, not yet having got upon their Land, many of them unprovided with a Blanket to cover Them, scarce any Turnip seed and neither Axes or Hoes for Half of them.'[12] Civilian settlers charged that Regimental Loyalists received favourable treatment and had been allotted the best land. Officers complained that the process had been too impartial and that special provision should have been made so that they were assured the prime parcels of land. Such were the divisions among the Loyalists that in the Royal Townships laid out along the St Lawrence settlers were divided, at their own request, according to their ethnicity and religion. The first township was consequently allotted to Catholic Highlanders, the second to Scottish Presbyterians, the third to German Calvinists, the fourth to German Lutherans, and the last to Anglicans.[13]

Once the Loyalists were settled, their economic and political behaviour was far removed from the cooperative and communitarian spirit idealized by Canniff. 'Disputes amongst the Loyalists frequently arise,' observed Major Ross in July of 1784.[14] Officers of the Loyalist regiments often complained that they were unable to exert any influence over those formerly under their command. Loyalist society was essentially atomistic. Settlers consistently acted as individuals, refusing to lay aside their self-interest for the common good or to merge their identity into some greater whole. In this respect, Loyalist society differed little from that in the United States.[15]

There is little truth in the image of the Loyalist as an Anglophile who venerated all things British and detested all things American. Governor Haldimand was shocked when Associated Loyalists insisted upon 'a form of government as nearly similar as possible to that which they Enjoyed in the Province of New York.'[16] Contemporary observers noted that 'passions mutually subsided' shortly after the Revolution and that 'the natural feelings of consanguinity, amnity, and personal friendship revived.'[17] Articulate Loyalist leaders, such as Richard Cartwright, were consciously Anglo-American and vigorously resisted efforts to transform the Upper Canadian wilderness into a little Britain. During the first session of the

Upper Canadian legislature in 1793, Cartwright complained that the province's lieutenant-governor, John Graves Simcoe, 'thinks every existing regulation in England would be proper here' and 'seems bent on copying all the subordinate establishments without considering the great disparity of the two countries in every respect.' Cartwright advised Simcoe that 'a government should be formed for a Country and not a country strained and distorted for the Accommodation of a preconceived and speculative scheme of Government.'[18] A Loyalist background did not provide a sure guide to political affiliation. While Loyalists of the officer class tended to be firm supporters of the social and political status quo, rank and file Loyalists were much more likely to advocate reform and support the opposition.[19] Preoccupied with carving out an existence on the Upper Canadian frontier, most Loyalists had neither the time nor the inclination to devote much attention to politics or abstract questions about the nature of government.

By the outbreak of the War of 1812, the Loyalist element was scarcely noticeable among the diversity of people that had come to the province to take up land or engage in trade.[20] The Loyalist response to the call to arms during the war was, at best, equivocal. A government report at the war's end declared that the son or daughter of a Loyalist would not be entitled to land grants unless able to demonstrate 'that the Parent retained his Loyalty during the late War, and was under no suspicion of aiding or assisting the Enemy – and if a Son, then of Age, that he was also Loyal during the late War, and did his duty in defence of the Province – and if a Daughter of an U.E. Loyalist married, that her Husband was loyal, and did his duty in defence of the Province.'[21] The government obviously had serious doubts about the contributions of the Loyalist community to the war effort. Contrary to conventional belief, the War of 1812 did not enhance or create a Loyalist identity in Upper Canada. Divided by race, origins, and religion before the war, Upper Canadians emerged from the war even more divided. Disputes over compensation, militia pay, land grants, pensions, and medals for heroism were the source of considerable postwar acrimony.[22]

The militia legend – the belief that the war was fought and won by the Upper Canadian militia – originated as a piece of wartime propaganda designed to cover up the extent of disaffection and desertion in the province and to encourage wavering elements within the population to respond to the government's call to arms.[23] For men like John Strachan, who were not of Loyalist background, the militia legend provided a usable past that was more inclusive and integrating than the Loyalist experience. After the war, the militia legend was used by members of the governing 'Compact' to justify their continued hold on the province's positions of privilege and authority. It was not until the 1850s, when the memory of wartime grievances began to fade and many of the remaining veterans had passed away, that the war began to be looked back upon as a great national achievement and to be interpreted as a Loyalist victory.[24]

The Loyalist reality differed significantly from Canniff's idealized treatment. The original Loyalist settlers of Ontario lacked a coherent and cohesive identity. Mixed motives, ethnic and religious diversity, preoccupation with the everyday work of surviving in the wilderness, frequent relocation, marriage into non-Loyalist families, and the influx of large numbers of American settlers all contributed to the failure of the Loyalists to develop a distinct self-awareness.[25] The question remains: when and why was the image of the Loyalist as an aristocratic, principled, Yankee-hating Anglophile invented?

If the original Loyalist settlers lacked a coherent and cohesive identity and ideology, they shared a fundamental common interest: land. It was land that attracted the Loyalists to Upper Canada in the first place or induced them to stay once they had arrived. Land was the main and for several years virtually the only source of wealth. For the Loyalists, land also had a symbolic value. Deprived of their landholdings during the Revolution, Loyalists viewed land grants from the Crown as recognition that their service and sacrifice had been worthy, their allegiance was legitimate, and their claims were valid. It was the successful battle to subdue the land, not the lost battles of the Revolution, that assumed the largest place in the reminiscences of the Loyalist pioneers. Not surprisingly, then, government land policy and the debates that it aroused played a critical role in the early evolution of the Upper Canadian Loyalist tradition.

It was land that initially set the Loyalists apart as a distinct group. In 1783 General Frederick Haldimand, governor of the Province of Quebec, received royal instructions directing him to allocate lands to all Loyalist refugees desiring to become actual settlers. Grants were to be free, unencumbered by survey and patent fees, and would vary according to rank and status. Heads of families were to receive 100 acres with an additional fifty acres for each member of the family. A single man was entitled to fifty acres. Grants to those who served in one of the Loyalist regiments ranged from 100 acres for privates to a 1,000 acres for field officers. An exception was the 84th Regiment, which had been recruited with the understanding that field officers would receive 5,000 acres, captains 3,000 acres, subalterns 2,000 acres, and non-commissioned officers 200 acres. In the face of considerable resentment over the 84th Regiment's favoured treatment, an order-in-council was passed in 1788 extending the 84th's generous terms to the other Loyalist regiments. In 1787 Lord Dorchester increased the grant by 200 acres to heads of families who had already improved their lands. 'Lord Dorchester's bounty' was interpreted by the Land Boards established to oversee the settlement process to mean that all those who had borne arms would be entitled to 300 acres or more, according to their rank, and that other Loyalists would receive an initial grant of 200 acres.[26]

It soon became obvious, however, that not all of the settlers flocking into the province were genuine Loyalists. Dorchester resolved in 1789 'to put a mark of honour upon the families who had adhered to the Unity of Empire and Joined the Royal Standard in America before the Treaty of Separation in the year 1783.' An order-in-council was passed directing the Land Boards to compile lists of Loyalists 'to the end that their posterity may be discriminated from future settlers ... as proper objects ... for distinguished benefits and privileges.' As a first step in this direction, it was resolved that the Loyalists and 'all their children and their Descendants by either sex are to be distinguished by the following capitals affixed to their names: U.E., alluding to their great principle, the Unity of Empire.' Although this 'mark of honour' was to appear in all parish registers, militia rolls, and other public documents, it was not consistently or widely used in the province.[27] A more tangible gesture was the decision that sons of Loyalists on their coming of age and daughters at the time of their marriage were to receive a land grant of 200 acres free of all survey and patent fees. Although the Loyalists were to be set apart from all subsequent settlers as a group deserving of special recognition, Dorchester was not very precise in his definition of who was a Loyalist. Acceptable wartime service remained unprescribed and no cut-off date for residence in the province was established. Given such loose definitions, inclusion on the U.E. List can hardly be said to identify committed Loyalists.

The text of Dorchester's order-in-council became the subject of considerable controversy over the next three decades. The terms of the order-in-council stipulated that such grants were limited to the children of Loyalists already in the province and would be made only if there were 'no default in the due Cultivation and Improvement of the Lands, already assigned to the Head of the Family, of which they were members.' It was also clear that the children were expected to conform to all settlement regulations and were thus expected to occupy and improve the grants.

Unlike the 'mark of honour,' the land grants to children, or 'U.E. Rights' as they came to be known, were never intended to be 'perpetual' or to constitute an imprescriptible right.[28] Loyalists and their descendants, however, imposed an entirely different construction upon the meaning of the order-in-council. It was repeatedly argued that Dorchester was simply implementing the royal will to recognize, reward, and compensate the Loyalists for their services and sacrifices on behalf of the Crown during the Revolution. All Loyalists, irrespective of their time of arrival in the province, it was maintained, were entitled to land free from all conditions and expenses for themselves and their children.

The controversy that came to surround these 'U.E. Rights,' perhaps more than any other single factor, accounts for the earliest attempts to transform the Loyalists into heroic figures who endured untold sufferings and privations on behalf of their unwavering allegiance to the Empire and British constitutional principles. Whenever the government attempted to put an end to Loyalist claims, to purge the U.E. List of fraudulent names or to impose settlement duties on U.E. grants, it was confronted by a storm of protest from surviving Loyalists and their disaffected offspring and descendants. The careers of early reformers such as Robert Thorpe and William Weekes were based to a considerable extent on the discontent arising from the government's handling of U.E. Rights. With each confrontation the Loyalists' sacrifices, their services to the Crown and Empire, in short, their claims to special status and recognition, reached new heights.[29]

In 1832 an order-in-council was issued stipulating that patents would not be issued for land held on location tickets until it was proved that a resident settler had been established on part of the grant. The following year even more stringent regulations were introduced: U.E. Rights were not to be located unless the original grantee was prepared to settle in person on the lot, and patents were not to be issued until two years' residence had been completed.[30] The government's actions produced a wave of dissent among speculators in U.E. Rights. The protests culminated with 'An Address to His Majesty on the subject of U.E. Rights' from the Assembly in 1834. The petitioners described the Loyalists as 'the most faithful and loyal subjects of His Majesty King George the Third.' 'Uncompromising' in their 'zeal and fidelity to His Majesty's cause, person, and government,' the Loyalists 'unhesitatingly sacrifice[d], not only their possessions and worldly effects, but also the peace and comfort of themselves and their families, by voluntarily joining the Royal Standard.' Land grants from the Crown, the petitioners insisted, 'were always considered and understood in the shape of a debt due by the government ... as a reward for meritorious services performed, and for which they considered they held the pledge and faith of government.'[31] Underlying the increasingly elevated rhetoric, however, was a very real economic interest. U.E. Rights had become the object of considerable speculation, and any restriction on their use or transfer threatened to reduce their value. Significantly, 1834 also marked the fiftieth anniversary of the Loyalists' settlement in the province. A year earlier, New Brunswick Loyalists had marked the occasion with a number of celebrations.[32] Despite the continuing debate over U.E. Rights, the anniversary passed without comment in Upper Canada.

Closely related to the land issue was the question of immigration. The desire to recognize the Loyalists immediately came into conflict with the imperatives of settling and developing the province. In the end, the forces of development prevailed. Upper Canada's first lieutenant-governor, John Graves Simcoe, lured settlers into the province from the United States with the promise of free grants of land. The Loyalist population soon found itself swamped and its power and influence reduced. By 1812 there were approximately 100,000 people in the province, 80 per cent of whom were recent arrivals from the United States.[33]

The Loyalist response to this influx was mixed. Many welcomed the Americans: without additional settlers, U.E. Rights had little speculative value. During the Alien controversy of the 1820s members of the House of Assembly of Loyalist stock and representatives from centres of Loyalist settlement were among the most vocal critics of the government's policy to prescribe the rights of Americans already in the province and to exclude additional American settlers from entering the province.[34] A Loyalist correspondent to the *Upper Canada Herald* insisted that American settlers were 'faithful subjects' and contributed as much as the first Loyalists 'to the clearing of the settlement, and improving of the country.'[35] Only the relatively few Loyalists who had entrenched themselves within the provincial establishment vehemently opposed the influx of American settlers. Opponents of American immigration portrayed Upper Canada as the exclusive preserve of those persons whose loyalty had been tested and found true during the American Revolution and subsequently in the War of 1812. Recent arrivals from the United States were described as radicals who threatened to subvert the very foundations of Upper Canadian society. Characteristic of this viewpoint were the words of a correspondent to the Kingston *Chronicle* of 1 February 1822 opposing the election of Barnabas Bidwell to the Legislative Assembly:

Well can I remember how I was driven from them [the scenes of my youth], and from the spot where my father fell, fighting for his King against rebels. By whom was I robbed of my patrimony – by whom was my parent deprived of life? Even by such as him who now claims equal privileges with the best of us. I was driven, like many of you, from my home, for I scorned to join the rebels, or to desert my King: – it makes my blood boil within me to think of it. Not only the leader of a violent democratic faction, one who had betrayed a public trust, who has committed crimes ... who held a seat in their House of Congress, and was amongst the loudest and most inveterate enemies of Great Britain ... comes now forward after a lapse of years, to enjoy one of your highest prerogatives, to amend and make your laws, to sit, cheek by jowl, with your honorable men, and like himself up in your Council Chamber as one whose hands are clean ... What are you about ye sons of U.E. Loyalists? What are you about? Will you suffer these things?[36]

Beneath such heated rhetoric lay questions of power, influence and income. On the one hand, American settlers threatened to undermine the power and privileges of the established leaders of the province. On the other, they promised to increase the speculative value of U.E. Rights.

As politics began to polarize around issues such as the Alien Question, the question of allegiance assumed a central position in the political discourse of the period. Loyalty, narrowly defined, became essential for entry into and advancement within the provincial power structure. The Tory establishment appropriated the example of the Loyalists as a weapon against the voices of opposition and reform. Every movement which questioned the position and privileges of the governing compact was dismissed as a manifestation of subversive republicanism and a deviation from Loyalist principles. An address delivered by Richard Cartwright to a Kingston town hall meeting in March of 1832 was typical of the manner in which the Loyalist experience was arrogated for partisan purposes during the divisive years prior to the 1837 rebellions. 'As the son and the grandson of an U.E. Loyalist,' Cartwright attacked 'the machinations of the disloyal and disaffected who are now industriously endeavouring to persuade the ignorant and unstable that certain weighty grievances exist.' Cartwright reminded his audience that the province 'owes its origins' to the Loyalists – 'a set of gallant men, many of whom were the greatest Landholders in the United States,' who 'contended for the constitution, and rights of the Crown' and 'hazarded their lives and fortunes, in attempting to put down Rebellion and preserve the unity of the Empire.'[37] As David Mills has noted, such rhetoric forced reformers to appropriate and reshape the language of Loyalism for themselves. In their defence, reformers claimed to be equally loyal to the British Crown and constitution, frequently claimed to be of Loyalist background, and often cited the Loyalists' dedication to principle to justify dissent against what they perceived to be the narrow and self-serving interests of the provincial administration.[38]

After the resolution of the land and Alien questions in the 1830s, the province's Loyalist origins became increasingly peripheral to political debate in Upper Canada. The experience and example of the Loyalists were rarely referred to following the 1837 rebellions and the subsequent debates over responsible government. By the 1840s the exclusive definition of loyalty that had been used by the governing elite to support its power and privileges was gradually displaced by an assimilative concept of loyalty that acknowledged the place of newcomers and of party in the political system. Loyalty ceased to be a birthright, but it could be earned through commitment to the community and the achievement of respectability.[39] No longer useful as a political or social weapon, the experience and example of the Loyalists became a distant memory throughout most of the 1840s and 1850s. Although the seventy-fifth anniversary of the arrival of the Loyalists was marked by substantial celebrations in New Brunswick in 1858, the milestone passed virtually unnoticed in Canada West.[40] Forces were building, however, that were to revive interest in the province's Loyalist past over the next few years.

2

'An ancestry of which any people might be proud': Official History, the Vernacular Past, and the Shaping of the Loyalist Tradition at Mid-Century

'No people,' the Toronto *Globe* observed in October of 1856, 'has made a figure in the life of nations, without its heroes.' Fortunately, Upper Canada could claim heroic foundations. 'United Empire Loyalists,' the *Globe* asserted, 'form an ancestry of which any people might be proud. They had every characteristic which can go to constitute an enduring substratum for a coming nation.' It was a matter of considerable concern to the *Globe*, however, that Upper Canadians displayed a decided 'ignorance' and 'indifference' towards the province's 'Loyalist Fathers.' 'No ignorance of history,' the *Globe* warned, 'can be more reprehensible than that which we now censure. It amounts to an utter obliviousness of our peculiar story ... Here, then, we are in the sixty-second year of our being in Upper Canada with the only men who would accurately inform, fast dying, if not already dead, and but grossly ignorant of our provincial parentage and birth ... such carelessness is a cruel injustice to our fathers.' The *Globe* urged the superintendent of education, Egerton Ryerson, to take immediate action to preserve and record the province's Loyalist history. 'Something must be done,' the *Globe* concluded, 'in justice alike to the past, and to coming generations.'[1] A small group of committed individuals, Ryerson among them, heeded the *Globe's* advice and set about collecting the reminiscences, memoirs, and papers of surviving Loyalists and creating a Loyalist history.

The *Globe's* interest in Upper Canada's history and its Loyalist origins attests to the emergence of a new historical consciousness in the 1850s. This development was largely a product of the nationalist sentiment and expansionist ambitions that accompanied the process of state formation and the province's economic growth. The past was invoked and recalled by provincial leaders interested in the creation of an official history that could be used to promote unity, build a national identity, and uphold social and political order. Promoters of Upper Canada's past sought a heroic and inspiring history that celebrated the province's past achievements and future potential. A concern with origins, the deaths of the last of the original Loyalists, the need to counter nationalist American histories, and the presence of Loyalist descendants in prominent positions of influence in the government ensured that much of this interest in the past became focused upon Upper Canada's Loyalist pioneers. The result was a concerted effort on the part of the state and Loyalist descendants to collect and preserve documents connected with the province's Loyalist origins and to construct a history worthy of the province's founders and its future aspirations. Creating an official history that preserved the memory of the Loyalists, celebrated their contributions, and pointed to a future of continued progress and achievement proved to be a difficult task. The papers and reminiscences of surviving Loyalists that were anxiously collected at the time were part of a vernacular past rooted in local conditions, personal recollection, and particular experience. As John Bodnar has demonstrated, the immediate concerns of the vernacular past frequently conflict with the abstract needs of official history.[2] This was certainly the experience in Upper Canada. The desire to create a heroic and forward-looking official history of progress and achievement confronted, in the reminiscences of surviving Loyalists, figures who were ambivalent and ambiguous rather than heroic, a nostalgic idealization of pioneer society, and a deep disenchantment with present conditions. Ignoring the reminiscences, the agents of official history recast the Loyalist pioneers of memory into a persecuted elite who heroically sacrificed their homes and comfort for the sake of principle. Ironically, the idealized past produced by Loyalist historians such as William Canniff and Egerton Ryerson was based to a considerable degree on the work of an American, Lorenzo Sabine.

By mid-century, Upper Canada was no longer an isolated colonial backwater but a self-governing and prosperous commercial society. A steadily rising population, the construction of railways, the beginnings of large-scale industry, and the growth of the professions, banking, and other financial institutions all provided evidence that the transition to a mature capitalist society was well under way.[3] A vigorous process of state formation followed the achievement of responsible government and resulted in a tremendous expansion in the size of the state and the scope of its activities.[4] At the same time, sectional conflict with Canada East and the expansionist sentiment that accompanied the province's economic growth and the disappearance of its agricultural frontier helped to define a distinctive Upper Canadian identity and sense of national destiny.[5]

The forces transforming Canada West gave birth to a growing historical consciousness among the province's political and social leaders. This development was not unique. A sense of continuity and identity with a national past, reverence for national heroes, and the commemoration of great national events were becoming commonplace in both Europe and the United States by the middle of the nineteenth century. The rise of mass democracy and the social changes wrought by the industrial revolution demanded new devices to ensure or express social cohesion and identity and to structure social relations. The result was a determined effort on the part of the state and other power groups to create what Benedict Anderson has termed 'imagined political communities.' According to Anderson, the creation of such 'imagined communities' required the active mobilization of periphery by cultural centre in order to create a shared history upon which a national identity could be erected. In this process, a particular view of the past is selected from all the different times and events possible in order to represent the nation. It is particularly important, Anderson asserts, to designate a founding moment of great significance from which a straightforward history of progress can be dated.[6]

Canadian legislators recognized the importance of the past in constructing community and a shared identity and actively supported the production of literary and historical works. A committee of the legislature was created to review applications shortly after the union of Upper and Lower Canada in 1841. In 1842 the Legislative Assembly made a grant to John Richardson to assist in the publication of his planned history of the War of 1812.[7] The committee responsible for the encouragement of 'literary enterprise in Canada' was dominated by members from Canada East, which ensured that most of the funds available were directed towards French-Canadian authors.[8] François-Xavier Garneau, G.B. Faribault, and Abbé J.B.A. Ferland all received parliamentary grants to assist in the collection, transcription, and publication of materials connected with French-Canadian history.

In 1855 John Mercier McMullen, an Irish immigrant and journalist, published the province's first narrative history, *The History of Canada from its Discovery to the Present Time*. For McMullen, the past was a guide to the future. 'To regard our national future with confidence,' McMullen insisted, 'an acquaintance with the past is an absolute necessity.' If Upper

Canadians understood the lessons of history, their future would be assured. McMullen's interest in the didactic uses of history was accompanied by an appreciation of the importance of the past in forging a national identity. In writing his history, McMullen hoped to overcome the ethnic, social, and political tensions that divided Upper Canadians and to create an 'identity of interests' by infusing 'a spirit of Canadian nationality into the people generally.'[9] Seeking to consolidate and celebrate the achievements of the past, McMullen used the rise of colonial self-government and the province's social and economic progress as the central themes of his narrative. McMullen's preoccupation with material progress and improvement reveals a great deal about the type of past Upper Canadians sought to create for themselves.[10]

The importance of the past in creating community and identity was appreciated by the founders of Upper Canada's system of public education. The province's public schools were designed to create social harmony and uphold the existing social structure and relations of authority by constructing a patriotic public with a common sense of identity.[11] To achieve these ends, the province's superintendent of education, Egerton Ryerson, sought to create a system that was 'not only British, but Canadian in form and content.'[12] The ability of the public schools to forge a common national identity was limited by the lack of domestically produced textbooks with local themes and illustrations. Concerned by the dominance of American textbooks, Ryerson authorized the adoption of the Irish National Readers. Although the readers better reflected the political, social, and religious values Ryerson felt should underlie Upper Canadian society, they did not satisfy the demand for Canadian texts.[13] Educators recognized the important role that history could play in fostering patriotism and inculcating moral lessons from the past. In 1849 the superintendent of common schools for the Ottawa district, Thomas Higginson, commented in his annual report on the urgent need for a Canadian history textbook. 'Such a work,' Higginson asserted, 'would be a secure basis whereon our young people could and would rest their loyalty and patriotism; such a work would develope [sic] events and circumstances around which the associations of heart and memory might cluster, as around a common centre, making us what we should be, what we require to be, and what we have never yet been – a united, a prosperous, and a contented people.'[14] Although Upper Canadian educators were astutely aware of the critical role that the study of history could play in creating the collective memory on which identity rests, it would be a number of years before a Canadian history text appeared for use in the public schools.

The appeal for Canadian history texts was finally answered by the publication of J. George Hodgins's *The Geography and History of British America and of the Other Colonies of the Empire* in 1857. Convinced that the British North American colonies were quickly emerging from their 'colonial infancy,' Hodgins saw the study of history as an essential element in forging bonds of unity and forming a national identity. He insisted that British North Americans could no longer rely on the 'uncertain and inaccurate' information contained in European textbooks and the 'unfriendly interpretations' found in American publications, but they must acquire 'a fuller acquaintance' with their own 'history, condition and capabilities.'[15] Hodgins's history portrayed Upper Canada as a distinct British American society built upon the loyalty, patriotism, industry, and self-discipline of its Loyalist founders. Presented in this fashion, the Loyalist past became a useful means of conveying the values and virtues educators hoped to instil in the province's students. The increased importance attached to the study of Canadian history was evident the following year, when Egerton Ryerson acquired a collection of Canadian historical materials to be used to train teachers at the provincial normal school.[16]

The Loyalist past became the focus of the growing historical consciousness that emerged in the 1850s. It was widely believed throughout the nineteenth century that origins played a critical role in establishing the character of a people and setting the future course of a nation's or a people's development. 'The beginnings of a nation, or even of a colony,' observed Nathanael Burwash at century's end, 'are always important. They are as the first track made across a hitherto untravelled prairie; they give direction to all that follows.'[17] An understanding of Upper Canada's destiny thus demanded an appreciation of its founders. 'If a man would know anything of the life of nations,' the *Globe* asserted in October of 1856, 'he should first know a little about the origins of his own.' There thus emerged a growing interest in recovering the Loyalist past and extolling the virtues, principles, and accomplishments of the province's 'Pilgrim Fathers.'[18]

Interest in the Loyalists received further stimulus from developments in the United States. The beginning of the nineteenth century witnessed the emergence of a highly nationalistic school of American historical writing, which exalted the nation's colonial and revolutionary founding fathers.[19] This history tended either to dismiss the Loyalists as an insignificant factor in the American Revolution or to portray them as unprincipled lackeys, calculating opportunists, or ruthless terrorists. Desiring to create a heroic history of origins of their own, Upper Canadians needed to vindicate the founders of their province. Ironically, the very history they denounced became a model for Canadian writers intent on creating their own myths, symbols, and traditions.

A sense of urgency surrounded the growing interest in the Loyalist past as the last of the Loyalists died. 'Our early settlers are fast passing away,' the Cobourg *Star* warned, 'and with them many invaluable records and instances of the past,' which 'must be secured very speedily or they will perish forever.'[20] This sense of irretrievable loss was reflected in the numerous obituaries that appeared throughout the press of the province during this period mourning the fall of 'another giant of the forest' or the removal of 'another landmark.' Loyalist descendants appear to have been especially influenced by the passing of the last of the Loyalist pioneers. Egerton Ryerson's lifelong interest in history did not become focused on the Loyalists until the death of his own father in 1854. Shortly after his father's death, Ryerson began to collect and compose Loyalist obituaries for publication in the *Journal of Education for Upper Canada.*[21]

Fearing that the opportunity to record and preserve Upper Canada's past was rapidly disappearing as the Loyalist generation died off, a number of concerned individuals urged the government to take immediate action to collect the recollections, memoirs, and family papers of surviving Loyalists. At the beginning of the 1859 sitting of the Legislative Assembly the Honourable William Hamilton Merritt presented a petition circulated by his son Jedediah calling on the government to support actively the collection of documents relating to Upper Canada's early history. The previous year, Jedediah had been frustrated in his efforts to copy previously inaccessible material in the Crown Lands Office by a lack of funds. In their petition the Merritts pointed out that the Literary and Historical Society of Quebec had received annual grants from the legislature since the union of Upper and Lower Canada in 1841 and that over the years special grants had been made to French-Canadian historians by the Legislative Assembly's library committee to collect and transcribe documents.[22] Feeling that Upper Canadian history was being neglected, William Hamilton Merritt used his political influence to displace the French-speaking majority on the library committee and managed to have his son Jedediah granted a sum of 200 pounds so that he could travel to England to collect documents.[23]

The Merritts' interest in the Loyalists was both personal and political. During the American Revolution, William Hamilton Merritt's father, Thomas, served under John Graves Simcoe in the Queen's Rangers. He moved to New Brunswick in 1783 but returned to the United States two years later. In 1796 the family settled in Upper Canada as late Loyalists.[24] A veteran of the War of 1812, William played a leading role in the erection of the second Brock monument on Queenston Heights and actively promoted the building of memorials on the sites of other battlefields.[25] Merritt's interest in the past was more than a little self-serving. A close friend observed that the Merritts did not hide their desire that 'posterity might know the energies pursued by them to establish an Independent Country and provide a good home as it had done to thousands of families now scattered throughout every portion of this Province.'[26]

Although such family egotism contributed to the Merritts' efforts to recover the Loyalist past, their historical interests also reflected their commercial and political concerns. Throughout his long career in business and politics, William Hamilton Merritt vigorously promoted efforts to improve Upper Canada's transportation system and enlarge its trade. Like many Upper Canadians, Merritt took pride in the growth of the province but feared that Upper Canada was outgrowing its boundaries. By the 1850s Merritt's interest in trade and transportation and his concerns for the future led him to take an active interest in the union of the British North American colonies and expansion into the northwest. Merritt's sudden interest in the province's past was closely linked to expansionist ambitions. He believed that history could play an important role in creating a shared sense of identity and destiny that would facilitate Upper Canada's political growth and national development within the British Empire. In the preface to Merritt's biography, Jedediah observed that his father was a man who 'loved Britain with a Briton's love, yet he loved Canada more' and 'longed for its prosperity.'[27] Such sentiments lay behind the Merritts' efforts to recover and preserve the Loyalist past.

William D. Eberts, Thomas D. Phillipps, and Duncan Warren presented another set of petitions to the Assembly in February and March, 'praying that an appropriation may be made out of the Provincial Treasury for collecting and re-printing original contemporary documents relating to the History of Upper Canada since its first settlement by the United Empire Loyalists.'[28] In April the Library Committee approved 'of the praiseworthy endeavours of those who have thus awakened public attention to the necessity of seeking to recover the lost fragments of our historical annals' and appropriated £100 for the collection of documents. George Coventry, a long-time associate of the Merritts, was engaged by the committee to collect and transcribe documents. Coventry and Jedediah Merritt received a further grant of 300 pounds in 1860 to continue their work.[29]

The English-born Coventry immigrated to Upper Canada in 1835. He settled in the Niagara district and soon became friends with William Hamilton Merritt, for whom he worked from time to time over the next two decades. A Tory in politics, Coventry was shocked by the events of the 1837 rebellions and developed an early interest in the Loyalists as exemplars of devotion to Crown and Empire. After an unsuccessful attempt at the newspaper business in Picton, Coventry secured a position as a customs broker at Cobourg in 1857. As a frequent contributor to the *Cobourg Sentinel*, he became acquainted with many of the old settlers in the region. Despite his position with customs and occasional newspaper work, Coventry experienced perennial financial difficulties. Aware of this situation, William Hamilton Merritt secured the appointment of his old friend by the legislature to collect and transcribe documents on the Loyalist pioneers.[30]

Inspired by the success of the Literary and Historical Society of Quebec and the formation of numerous historical and patriotic organizations in the United States, Jedediah Merritt and George Coventry circulated a 'Prospectus for the Formation of an Upper Canadian Historical Society' in 1861. Contending that 'the rise and progress of nations' depended on an appreciation of the past, Merritt and Coventry urged that a society, free of 'party politics' be formed to 'collect material and information relative to our early history.' 'The old settlers are year after year, quitting the scene of their labours,' Merritt and Coventry warned, 'and whilst any remain, our object will be to collect from them the Reminiscence of their early days and the path they trod, to acquire, by industry and perseverance, comfortable homesteads for themselves and [their] families.'[31] The movement to form a provincial historical society was endorsed by many of the province's leading political, business, and cultural leaders. The names of Egerton Ryerson, Chief Justice John Beverley Robinson, Sir Allan MacNab, Hon. W.H. Dixon, Rt Rev. John Strachan, J. George Hodgins, William Boulton, Hon. George Boulton, and Hon. Sydney Smith were listed among 'the gentlemen favourable to the formation of an historical society for Upper Canada' on a circular promoting the new association.[32] The society's inaugural meeting was held on 14 November 1861 in Toronto. At the meeting it was resolved that members of the society should collect the reminiscences of the surviving pioneers of the province and furnish them to the society to be examined by a committee, which would publish the most 'worthy' manuscripts. It was hoped that the province would support the society in its endeavours to publish a documentary history of the province that would help to instil a 'sentiment of nationality' among the people of Canada West.[33]

The Historical Society of Upper Canada played a key role in the development of the Loyalist tradition. At the urging of the society, Egerton Ryerson issued a circular in 1861 addressed to the 'descendants of the British United Empire Loyalists' soliciting 'any Documents, Journals, Letters or other Papers which may relate to the Lives and Adventures of their forefathers and of their settlement in Canada, or any facts or information which may afford materials for a history of the venerated founders of our country.'[34] The work begun in 1861 for the Historical Society of Upper Canada culminated with the publication in 1880 of Ryerson's 'monument to the character and merits of the fathers and founders of my native country,' *The Loyalists of America and Their Times from 1620–1816.*[35] It was also at that request of the society that the Belleville physician William Canniff undertook to interview surviving Loyalists and to write the paper upon the settlement of the Bay of Quinte that was the genesis for his influential study, *The History of the Settlement of Upper Canada.*

A number of forces coalesced in the 1850s to generate an official interest in Upper Canada's past generally and the Loyalist past in particular. Economic growth and sectional tensions fostered expansionist ambitions and nationalist sentiment. The expansion of the state and the need to create a public produced an appreciation of the usefulness of the past in constructing a shared sense of identity, promoting patriotism, and instilling common values. The death of the last of the Loyalists and the desire to vindicate the province's founders in the light of nationalist American histories focused this growing historical consciousness on the Loyalists. All of these elements contributed to official efforts to construct a heroic history of origins that celebrated the achievements of the past and looked forward to a future of continued accomplishment. The attempt to construct an official history along these lines confronted a serious challenge in the reminiscences, memoirs, and documents collected at the time. Rooted in local particularities and personal experience and memory, the memoirs and reminiscences collected by Coventry, Merritt, Canniff, and Ryerson were part of a nostalgic vernacular past that lamented the loss of a simpler and purer world.

For those hoping to create a forward-looking history that presented the province's founders in heroic terms, the reminiscences were disappointing. Descendants did not dwell on the principles of their Loyalist parents or grandparents or the role they had played in the Revolution. The son of a Dutch Loyalist, James Dittrick, simply stated that his father was a 'strict Loyalist' and that the Revolution was 'a momentous struggle, a frightful warfare, where two parties were fighting to obtain ascendancy.'[36] Henry Ruttan asserted that his Huguenot grandfather was 'loyal to the backbone,' but he did not elaborate on the reasons behind his grandfather's attachment to the Crown.[37] The Loyalists' mixed motives are evident in the reminiscences of Catharine White, the daughter of a Thurlow Loyalist. White recalled: 'hearing that sugar was made from Trees in Canada, and being thorough Loyalists, and not wishing to be mixed up with the Contest about to be carried on, we packed up our effects and came over to Canada.'[38] There were few stories of individual bravery and heroics, but bitter accounts of the losses endured by the Loyalists were plentiful. Such material did not lend itself easily to the portrayal of the Loyalists as heroic defenders of principle.

While the reminiscences provided little insight into the Loyalists' role in the Revolution, they did present the Loyalists as a group of hardworking men and women who toiled and suffered and triumphed over the obstacles of nature and in so doing laid the foundations of the province's progress and prosperity. Henry Ruttan recalled that 'our family, like all settlers in the Wilderness experienced at first incredible hardships.'[39] Wolves, wildcats, 'savage' Indians, swarms of mosquitoes, fever-infested swamps, and poisonous snakes were all mentioned as dangers encountered by the Loyalists. Particular attention was paid to the 'Hungry Year,' days of 'dearth and famine' during which many were said to have been reduced to surviving on the leaves of trees, herbs, and ground nuts, or soup bones passed from family to family. James Dittrick maintained that such hardships were character building, instilling industrious habits and trust in Providence. 'Perseverance and industry,' Dittrick observed, were soon rewarded and the wilderness replaced by 'thriving homesteads.'[40]

The contributions made by Loyalist women during the Revolution and resettlement in Upper Canada received comment in many reminiscences. Roger Bates of Cobourg recalled that his grandmother was an 'active,' 'intelligent,' and 'wonderfully industrious' woman, who shared his grandfather's 'indomitable courage' and 'love of the British Constitution' and happily left the comforts of her former home to begin life anew in the wilderness.[41] While their husbands served in the Loyalist militia or sought refuge from Patriot harassment, many women found themselves solely responsible for the care and maintenance of their homes and property. 'The farms,' James Dittrick asserted, 'were left to the care of the women, who seldom ate of the bread of Idleness.'[42] The many demands placed on Loyalist women during resettlement were described by Catherine White, who recollected that her mother 'used to help chop down trees' as well as attend to 'household duties.'[43] Life in the pioneer family was often characterized by mutual dependence, as husbands, wives, and children laboured together to fulfil the family's needs. John Clark asserted that 'everything was performed by a division of labour so that all performed their parts and imbibed a spirit of industry.' The importance of women's work to the economic success of the family was also noted by Clark, who observed that 'wherever the spinning wheel and loom were at work that family was industrious and prosperous.'[44] Women were especially commended for their ingenuity and resourcefulness and their ability to persevere in difficult circumstances.

Descriptions of pioneer achievement and ingenuity served the interests of official history well and became an integral part of the Loyalist tradition. The utility of the reminiscences was severely limited, however, by a pervasive nostalgia that idealized pioneer society and denigrated the present. Pioneer society was repeatedly asserted to have been free of 'unsettled minds,' 'political strife,' and 'squabbling.'[45] Amelia Harris, the daughter of Long Point Loyalist Captain Samuel Ryerse, professed that during those 'halcyon days' the 'greatest good feeling existed amongst the settlers, although they were of all nations and Creeds, and no Creeds ... Crime was unknown in those days, as were locks and bolts. Theft was never heard of, and a kindly, brotherly feeling existed among all.'[46] Notwithstanding the 'numerous privations' suffered by the Loyalist pioneers, John Clark referred to the period as 'the happiest hours of existence.'[47]

The idealization of the past was frequently followed by a profound sense of loss and declension. John Kilborn, the son of a Brockville Loyalist, insisted that 'At this early date, the State of Society, however humble, was in many respects I think superior to the present. All the parties then were more or less dependent on each other for favours and occasional assistance, and all felt more or less interested in each other's condition and prosperity ... all were acquainted and were friends, entirely unlike our present position.'[48] The loss of community was also lamented by James Dittrick. 'We visited one another,' Dittrick asserted, 'and all appeared like one family. There was then no distinction, as is the case nowadays – all were on an equality and ready to do any kind acts and services for one another.' 'I am decidedly of the opinion,' Dittrick concluded, 'that true happiness, as far as human nature has the privilege of enjoying it, was far more abundant then than the present frivolities of the age.'[49]

To many of the Loyalist generation it appeared that the industry and perseverance that had built the province had been replaced by extravagance and false pretensions. Thomas Gummersal Anderson, the son of a lieutenant in the British army, recalled that 'in these primitive times every inhabitant in the country was striving might and main to earn an honest and comfortable living. None was idle. People were honest, attended to their own business and were kind, accommodating and friendly to each other. No banks to encourage extravagance and indolence with the proud spendthrift, or to excite envy in the breasts of his less presuming, though perhaps more worthy, neighbours'. Anderson had few doubts about the forces that had produced such degeneration. 'The young of the present day wallowing in wealth, yes, the hard-earned wealth of their forefathers,' Anderson insisted, 'have became such lumps of stalking pride and arrogance, that to remind them of old times, when their fathers gained an honest livelihood by holding the plough and their mothers by household economy assisted in providing property for their offspring, is to bring upon your head every evil their weak minds can invent or command.'[50] Many contrasted the hardiness of pioneer wives, who 'gloried in their occupations,' with the frivolous fashion concerns of the current generation of women.[51] Such sentiments conveyed a fear that the accomplishments of the Loyalists were in danger of being lost and forgotten in the prosperity and materialism of the present.

Although the vernacular past is based in personal experience, it needs to be stressed that recollections are malleable and undergo constant revision in the light of subsequent knowledge and present need. The reminiscences thus reveal as much, if not more, about the contemporary position and condition of the individuals concerned as they do about the reality of the past. The individuals contacted by Coventry, Ryerson, Merritt, and Canniff were well into their seventies, eighties, and nineties, usually of modest means, and typically lived in older rural areas of the province that were in a state of decline. The feelings of disenchantment with the present and idealization of the past expressed in the reminiscences are typical of the elderly and individuals and groups that feel marginalized by society. Psychologists attribute the nostalgia of the elderly to a naturally occurring mental process termed the 'life review.' Awareness of 'approaching dissolution and death' results in 'a progressive return to consciousness of past experience,' which 'absorbs one in attempts to avoid the realities of the present.'[52]

'The nostalgic evocation of some past state of affairs,' sociologist Fred Davis maintains, 'always occurs in the context of present fears, discontents, anxieties or uncertainties, even though they may not be in the forefront of awareness.'[53] The pervasive nostalgia of the reminiscences represented a search for continuity amid the discontinuity and disorientation that accompanied the transformation of Upper Canada into an increasingly complex commercial society. Such sentiments were not confined to the passing Loyalist generation. William Canniff observed that 'there exists, as one characteristic of the nineteenth century, an earnest desire on the part of many to recall, and, in mind, to live over the days and years that are past.'[54] A few voices began to raise concerns about the increasing complexity of society and the growing influence of urban centres, institutions, and classes. Among the most prominent of these was the Niagara journalist and man of letters William Kirby.

In 1859 Kirby published an epic poem, *The U.E.: A Tale of Upper Canada*, to honour 'the noble Patriarchs of Upper Canada,' who 'with this goodly land, the fruit of their early toils and almost incredible hardships, have left us the still nobler inheritance of their patriotic and loyal example.' A nostalgic ode to a simpler agrarian past, the poem tells the story of Walwyn, an English yeoman who leaves England following the Napoleonic wars in order to escape the social and political upheavals accompanying the industrial revolution. Shortly after his arrival at Niagara, Walwyn meets an old Loyalist, Ranger John, who recounts his experiences during the Revolution:

> I sought but truth and rights; I was a man
> When first those loud complaints of wrong began.
> I loved my king and boldly dared despise
> Their factious tales and base, disloyal lies.
> For we had lived an honest country life,
> Apart from towns and politics and strife,
> Felt no oppression and perceived no ill
> That peaceful means might not redress at will.

Walwyn and his sons settle among the farmers of Niagara and quickly are assimilated into the Loyalist community. When news of the Rebellion of 1837 reaches Niagara, it is Walwyn and his sons who are first to answer Ranger John's call to arms.[55] For Kirby, Loyalism was not the exclusive domain of the Loyalists of 1784 and their descendants, but rather the product of a particular social outlook.

Kirby's disdain for industrialism and his attraction to a romanticized Loyalist past were rooted in personal experience. Kirby was born on 23 October 1817 at Kingston-upon-Hull, Yorkshire. His father, a journeyman tanner, was among those traditional craftsmen whose skills had been devalued by the introduction of machines. Like many others whose trade and status had been undermined in the evolving industrial order, the Kirbys emigrated to America in 1832. After a brief stay in New York City, the family moved to Cincinnati, Ohio, where Kirby was enroled in Alexander Kinmount's school before entering his father's trade. In 1839 Kirby left the family home in Cincinnati, Ohio, and moved to Canada. Kirby later recollected that he 'came to a resolution to go to Canada and aid in the defence of the Provinces' when he learned of the formation of Hunter's Lodges sympathetic to Rebels of 1837. 'I had a tincture of U.E. Loyalist blood in my veins and the spirit of it in my heart,' Kirby explained. It was with a loyal heart, that Kirby set foot in Canada, 'being the last almost ... of the U.E. Loyalists who came in.'[56] Kirby's account of his decision to move to Canada, written over sixty years after the fact, is largely apocryphal. Just as his father found it difficult to practise his trade in England, tough times likely forced Kirby to look for work elsewhere, first in Toronto, then in Montreal and Quebec, before finally settling in Niagara-on-the-Lake and setting up his own tannery.

A man of great ambition, Kirby earnestly desired to rise above his plebeian rank. Regarded by many as 'a handsome upstart and adventurer,' Kirby 'acquired the aims and habits of the learned and exclusive.' It was his marriage to Eliza Madeline Whitmore in 1847, however, that 'put his feet upon the social ladder.'[57] The daughter of John Whitmore and granddaughter of Captain Daniel Servos, Eliza came from pure Loyalist stock. Significantly, Kirby began work on *The U.E.: A Tale of Upper Canada* during his courtship of Eliza and devoted much of his spare time in succeeding years to researching the Whitmore and Servos family histories.[58] Kirby appears to have discovered in his own distant Loyalist ancestry and marriage into the local Loyalist establishment a ready-made and long sought-after social niche. How much of Kirby's 'quasi-professional' Loyalism was in fact deliberately cultivated for these reasons is of course difficult to determine. Dennis Duffy has observed that there is a 'compensatory quality' to Kirby's writing that suggests an all too earnest desire to cultivate a personal association with the Loyalist past.[59]

As society underwent increasing change, there was a sense that the contribution of the Loyalist pioneers would be lost and forgotten. Throughout the reminiscences collected by Coventry, Ryerson, Merritt, and Canniff, the current generation was repeatedly reminded of their indebtedness to the Loyalist pioneers and admonished to 'cherish the remembrance, and imitate the example of their forefathers.'[60] Roger Bates, the grandson of a late Loyalist, called upon Upper Canadians to 'forever remain faithful and loyal' and 'pursue the old beaten track of their fore-father[s].'[61] Henry Ruttan urged the 'rising generation' to 'remember the apparent hardships their ancestors had to undergo to obtain their present goodly heritage.'[62] In collecting Loyalist materials and chroni-cling their history, Loyalist descendants hoped to fulfil their filial obliga-tions to preserve the memory of their forefathers' accomplishments.[63] Some became obsessed with the task. Egerton Ryerson dedicated much of the last twenty years of his life to completing his history of the Loyalists. 'I am so absorbed in my historical work,' Ryerson wrote to his daughter, 'that I have little inclination to talk or write to anybody.'[64] The fear that he might not complete 'the chief legacy I can leave after me' weighed heavily upon Ryerson and was one of the principal reasons he finally decided to retire in 1875. 'I feel,' Ryerson wrote to his daughter, 'that my retirement from office is indispensable to my completing my history, & not losing the labours of years in the preliminary part of it.'[65] When Ryer-son finally completed *The Loyalists of America and Their Times* in 1880, he thanked God 'for sparing and enabling me to complete a work which has weighed upon my mind and occupied so much of my time and labour for more than a quarter of a century, and which I hope may do some honour to the fathers and founders of our country.'[66]

While the descendants of Loyalists felt compelled to persevere in their efforts to record and preserve the Loyalist past, official support for this work quickly evaporated. In May of 1862 George Coventry presented a report of his progress and a large collection of papers to the Legislative Assembly's Library Committee. On the basis of Coventry's report, the committee renewed his grant for another year. In September of 1863, however, the committee had second thoughts. 'After an examination of the material already collected' the committee reported that it did 'not think it advisable to recommend that his engagement should again be renewed.' Dissatisfied with the results of Jedediah Merritt's labours, the committee requested that he return the grant he had received in 1859 to collect documents in England.[67] The fortunes of the Historical Society of Upper Canada also suffered. Despite repeated attempts, the society was unable to secure government financing for the collection and publica-tion of documents. Unable to live up to the expectations of its founders, the society quickly dissipated.[68] The government's decision to withdraw its support appears to have been based largely on the content of the mate-rials already collected. Ambivalent in their description of the Loyalists' motives and ideas, nostalgic in tone, and pessimistic about the province's present and future prospects, the reminiscences and memoirs simply did not lend themselves to the creation of a heroic, unifying, and future-oriented official history that legitimized the ambitions and aspirations of the province's political and economic elites.[69]

Although the state could simply withdraw its financial support when it became evident that the materials being collected did not support its official agenda, Loyalist descendants could not ignore the voices of their forebears so easily. A sense of filial duty obliged them to preserve the memory of their ancestors by writing their history. Loyalist historians such as Egerton Ryerson and William Canniff, however, shared the aims and objectives of official history. The imperative to create a history that was heroic, celebratory, and forward looking dictated that the vernacular past of the reminiscences would be largely ignored and forgotten in a deliberate act of historical amnesia. Despite the considerable time and effort each had devoted to the collection of documents and reminiscences, in their respective works Ryerson and Canniff made little use of the reminiscences and memoirs they had collected from surviving Loyalists. Canniff cited the popular folklore surrounding incidents such as the Hungry Year, and Ryerson published excepts from several memoirs, but neither integrated the material into his central argument. In place of the vernacular past of the reminiscences Canniff and Ryerson constructed an invented past that satisfied the needs of official history.

William Canniff's *The History of the Settlement of Upper Canada*, first published in 1869, and Egerton Ryerson's *The Loyalists of America and Their Times*, completed in 1880, represented the culmination of the research they had begun on behalf of the Historical Society of Upper Canada. Although their works differed in style and organization, Canniff and Ryerson each wrote a history of the Loyalists designed to 'vindicate their character as a body, to exhibit their principles and patriotism, and to illustrate their treatment and sufferings.'[70] In both histories the Loyalists are portrayed as a noble elite persecuted for their principles. Adhering faithfully to their convictions, the Loyalists took up arms for the king, passed through the horrors of civil war, sacrificed their homes and possessions, endured the hardships and privations of the Upper Canadian wilderness, and laid the foundations for the nation's future progress and prosperity.

The forms and structures of historical writing have recently attracted a great deal of attention from literary critics. Theorists such as Hayden White and Dominick LaCapra have demonstrated the important role of language and form in the creation and description of historical reality.[71] When analysing the Loyalist histories written by Canniff and Ryerson, it is thus essential that we distinguish between 'story,' the sequence of events to which historians refer in constructing their narratives, and 'discourse,' the rhetorical overwriting that colours and shapes the direction of the narrative. Throughout most of the nineteenth century, history was viewed as a branch of literature rather than a science. As a branch of literature, history was expected to conform to the literary form and style of the period. The idealized portraits of the Loyalists drawn by Canniff and Ryerson were greatly influenced by the literary conventions of their day. The most important of these influences came from the romantic movement, with its emphasis on the struggle between the forces of light and darkness, the role of great men, and its vivid pictorial descriptions. Sir Walter Scott's national romances attracted a large audience in English Canada and exercised a significant influence on the writing of Canadian history.[72] Canniff and Ryerson drew upon the conventions of romance in order to fit the Loyalist past into a 'master narrative' that generated meanings on both a literal and an allegorical level. The 'story' of the Loyalists was overlaid with a discourse that appealed to the emotions and attempted to create the same sense of ancestry and unimpeachable morality and character that were distinctive features of Scott's historical romances.

Both Canniff and Ryerson cast the American Revolution as a struggle between noble and principled Loyalists motivated by 'all the ardor of a lofty patriotism' and a rebel minority 'actuated mainly by mercenary motives, unbounded selfishness and bigotry.'[73] Ryerson traced the struggle back to the original settlement of New England by the Puritans and Pilgrims. 'The government of the Puritans,' Ryerson maintained, 'was deceptive and disloyal to the Throne and the Mother Country from the first, and sedulously sowed and cultivated the seeds of disaffection and hostility to the Royal government, until they grew and ripened into the harvest of the American revolution.' 'The government of the Pilgrims,' on the other hand, 'was frank and loyal to the Sovereign and people of England.'[74] A graphic description of the persecution endured by the Loyalists followed both authors' assessment of the causes of the Revolution. Ryerson condemned the Loyalists' 'cruel treatment from the professed friends of liberty,' and Canniff denounced the rebels' 'bloodthirsty and vindicative' treatment of 'innocent old men, women, and children.'[75] The depiction of the Loyalists as 'men of property and character' drawn from the ranks of the 'most wealthy and intelligent' inhabitants of the colonies further emphasized the degree to which the they suffered for their convictions.[76] Both Canniff and Ryerson contrasted the Loyalists' comfortable lives in the American colonies with the 'hardships, exposures, privations and sufferings' encountered in the Upper Canadian wilderness. The 'spirit and determination' displayed by the Loyalist pioneers, however, transformed the primeval forest into 'a fruitful field' and laid the foundation of the province's 'growth and prosperity' and 'future greatness.'[77] Both Canniff and Ryerson included a large section on the War of 1812 in their histories. For both historians, the War of 1812 vindicated the defeat of 1783. 'The true spirit of the Loyalists of America,' Ryerson concluded, 'was never exhibited with greater force and brilliancy than during the war of 1812–15.'[78] In constructing their discourse in this fashion, Canniff and Ryerson fit the Loyalists into a master narrative of progress and redemption in which the Loyalists' convictions, heroic fortitude, and sufferings and privations were ultimately rewarded as they overcame adversity and succeeded in creating a prosperous society built upon noble principles of honour, loyalty, and patriotism.

Although the vital contribution of women to the Loyalists' settlement and success in Upper Canada was frequently commented on in the reminiscences of Loyalist descendants, women did not figure prominently in the histories written by Canniff and Ryerson. Both authors produced a gendered past that emphasized the strength, courage, endurance, and dedication of the province's heroic 'founding fathers.' When women were mentioned at all, they were typically portrayed as fragile victims of Patriot harassment or as helpless refugees in need of protection and assistance. Men, in contrast, were depicted as brave defenders of the Empire and industrious pioneers. The masculine images that filled the histories written by Canniff and Ryerson reflected the assumptions of female frailty and domesticity that characterized the period. As Janice Potter has pointed out, the manly patriotism attributed to the Loyalists had 'obvious and unequivocal gender implications' in a society that excluded women from politics and confined them to the domestic sphere – a fact recognized by advocates of women's rights, who set out at the end of the nineteenth century to reclaim a place for women in Loyalist history.[79]

One of the most striking features of both Canniff's *The History of the Settlement of Upper Canada* and Ryerson's *The Loyalists of America and Their Times* is the degree to which their characterizations of the Loyalists are based on American paradigms and sources. Each author refers to the Loyalists as 'Canada's Pilgrim Fathers.' Much of the material used by Canniff and Ryerson was drawn from the works of an American historian,

Lorenzo Sabine. Sabine was born in 1803, the son of a Methodist minister. In 1821 he moved to Eastport, Maine, where he was employed as a clerk. After several initial set-backs, Sabine eventually became editor of the Eastport *Sentinel*, a justice of the peace, and a member of the Maine House of Representatives. He had an avid interest in history. A close friend recalled: 'His business brought him into intercourse with the neighboring provincials, many of whom were descendants of the American loyalists. From them he learned much of the fortunes of their fathers that had been entirely unwritten, and which led him to a course of inquiry in a field of interest to him. He interviewed every old man and woman, though it took a journey to do it; searched parish records and explored graveyards.'[80] Proximity to the Canadian border was not the only reason Sabine took an interest in the Loyalists. Sabine was a Whig in a frontier town at the time Jacksonian democracy was at its height. As men of education and property, Whigs believed themselves to be worthy of emulation and electoral deference from the majority. Sabine saw a parallel between the position of the Loyalist elite and that of the Whigs.[81] Sabine's interest in the Loyalists resulted in a review of Simcoe's military journal in October of 1844 for the *North American Review* and ultimately in the publication of *The American Loyalists, or Biographical Sketches of the Adherents to the British Crown in the War of the Revolution* in 1847. A two-volume, enlarged edition, retitled *Biographical Sketches of the Loyalists of the American Revolution*, appeared in 1864.

Sabine set out to challenge the popular mythology that surrounded the American Revolution. The Revolution, Sabine insisted, was not a conflict rooted in 'fixed principles,' but rather one that arose from 'practical' and material considerations. Nor was the Revolution a spontaneous uprising of the whole of the American people. 'Those who have not been at the pains to investigate the matter may be surprised to learn,' Sabine asserted, 'that the opponents of the Revolution were powerful in all the thirteen Colonies; and that, in some of them, they were nearly, if not quite, equal in number to its friends, the Whigs.'[82] Not only were the Loyalists numerous, they included 'some of the most respectable persons' in the colonies. Sabine was especially critical of the treatment of the Loyalists. He condemned the acts of proscription and banishment and the seizure and forfeiture of property, which had forced many Loyalists to flee the republic, as excessively harsh and unnecessary.[83]

Sabine's attempt to provide a balanced treatment of the Revolution and the Loyalists was widely condemned in the United States.[84] While he argued that the Loyalists deserved better treatment than they had received at the hands of most American historians, Sabine was by no means pro-Loyalist and was equally determined to expose Loyalist mythology. 'The Loyalists, and those of their descendants who repeat their fathers' accusations' that the Patriots 'were mere needy office-seekers,' Sabine asserted, 'are to be turned upon in quiet nature, and to be put upon their own defence.'[85] 'Place and patronage,' 'timidity of character,' 'the dread of bloodshed,' and 'a sense of the overpowering strength and resources of England, and of the utter impossibility of successfully resisting her,' he concluded, 'appear to have been general among those who made shipwreck of their patriotism.' Those Loyalists who 'clung to the cause of the King' because of 'a calculation of personal advantage, or from the love and expectation of place and power,' Sabine insisted, 'deserve to be held up to public scorn,' as did those who entered the British service and 'fought against their brethren.'[86]

In his analysis of the causes of the American Revolution and the motives of both Patriots and Loyalists, Sabine displayed a sophistication and balance unique in his generation. His revisionism did not have a significant impact on American historiography. Nationalist historians such as George Bancroft had little use for his attempt at even-handedness. It was not until the 1920s and publication of the writings of Progressive historians such as Charles Beard and Vernon Parrington that the arguments enunciated by Sabine gained any significant following in the United States. The story was different in Canada, where Sabine's *The American Loyalists* had a considerable impact on the development of the Loyalist tradition. Canniff and Ryerson found in Sabine an American acknowledgment of the position and plight of the Loyalists. 'It is a matter for grateful recognition,' William Canniff asserted in *History of the Settlement of Upper Canada*, 'that a native of New England should take up his pen to write redeeming words on behalf of the Loyalists' that contradicted the 'distorted history and hifalutin panegyrics' typical of American school texts and Fourth of July orations. In *The Loyalists of America and Their Times*, Egerton Ryerson praised Sabine for presenting the 'true history' of the Loyalists.[87] Although Ryerson and Canniff were critical of the one-sided view of the American Revolution presented by nationalist historians such as George Bancroft, they shared with American writers a belief that history played an essential role in creating a national identity and producing a common sense of purpose and destiny among a people. A selective reading of Sabine provided exactly the kind of material lacking in the Loyalist reminiscences and memoirs and from which a heroic and redemptive narrative could be constructed.

The version of the Loyalist past constructed by Canniff and Ryerson became increasingly politicized in the years following the publication of their histories. Advocates of closer ties to the Empire such as Alpheus Todd looked to the Loyalist example to further the cause of imperial unity. In an 1881 article entitled 'Is Canadian Loyalty a Sentiment or a Principle?' Todd praised the 'wisdom and foresight' of the Loyalist founders of Upper Canada who 'deliberately preferred the loss of property and the perils incident to their flight into the wilderness, rather than forgo the blessings of British supremacy and monarchical rule.' By refusing 'to relinquish their cherished convictions,' the Loyalists avoided the 'excesses' of republicanism and preserved for future generations all the benefits of 'stable Christian government,' 'the supremacy of British law,' and 'free institutions.' Todd denounced the 'crafty or thoughtless propagandists' who advocated independence, and he appealed to Canadians to remain true 'to the lessons of their past history.'[88] W.D. LeSueur challenged Todd's interpretation of the Loyalists' devotion to the Empire a few months later in an article entitled 'The True Idea of Canadian Loyalty.' LeSueur condemned the Loyalists' 'submission to arbitrary authority' and suggested that they would have abandoned their allegiance to the Crown and remained in the United States but for the 'odium into which they had fallen with their neighbours.' LeSueur warned Canadians not to be misled by exaggerated claims of the Loyalists' dedication to the Empire and insisted that 'true loyalty' was to be found in patriotic allegiance to one's own country and in support for greater independence.[89] It was not until the 100th anniversary of Loyalist settlement in 1884, however, that the Loyalist past became the subject of intense interest and debate.

The publication of William Canniff's *The History of the Settlement of Upper Canada* and Egerton Ryerson's *The Loyalists of America and Their Times* marked the culmination of the efforts begun at mid-century to create a history for the province. With the appearance of both works, all of the constituent elements of the Loyalist tradition were in place: the Loyalists' dedication to the British Empire, the persecution they suffered for their principles, the hardships and privations they endured in the Upper Canadian wilderness, their vigilant anti-Americanism, and finally, their elite social status. The forces underlying this process of transformation were complex. The province's economic growth, expansionist ambitions, and sectional tensions combined to produce a growing national sentiment and a desire for a celebratory history of origins that would sanction future aspirations. At the same time, the growth of the state and the need to construct a public out of the province's diverse population contributed to official interest in the production of a unifying and future-oriented past. The anxiety produced by the passing of the last of the Loyalist pioneers, the vilifying treatment of Upper Canada's founders presented in nationalist American histories, and the filiopietism of Loyalist descendants ensured that much of this emergent historical consciousness was focused on the province's Loyalist origins. Although the legislature financially backed the first efforts to collect and preserve historical materials connected with the province's Loyalist founders, state support for Loyalist history was withdrawn when it became evident that the nostalgic and idiosyncratic vernacular past contained in the reminiscences and memoirs of surviving Loyalists did not meet the needs of official history. A sense of filial obligation compelled Loyalist descendants such as Canniff and Ryerson to persevere in their work. Heavily influenced by the conventions of romance and the works of the American historian Lorenzo Sabine, Canniff and Ryerson produced an idealized version of the Loyalist past that greatly influenced the way in which the Loyalists were portrayed by publicists and promoters in later years.

3

'Loyalism is not dead in Adolphustown': Community Factionalism and the Adolphustown Loyalist Centennial Celebrations of 1884

Throughout the summer of 1884 celebrations were held in Adolphustown, Toronto, and Niagara to commemorate the centennial of the settlement of the Loyalists in what is now Ontario. In the past, historians have frequently looked to the celebrations surrounding significant anniversaries of individuals and events to provide insight into the mind-set of a period or people. Treated in this fashion, celebrations often appear as public expressions of a widely accepted popular consensus. This approach has been challenged in recent years by historians such as Eric Hobsbawm and George Mosse who interpret such events as exercises in political and cultural hegemony. According to this view, the past is celebrated in the present to lend authority and legitimacy to the positions of individuals, organizations, occasions, morals, values, and views of the world. The ritual and ceremony employed on such occasions serve to structure and present particular interpretations of social reality in a way that ascribes permanence to what are actually evanescent cultural constructs. Although the concept of hegemony deepens our understanding of the ways in which the past is called to serve various interests, the proponents of this interpretative framework have been too quick to attribute the organizers of celebrations with a single mentality and to equate intentions with effects. An in-depth examination of the 1884 Loyalist centennial celebrations reveals a much more involved situation as different groups and interests competed with each other for control over the content, meaning, and uses of the past.

In analysing commemorative celebrations, it is imperative that we go beyond their rhetorical and ideological content and give careful consideration to the internal process of cultural construction to see how, when, and at whose instigation the celebrations came about. It is only by placing

such events in their social context, establishing the intentions of the organizers, and carefully examining the responses of the public that they can
be fully appreciated. Approached in this way, the meaning of commemorative celebrations appears much less unified than many studies of events
of this sort have acknowledged. The celebration of important anniversaries in a nation's, people's, or community's past is rarely the product of a
common outlook and objective, nor are the intended audiences passive
recipients of the messages conveyed on these occasions. The tensions and
conflicts that surround commemorative celebrations demand a more
complex understanding of the invention of tradition as a set of heteroge-
neous interactions in which hegemonic intentions are accommodated,
resisted, and reshaped in a variety of ways.

In *The Sense of Power* Carl Berger interpreted the 1884 Loyalist centennial celebrations as significant indicators of the emergence of a popular
and 'indigenous variety of Canadian imperialism.'[1] A careful examination
of the conception, organization, and reception of the 1884 celebrations
reveals a far more complex range of motivations and ideas. The organizers of the Adolphustown, Toronto, Niagara, and Six Nations celebrations
used the Loyalist centennial as a vehicle to serve a number of causes and
interests, not simply those of imperialism and nationalism. Underneath
the imperialist and nationalist political rhetoric of some organizers,
moreover, lay larger social concerns. While there was a general consensus
about the need to commemorate the centenary of the Loyalists' arrival in
the province, there was little agreement about the nature of the Loyalist
past or the most appropriate means of celebrating the event. The Loyalist
centennial consequently became a battleground where competing
groups and localities vied with each other to shape the past according to
their own interests and purposes. Although organizers hoped to use the
Loyalist centennial to win public attention and support for their various
causes, the celebrations had the unintended result of alienating many
people, who criticized efforts to present the Loyalists in socially exclusive
or politically narrow terms. Among the general public, the pioneer tradition remained more popular than the official lines taken by the organizers of the 1884 celebrations.

Regimental bands, patriotic addresses, the laying of cornerstones, torch-
light parades, fireworks, costumed cavalcades, historical displays, and athletic games: these were just some of the events scheduled for the three-
day celebration of the Loyalist centennial held at the small Bay of Quinte
community of Adolphustown in June of 1884. The Adolphustown event

was the most ambitious and extensive of the celebrations organized in 1884 to mark the centenary of the arrival of the main body of Loyalists to Ontario. Prior to 1884, however, the approaching Loyalist centennial was little more than an occasional topic of conversation in Adolphustown. A prominent Picton Loyalist, Elisha Sills, initiated a campaign in the pages of the Kingston *Daily News* as early as 1880 to erect a monument to commemorate the arrival of the Loyalist pilgrim fathers. Sills's repeated calls to pay homage to the Loyalists aroused little interest or response.[2] It was not until the late fall of 1883 and the appointment of the Reverend Richard Sykes Forneri as Anglican rector of Adolphustown that the topic of the Loyalist centennial engaged the attention of the community.

Shortly after his transfer to Adolphustown, the Reverend R.S. Forneri began to write letters to the editors of the local newspapers calling for the erection of some sort of monument to the United Empire Loyalists.[3] The first of these letters appeared in the Kingston *Daily News* on 20 November 1883. In the letter, Forneri related how 'at the earliest opportunity' he had visited the old Loyalist cemetery in Adolphustown and was appalled by its 'deplorable condition.' Forneri urged the community's Loyalist descendants 'to do honour' to the memory of 'their sturdy fathers, who made the wilderness a fruitful field and laid the foundation of the comfort and influence' they now enjoyed. He suggested that 'at the very least' a wall be built around the cemetery to protect it from further desecration, but hoped that the community would join together and erect 'some worthy and enduring monument' to the memory of their Loyalist ancestors.[4] The type of 'enduring monument' Forneri had in mind became clear a few days later in a 27 December 1884 letter to the Belleville *Intelligencer* in which Forneri envisioned the erection of a church of 'modest dimensions and appearance, in the early English style, built of stone from the Kingston quarries with a massive tower surmounted with turrets and battlements' situated on a ridge overlooking the Bay of Quinte.[5]

Forneri's interest in the Loyalists is at first glance rather surprising. He himself was not of Loyalist descent. The son of James Forneri and Elizabeth Wells, Forneri was born in Belfast, Ireland, on 19 November 1836. The family emigrated to Nova Scotia in 1851 when James resigned as chair of Modern Languages at Queen's College to accept a position at Windsor Collegiate school. James Forneri was offered a professorship in modern languages at University College, and the family moved to Toronto in 1853. It was his family's history of political persecution and experience as refugees that attracted Forneri to the Loyalists. His grandfather David Emmanual DeForneri was a wealthy lawyer and civil servant.

Because of his connections with the Italian Royalists, DeForneri was forced to flee the persecution that spilled into northern Italy at the time of the French Revolution, and he eventually died of exhaustion. Although originally destined to become a priest, Forneri's father, James, earned a doctor of laws degree at the University of Della Sapienza in Rome. James became actively involved in the Risorgimento, the liberal movement led by Italy's enlightened and professional classes to unite the nation, free it from foreign rule, and establish a secular constitutional government. A member of the revolutionary Carbonari and an officer in the students' volunteer corps, the Veliti Italiana, he was forced to flee Italy in 1821 following the defection of Prince Carignan and the invasion of Austrian troops. Exiled in Spain, James readily joined with Spain's liberal forces to defend the country's constitution against the machinations of Ferdinand VII. He was again forced to flee and sought refuge in England in 1824.[6] Richard claimed that his interest in the history of the Loyalists was a product of 'heart felt sympathy.' 'I take more than a passing interest in the story of those noble sleepers,' he confessed in the Kingston *Daily News*, 'for my father was an Italian refugee from political tyranny, who staked and lost all he had in one brave blow for freedom, and who found under the flag of England that liberty which satisfied his aspirations.'[7]

There was more to Forneri's efforts to erect a memorial church dedicated to the Loyalists than personal empathy with the plight of refugees. When he arrived in Adolphustown, Forneri found his church in a 'dilapidated condition' and the parish in a 'state of indifference and apathy.' He also discovered that many of his parishioners had been attracted to Methodism and were 'lost to the Church.' 'This new project,' Forneri wrote in a letter to the Society for the Propagation of Christian Knowledge, 'is not only necessary for use, and in view of Methodist efforts, but as a means of raising the parishioners to animation and beginning a better state of things.'[8] Forneri clearly hoped to appropriate the community's Loyalist past in order to boost the fortunes of a declining Anglican church. 'I know not of a church which should more properly be foremost in rearing such a memorial edifice,' Forneri wrote in the Belleville *Intelligencer*, 'than the church of that country and sovereign for whose sake they "counted not their lives dear unto them," the church to which so many of them and of their children adhered, as a necessary part of their Loyalty to the British Crown.' Forneri wistfully concluded: 'I do not think any denomination of Christians will be jealous of the old Church of England taking in hand this work.'[9]

Forneri's suggestion that virtually all Loyalists were members of the Church of England and that Anglicanism was a necessary attribute of Loyalism produced an immediate response in the predominantly Methodist community of Adolphustown.[10] In a letter to the Napanee *Standard*, the Reverend M.L. Pearson, a local Methodist minister, agreed that 'to permit 1884 to pass without a celebration would prove us unmindful of one of the greatest events in our country's history' and that 'an appropriate monument should be erected.' He was absolutely opposed, however, to the idea that an Anglican church constituted a suitable memorial. Forneri's 'chief design,' Pearson charged, was 'to take advantage of the centennial celebration to accomplish a sectarian purpose.'[11] Similar views were expressed by W.S. Griffen in the Toronto *Mail*. Griffen accused Forneri of attempting to make use of 'this Loyalist enterprise to build up mere denominational interest.' He reminded Forneri that among the Loyalist pioneers 'none had so few representatives as the Church of England.'[12] The suggestion that the Loyalist centennial should be observed at all was denounced in the Kingston *Daily News* by 'Kanuck.' 'Kanuck' denied that Anglicans and Loyalists were 'the only ones that first set foot in the province as settlers' and charged that much of the 'twaddle' about the Loyalists emanated from persons who 'would find it very difficult to trace any part of their origins to a UE.' 'Kanuck' advised Forneri to put his 'visions of "castles of the air"' on 'canvas and hang then up in his study.'[13]

Forneri was not without his supporters. A letter to the Napanee *Beaver* signed simply 'UEL Friend' accused the critics of the memorial church project of attempting to 'throw the apples of discord and jealousy among the simpleminded friends of the memorial church of Adolphustown.' M.L. Pearson was described as 'one of those unhappy people affected with a green eye, that looks askance at every proposition not imanating [*sic*] from themselves.'[14] Another letter signed 'A Loyalist' accused Pearson of being one prone 'to air his party politics' and afflicted with 'sectarianism and jealousy.' The letter concluded that 'no faithful minister of Christ' would attempt to invoke such discord, but would 'unite in a patriotic spirit in commemoration of those men who preserved a noble heritage to the British Crown and laid the foundations of the great and free institutions we now enjoy.'[15]

Despite the mixed reception, Forneri pressed ahead with his plans to erect a memorial church. In December he met with prominent local Anglicans in Napanee and Kingston, sought support from his bishop, John Travers Lewis, repeated his call for a Loyalist memorial in the Napanee and Belleville newspapers, and even contacted a Toronto architect.[16] Also in December a notice appeared in the local press announcing a public meeting to be held on 10 January at the Adolphustown Town Hall to 'consider the subject of a UE Loyalist Centennial Celebration in June next on the spot where our pilgrim fathers landed.' Although Forneri's name did not appear on the notice, he was in fact its author and responsible for its circulation in the local press. With one exception, all of the individuals named as sponsors of the meeting were members of Forneri's congregation.[17] Forneri clearly expected that the proposed memorial church would be the central topic of discussion at the meeting and would receive an enthusiastic endorsement from the community. In a letter to the *Intelligencer* he naïvely enthused that 'the meeting and the object of it ought to be a grand success.'[18]

The meeting called for 10 January was cancelled because of bad weather, however, and was rescheduled for 23 January 1884. The postponement gave Forneri the opportunity to respond to the charges of his critics. In a letter to the *Intelligencer*, Forneri denied that the memorial church was 'a sharp scheme on my own part to raise money from the public for a new place of worship in my parish by taking advantage of the feeling of the hour on UE Loyalist matters.' He insisted that he had never intended the memorial church to be 'a substitute for some general or provincial monument' and was merely acting according to the 'wishes of numbers of their [the Loyalists'] descendants.'[19] The township's Methodists in the meantime had resolved that the time was right to put into action their long-laid plans to build a new church and had decided that it too should be dedicated to the memory of the Loyalists.[20]

The depth of division in the community immediately became apparent at the public meeting held on 23 January 1884. According to Forneri's account of the proceedings, M.L. Pearson attempted to take over the meeting.[21] A heated exchange over the right of anyone not of Loyalist descent to participate in the proceedings prompted Forneri and William Dougall of Picton to walk out of the meeting.[22] 'We had barely commenced,' P.D. Davis later recalled, 'when religious bigotry and political jealousy showed themselves plainly by the treatment of the Rev. Mr Forneri from those belonging to a different church, which compelled him, from a sense of honor, to retire from the meetings.'[23] In order to defuse the situation, Davis and H.H. Allison moved that 'no political or sectarian questions be discussed.' A committee was then appointed to make the necessary preparations for holding a centenary celebration on 16 June 1884 and to consider the erection of 'a suitable monument.'[24] Pearson's efforts to take over the meeting and to discredit Forneri's plans appeared to have succeeded; Methodists occupied most of the positions on the committee appointed to oversee the centennial celebrations.

The centennial committee met on 2 February 1884. The February meeting proved as contentious and unproductive as the first. The committee became embroiled in controversy over a suggestion to add members to its ranks. On this occasion, however, the divisiveness appears to have been triggered by politics rather than religion. A 'hot discussion' erupted when Parker Allen boasted to J.J. Watson that there were more Conservatives on the committee than Liberals. Both Allen and Watson were active Conservatives, Anglicans, and among the early supporters of Forneri's Loyalist memorial church. Liberal Methodists sensed a conspiracy to infiltrate the committee. Mired in suspicion and mutual recriminations, the meeting adjourned without anything being accomplished.[25]

It is not surprising that the discussion of the Loyalist centennial was dominated by religious and political discord. Adolphustown had a long history of Anglican-Methodist tension, which extended back to the earliest days of the community. In 1788 Charles Justin McCarty began holding Methodist meetings in the Adolphustown area. The local Anglican clergyman, John Langhorn, confirmed the popularity of Methodism, reporting that less than one-fifth of the area's residents belonged to the Church of England. McCarty was arrested and charged with vagabondism in Adolphustown in 1790. Ordered to leave the district, the popular McCarty did so, but he returned and was again arrested. Local legend stated that McCarty was abandoned on an island in the St Lawrence River, where he died of starvation and exposure. McCarty more likely removed himself down river to Montreal or returned to New York. Tensions remained high between Anglicans and Methodists during the early decades of the nineteenth century. In 1810 John Roblin, a local Methodist, was prevented from taking a seat in the provincial assembly because he served as a lay preacher. Methodists particularly resented the fact that only the Anglican church could solemnize marriages. Although the Presbyterian and Lutheran churches were eventually permitted to perform weddings, it was not until 1831 that Methodists were granted the same right. All of these episodes passed into local mythology and continued to excite religious feelings late in the century.[26]

Local religious discord was compounded by the intense partisan divisions that characterized politics in Adolphustown, a legacy of Sir Richard Cartwright's desertion of the Conservative party during the Pacific Scandal of 1873 and his subsequent appointment to Alexander Mackenzie's cabinet. The electoral contest that followed Cartwright's shift in allegiance was extraordinarily bitter and divisive. Despite the efforts of Sir John A. Macdonald to array all the resources available to him against Cartwright, Cartwright managed to retain the riding. The Conservatives avenged their humiliation during the elections of 1878, when Edmund Hopper, a Camden East merchant and county treasurer, narrowly defeated Cartwright. The Conservatives' euphoria, however, was short lived. In 1879 Hopper was forced to resign his seat after funds were found missing from the county coffers. Local Conservatives immediately launched a movement to convince Macdonald to stand in the subsequent by-election. Macdonald resisted these efforts at first but finally succumbed to the enthusiastic campaign to draft him. No doubt the prospect of holding the seat formerly held by Cartwright had an irresistible appeal. Macdonald's opponent during the 1882 campaign was D.W. Allison. Again, the campaign proved acrimonious. Conservatives charged that Allison had agreed to support Macdonald if he could be convinced to stand for Lennox. The Conservative Napanee *Standard* labelled Allison a 'double dealing and unscrupulous intriguer.' Although Macdonald held the riding for the Conservatives, he did so by only 201 votes. The Conservatives' jubilation was once again short lived. Within a few weeks, Macdonald's election was declared void after thirty charges of bribery were levelled against him. In the subsequent by-election Allison again stood for the Liberals. Mathew J. Pruyn carried the Conservative banner. Allison defeated Pruyn by the narrowest of margins with only a four-vote plurality. Throughout 1884, however, Liberals and Conservatives accused each other of electoral impropriety and Allison's election was eventually declared void. Divided as the public was by a long history of religious and political dissension, it is hardly surprising that local tensions should dominate the efforts of the people of Adolphustown to organize a centennial celebration.[27]

The organizing committee next met on 29 February 1884. Although two meetings had already been held, it was not until this third meeting that the committee got around to electing officers. L.L. Bogart was selected president, probably for no other reason than the fact that he was the oldest living Loyalist descendant in the community. A.L. Morden, Parker Allen, and D.W. Allison were appointed vice-presidents and S.W. Trumpour was chosen treasurer. J.J. Watson, A.C. Davis, W.H. Ingersoll, and J.B. Allison were selected to be corresponding secretaries.[28] The election of officers clearly revealed that by this point the anti-Forneri group had taken command. Of the eight men who sponsored the original meeting, only D.W. Allison, Parker Allen, and J.J. Watson filled committee offices. Although Allen and Watson were both Anglican and Conservative, neither could easily be excluded from positions given their prominence in the community and the committee's need to have someone available to approach the Conservative government of Sir John A. Macdonald for financial support.[29] All the remaining officers were Methodists and, it would appear, of a Liberal political persuasion.

Once the anti-Forneri group assumed control of the centennial committee, it became clear that they did not have a clear idea what form they wanted the celebration to take. Although united in their opposition to Forneri's proposal to erect a Loyalist memorial church, there was little consensus about an alternative tribute. Some favoured the erection of a monument, others preferred a simple gathering of local Loyalist descendants for a picnic, and still others advocated a much grander affair. Not surprisingly, confidence in the committee's ability to organize any sort of celebration soon began to wane.

On 9 February 1884 a public meeting was held in Picton to discuss the upcoming centennial. After considerable debate a resolution was passed supporting Adolphustown as the site of the centennial celebrations. The meeting took the extraordinary step of appointing its own committees of correspondence and reception.[30] An editorial in the Picton *Gazette* intimated that this action reflected a lack of confidence in the competence of the Adolphustown committee. 'The plain duty of all in the neighbouring districts,' the *Gazette* asserted, 'is to work with a will and aid by every legitimate means to make the celebration a pronounced success.' The *Gazette* urged, however, that 'strong committees be appointed, where such has not been already, whose duty is shall be to get up such a programme as will attract a large gathering.'[31] Similar concern was expressed by the Belleville *Intelligencer.* With only three and half months remaining before the celebration was to take place, the *Intelligencer* suggested that 'should Adolphustown fail in its duty, then Belleville should organize a grand celebration.'[32] The Native Canadian Society of Belleville went even further. The 'unanimous' opinion of the society was that the celebrations should be held in 'some prominent location' and that a monument 'worthy of the Fathers of our Province' be erected instead of Forneri's proposed memorial church.[33] In its only editorial on the centennial celebrations, the Kingston *British Whig* claimed that Kingston was 'a locality quite as prominently associated with the first settlement by the Loyalists as is Adolphustown' and unlike Adolphustown was able to offer 'ample accommodations and added attractions.'[34]

Confronted by growing doubts in its ability to organize a suitable celebration, the centennial committee sent a circular to the local press assur-
ing the public that 'arrangements are being perfected, committees are
fast being appointed, working with a zeal and determination that can no
failure know.' Despite the fact that the committee had not yet discussed,
let alone agreed upon, an agenda, the circular promised that the Adolphustown celebrations would be 'the grandest affair, attended with the
largest gathering of people, ever witnessed in central Ontario.'[35] The
centennial committee also attempted to firm up support in the surrounding area for the Adolphustown celebration. At the meeting held
on 8 March 1884 Mayor R.R. Lascombe and James Cryenham of Bowmanville, the Reverend E. Loucks and J.S. McQuaig of Picton, Thomas
Claus of Tyendinaga, and Rural Dean Baker of Desoronto were made
members of the general committee.[36] Further steps were taken at the
next meeting on 12 March 1884. The committee reversed its earlier decision to exclude those not of Loyalist descent from its ranks and passed a
resolution extending 'a cordial invitation to all parties, whether UEL
descendants or not, in this and adjoining townships, for the purpose of
taking into consideration the best means of celebrating the centenary
anniversary.'[37]

The committee's efforts to extend its membership were in part a product of its precarious financial position. In March J.J. Watson and J.S.
McQuaig met with Sir John A. Macdonald and presented him with a petition urging the dominion government to direct funds to the erection of a
monument to the 'Fathers and Founders of Canada' to commemorate
their 'sufferings and privations.'[38] Macdonald turned down their appeal,
however, on the grounds that contributions would then be sought in aid
of similar celebrations elsewhere.[39] The decision disillusioned local Conservatives. 'When Sir John, himself a Canadian boy, came into power,'
Elisha Sills complained, 'we thought he would remember the poor old
UEL's, but he has so far disappointed us.'[40]

In an ingenious attempt to raise funds, the committee decided to make
all local town and county councillors members of the executive committee. As members, all councillors were expected to contribute $5 towards
the celebrations. It was also expected that as members of the centennial
committee they would respond favourably to petitions for financial assistance. The results of this appeal were less than gratifying. The Napanee
town council turned down outright the centennial committee's request
for funds.[41] After considerable debate, the finance committee of Frontenac county council recommended a contribution of $40. While some

councillors felt that such a small amount was 'an insult,' most members of the committee shared Councillor Hogan's conclusion that the county should not be using public funds 'to enable people to air themselves in Adolphustown.'[42] These sentiments were shared by the Lennox and Addington county council. Despite the objections of some councillors that public money should not be 'expended in fireworks and other frivolous pastimes,' the council approved a token sum of $30.[43] Prince Edward county proved more forthcoming, granting $100 to the centennial committee. The niggardly response of area councils reflected the widespread indifference to the celebrations beyond the immediate environs of Adolphustown.

Few local newspapers took as active an interest in promoting the Loyalist centennial as the Belleville *Intelligencer*. The *Intelligencer's* efforts, however, belie a general apathy and lack of interest. Shortly after R.S. Forneri's proposal to erect some sort of 'enduring memorial' to the Loyalists, the *Intelligencer* urged that 'Belleville, Napanee, Trenton, and other places in this district' take up the project. The *Intelligencer* had no doubt that the public would respond enthusiastically and liberally, but warned that there were just six months remaining before the scheduled celebration and that it was 'therefore absolutely necessary that what is done towards a celebration must be done quickly.' The *Intelligencer*, seemed a little less assured two months later. 'When are the descendants of the Loyalists who reside in this city going to take action on this matter?' the *Intelligencer* enquired?[44]

By mid-February the *Intelligencer* felt compelled to go to the extraordinary lengths of naming the constituency from which it expected action. The *Intelligencer* exhorted 'Belleville and vicinity' not to 'be last to organizing for the celebration' and called upon the 'Meyers, Gilberts, Ketchesons, Ostroms, Bleeckers, Farleys, Taylors, Badgleys, Canniffs &c' not to be 'indifferent to the virtues of their forefathers' and not to 'neglect to testify their respect.' The editorial concluded by warning the citizens of Belleville and area that 'procrastination is the thief of time.' Only a month before the Adolphustown celebrations were to begin, the *Intelligencer* was still reminding its readers that interest in the Loyalists should not be confined to Adolphustown. Again, readers were exhorted to take part in the 'manifestation of respect.' Despite its constant assurances that 'all are equally interested in the proposed demonstration,' the *Intelligencer's* repeated attempts to goad its readers into active support of and involvement in the centennial celebrations testify to a much different reality.[45]

The centennial committee did not actually begin to discuss, let alone plan and organize, the actual centennial program until April. Without a clear objective, the vacuum was easily filled by an overly ambitious and unrealistic agenda. Although arrangements were still at the planning stage, the committee released a program to the local press. The celebrations were to begin on 16 June 1884 and continue through to the evening of 18 June. An impressive list of speakers, including the prime minister, the premier, the Speaker of the House of Commons, and Edward Blake, was promised. On the 16th the lieutenant-governor was to lay the cornerstone to a monument dedicated to the Loyalist 'pilgrim fathers.' The remaining days were to be taken up with regattas, hot-air-balloon rides, bicycle races, baseball and lacrosse tournaments, fireworks, processions, and a sculling demonstration by world champion 'Ned' Hanlan.[46] R.S. Forneri was sceptical of the committee's ability to deliver. 'The committee have drawn up a grand programme,' he wrote William Canniff; 'in which *Hanlan, regattas,* and the *Volunteers* with their bands, figure. But there is no money to provide for expenses or prizes. Nothing really has been done or decided and the month of May is the most busy for the farmers. They have no time to devote to the arrangements.'[47] Forneri also observed that the committee continued to be plagued by internal divisions. There was considerable debate between Liberals and Conservatives over whether Richard Cartwright or Sir John A. Macdonald would be the main speaker on the first day of the celebrations.[48]

Very little of the centennial committee's ambitious program actually materialized. Macdonald, Mowat, Blake, and Kirkpatrick did not attend, nor did the lieutenant-governor lay the cornerstone to the Loyalist monument. There were no hot-air-balloon rides, bicycle races, or regattas, and the lacrosse and baseball tournaments did not go ahead as planned because the committee lacked the money to award prizes. Burdened by internal division, lack of finances, and inexperience, it is hardly surprising that the Adolphustown celebration failed to live up to its billing as the 'grandest affair ... ever witnessed in central Ontario.' The Kingston *British Whig* reported that by the third day, 'the multitude had got their fill of dust, heat, and oratory, of which the celebration chiefly consisted' and that the 'general opinion was that the demonstration was a decided failure.'[49] 'Most people thought the whole affair very tame and spiritless,' the Belleville *Daily Ontario* insisted, and they displayed 'positively no enthusiasm whatever.' The *Daily Ontario* concluded that the whole affair was '"stale," "flat," and "unprofitable."'[50] Even the usually supportive Belleville *Intelligencer* admitted that 'the celebration was not a success' and that 'we have heard numerous complaints of the manner in which the affair was managed.'[51]

The failure of the centennial celebrations to live up to expectations resulted in a series of accusations and counter-accusations as each faction attempted to blame the other. In a letter to the Belleville *Intelligencer* P.D. Davis charged that after Forneri's ostracism the centennial movement was taken over by those 'who had no sympathy with the object we had in view' and 'whose object seems to have been to make themselves conspicuous at the celebrations, and charge extravagant prices for their services.' He concluded, 'such is Gritism in Adolphustown.'[52] The Napanee *Express* responded to the charge that the celebrations were 'a Grit affair' by claiming that 'nothing could be farther from the truth' and that 'the men who put themselves most prominently in the management were Conservatives.'[53] Sir John A. Macdonald's absence became a topic of heated debate in the pages of the local press. Local party president, J.J. Watson, insisted that ill health and urgent state business had kept Macdonald in Ottawa.[54] The Liberal Napanee *Express* suggested that Macdonald 'found that it would be very dangerous for him to attempt to make political capital of his party in the presence of Sir Richard Cartwright, and in a county where he was so recently unseated for corrupt practices, and where his candidate was afterwards beaten.'[55] Elisha Sills of Picton denounced the event as 'a money grab' organized by 'bogus UE's.' He hoped that those 'who wore the mantles the old UE's had thrown over their sons' could yet meet 'before 1884 is gone.'[56]

The Adolphustown centennial celebrations were the product not of a broadly felt revival of interest in the Loyalists and Loyalism, but rather of local political and religious tensions. Indeed, throughout the entire period leading up to the celebrations, the supposed object of those celebrations, the Loyalists, remained very much in the background. Without Forneri's memorial church proposal and the reaction it provoked, the Loyalist centennial would have continued to be something about which the people of Adolphustown occasionally spoke but never felt strongly enough to take concrete action.

The much debated celebrations finally commenced on Monday, 16 June 1984. Throughout the morning, hundreds of people arrived by steamer from Belleville, Picton, Kingston, and all points in between. The crowds eagerly moved from the Adolphustown wharf to the nearby field set aside for the celebration. Row after row of refreshment stalls and tents and the loud cries of fakirs, pitchmen, and rifle gallery men gave the scene a carnival atmosphere. As the 15th Battalion from Belleville performed appropriately festive and patriotic music, the anxious multitude congregated around the banner-festooned grandstand and intently awaited the official opening.

Over the next three days, the crowds were repeatedly reminded that the Loyalists were men not afraid to 'sacrifice everything that men commonly hold dear' in order to remain true to their 'convictions' and that the 'sacrifices and labours' endured by the Loyalists were responsible for their current freedom and prosperity. Time and time again, speakers returned to the Loyalists' example and called upon their audience to 'imitate the heroism of their ancestors.'[57] There was little agreement, however, about the nature and implications of the principles that the Loyalists were said to have sacrificed so much for and that the present generation was called upon to uphold.

No speaker created as much interest or comment during the Adolphustown celebrations as did Sir Richard Cartwright, the controversial Liberal member of Parliament. Cartwright had impeccable Loyalist credentials. His grandfather the Honourable Richard Cartwright (1759–1815) had fled the rebellious American colonies in 1777 and served as a secretary to Colonel John Butler of the Queen's Rangers. After the Revolution, he became a prominent member of Upper Canada's Tory elite, holding influential positions in government, business, and law. Richard seemed destined to follow in his grandfather's footsteps. He sat as the Conservative member for Lennox in the Canadian Assembly from 1863 until 1867, when he was elected to the new federal Parliament. By 1869 Cartwright was disenchanted with the governing Conservatives and declared himself an independent. He joined Alexander Mackenzie's Liberals in 1873 and was appointed to the cabinet as minister of finance. Comments made during a meeting of the Reform Association of Toronto in the spring of 1884 put Cartwright at the centre of the heated debate over Canada's destiny. In the speech, Cartwright dismissed imperial federation as unrealistic and endorsed Canadian independence. He urged all Canadians, however, to aspire to 'another, nobler plan': the reconciliation of Britain and the United States and the confederation of all English-speaking peoples.[58]

Cartwright began his Adolphustown speech by praising the Loyalists for not being afraid to 'fight, if need be suffer and die for their convictions.' He challenged Loyalist descendants to consider 'what induced our grandfathers to make the sacrifice they did.' 'It would be a mistake to suppose [the Loyalists] wholly approved of the course of the British government,' Cartwright insisted. The Loyalists were motivated not by a blind attachment to Britain, but rather by the conviction that an 'enormous future ... awaited the English race in North America' and that it 'would be a thousand pities and a disgrace' for the English race to 'allow itself to split into fragments.' Cartwright advised Loyalist descendants that they 'can best do justice to the spirit of their forefathers by doing what they can to bring together in a union all the English-speaking races in the World.'[59]

Cartwright's remarks outraged several of the speakers who followed. The Reverend D.V. Lucas, a Methodist minister from Montreal and a descendant of Loyalists who had settled in Halton County, dismissed Cartwright's call for British-American union as impractical and contrary to the feelings of most Canadians. Observing that Canadians were proud of their ancestry and loath to sever those ties that bound them to the motherland, Lucas declared that 'the institutions of the two peoples are too diverse to admit to a political amalgamation' and their loyalty was too strong 'to admit any action which implies dismemberment of that mighty empire.' 'As Canadians,' Lucas concluded, 'this is our boast, we are a part, and we hope no insignificant part, of the British Empire, and our prayer is that nothing may ever occur, to the end of time, to sever those ties which bind our favoured and happy country to the motherland.'[60] Similar sentiments were expressed by Rev. C.E. Thomson, rector of St Mark's Church, Carleton West. Thomson exhorted the crowd 'to be true to the traditions of their forefathers, and to maintain, unbroken, their connection with the great and glorious empire for whose integrity their ancestors had so greatly suffered.'[61]

Still others advocated Canadian independence. Dr J.H. Sangster of Port Perry spoke on the final day of the celebrations. He pursued a theme of national development, describing the Loyalists as founders of the nation. Adolphustown was portrayed as Canada's 'Plymouth Rock' and the Loyalists as her 'Pilgrim Fathers.' According to Sangster, the 'tears and sighs and sweat and suffering' of the Loyalists had laid the basis for the creation of a great country. Asserting that independence was Canada's ultimate destiny, Sangster urged all Canadians to do what they could to assure the country of a future equal to its potential. Separation from the mother country, however, could not be achieved 'except in the natural way without straining or undue haste.'[62]

With a few notable exceptions, such as D.V. Lucas, there was a noteworthy lack of the vituperative criticism of the United States that historians have found inherent in the Loyalist tradition. William Canniff observed that there is much that 'is good and noble in our kinsmen over the bor-

der' and assured his audience that 'the bitterness of the last century is all
buried.' 'We are assembled to-day to celebrate the settlement of this province,' Canniff asserted, 'but we do so with no narrow feeling of sectional-
ism.'[63] The third day's activities concluded with a few warmly received
congratulatory remarks from R. Clapp, the American consul in Picton.
Despite the frequently made claim that the 'militia legend was the very
heart of the loyalist tradition,' very few references in fact were made to
the War of 1812 or the role of the Loyalists in defending Canada from
aggressive American encroachments.[64]

Significantly, most of the natives of Adolphustown who spoke during
the celebrations did not address the political issues raised by Cartwright. Rather than debate the principles for which the Loyalists had
supposedly suffered and sacrificed so much, this group dwelt almost
entirely upon the Loyalists as pioneers and the founders of the current
prosperity of Ontario. In his opening remarks, the president of the centennial committee and the area's oldest resident, L.L. Bogart, asked his
audience to transport themselves in their imagination back 'to that
time when the little company who had left all for king and country ...
came here to hew out for themselves new homes in this vast primeval
forest.' Contrasting the sufferings and hardships of the Loyalist pioneers with the comforts of today, Bogart noted that 'we would be very
ungrateful indeed did we not appreciate the sacrifices and labours of
our pioneer ancestors in procuring for us so goodly a heritage.'[65] Similar sentiments were expressed by Parker Allen and the area's Liberal
member of Parliament, D.W. Allison. Although all these speakers made
brief reference to the Loyalists' sacrifices on behalf of king and country,
they did not elaborate to any great extent upon the nature of the Loyalists' revolutionary experience, or upon the political implications of the
'principle' on whose behalf they were said to have acted. To this group,
the Loyalists' real significance was as pioneers. The principles they were
called to emulate included hard work, community cooperation, thrift,
and self-control, not the abstract concepts of constitutional liberty and
imperial organization.

One of the celebration's most popular attractions was a collection of
pioneer relics. Many local families donated artefacts for the exhibit,
which included an iron band from the first bateau built on the Bay of
Quinte, a 200-year-old pewter plate, a shoe hammer, a pair of scissors, and
a number of flints, muskets, and pocketbooks belonging to the Loyalist
settlers.[66] The public exhibition of artefacts put the lessons of history in
tangible form, authenticating the historical account presented in many of

the orations. The widespread community participation in gathering the exhibits and the interest shown in the display testified to the continuing influence of a vernacular pioneer tradition that had little to do with the Loyalist-imperialist tradition expressed by so many of the speakers imported for the occasion.

The pioneering image of the Loyalists also dominated the editorial pages of the newspapers in the region. In December of 1883 the Belleville *Intelligencer* began a three-part series of editorials entitled 'Why We Should Honor Their Memory.' The emphasis throughout these articles was on the Loyalist as pioneers. The first article dealt with the hardships the Loyalists pioneers endured during the early years of settlement. Responding to charges that the Loyalists' difficulties had been exaggerated and that they had received free land, food, tools, and seed, the *Intelligencer* reminded its readers that many of the Loyalists were soldiers with little experience of farming and few possessions. The *Intelligencer* recalled that during the Hungry Years many families 'were reduced to roots, leaves, and bark to sustain life' and that men 'wandered for miles in search of a crust of bread, or a beef bone to make soup.' The second article contained detailed descriptions of the difficulties experienced by the settlers in getting their meagre crops to mills fifty or sixty miles away over roads that were little more than blazed 'bridle paths' through the woods. The *Intelligencer* praised the ingenuity of the Loyalist pioneers in overcoming these difficulties and the cooperative spirit of the community as all banded together to secure each other's welfare. The final instalment in the series called upon the descendants of these 'noble Pilgrims' to emulate their pioneer forefathers and to do honour to their memory by organizing a 'demonstrative tribute' in appreciation of their 'heroic labors.'[67] In an article entitled 'Looking up the History' in the Kingston *British Whig* the hardships of settlement experienced by the 'noble Pilgrims also were described at length.'[68] Among local papers, only the Napanee *Standard* emphasized the Loyalists' role in the American Revolution and insisted that it was their commitment to principle that 'prompted them to give up lands and homes and comforts rather than forswear allegiance to sovereign and country.'[69]

The tendency to look back upon the Loyalists primarily as pioneers disturbed men like D.V. Lucas. He insisted that 'however much we may admire [the Loyalists'] courage and fortitude in braving the vigours of Canadian winters, and the difficulties of making homes for themselves and their posterity in the Canadian forests,' the 'spirit which brought them hither' was of infinitely greater significance.[70] According to Lucas that spirit consisted of an unwavering allegiance to the British Empire and British constitutional principles. The press and area residents, however, were clearly more interested in celebrating the Loyalists as local pioneers.

At a February meeting of the committee organizing the 1884 Loyalist centennial celebrations in Toronto, the Reverend R.S. Forneri jested: 'Loyalism is not dead in Adolphustown, though it may be in a state of suspended animation.'[71] Forneri's quip provides an appropriate epithet for the Adolphustown celebrations. Although the approaching centennial had been an occasional topic of discussion in the town, it was not until the arrival of Forneri and his controversial proposal to erect a memorial church that the local population was awakened from its lethargy. A complete understanding of the significance of the Adolphustown celebrations must take into account local divisions. Long-standing religious and political rivalries between Methodists and Anglicans and Liberals and Conservatives dictated the dynamics that shaped the centennial celebrations as various factions attempted to appropriate the Loyalist past for their own purposes.

Although it has been argued that 'the literature of the centennial celebrations contained the quintessence of the Loyalist tradition and confirmed that an indigenous variety of Canadian imperialism had appeared,' there was in fact little agreement on the consequences of the Loyalists' dedication to principle.[72] Men like Sir Richard Cartwright claimed that Canadians could remain true to their Loyalist heritage only by pursuing friendly relations with the United States and promoting Anglo-American reconciliation. Such suggestions were heresy to men like D.V. Lucas who insisted that the Loyalists were a divinely chosen, superior class of men who demonstrated unfailing loyalty in the face of untold suffering and persecution because of their steadfast devotion to British constitutional principles and the British Empire. Others openly advocated Canadian independence. Most, however, showed little interest in the ideological debate surrounding the Loyalists and were satisfied simply to celebrate their contributions as local pioneers. To a large number of those gathered the celebration was essentially an occasion for recreation and amusement. It is thus incorrect to talk of a single Loyalist tradition. There was not one tradition but rather a wide range of viewpoints. Significantly, the view of the Loyalists held by the population at large differed considerably from the tradition usually described by historians. When not completely indifferent, most people thought of the Loyalists in terms of their pioneer experience, not in terms of the American Revolution, British constitutional principles, or the British Empire.

The 1884 Loyalist centennial celebrations passed quickly from the public consciousness in Adolphustown. In an 1896 pamphlet, 'Adolphustown Ramblings,' local journalist and amateur historian T.W. Casey complained that the Old Loyalist burying ground was once again in a state of disrepair. 'It is much to be hoped,' Casey concluded, 'that some movement may yet be made to better preserve and guard their last resting place.'[73]

William Hamilton Merritt

William Kirby

Egerton Ryerson

William Canniff

Sketch of R.S. Forneri's planned Loyalist memorial church in Adolphustown

Unveiling of Loyalist monument, Adolphustown

George Taylor Denison III, one of the principal organizers of the
Toronto Loyalist centennial celebration

1784. 1884.

CENTENNIAL
CELEBRATION
OF THE
SETTLEMENT OF THIS PROVINCE
BY THE
U. E. LOYALISTS
WILL BE HELD AT
NIAGARA,
UNDER THE PATRONAGE OF THE COUNTY COUNCIL OF LINCOLN, ON THE
FOURTEENTH OF AUGUST, 1884

The following Gentlemen form the GENERAL COMMITTEE for the Celebration:

His Honor J. B. Robinson, Lt. Governor of Ontario; the Warden, Reeves and Deputy-Reeves of the County of Lincoln; R. H. Smith, Mayor of St. Catharines; H. S. Garrett, Mayor of Niagara.

Rt. Rev. T. B. Fuller, Bishop of Niagara.
Hon. W. H. Dickson, ex-Senator
Hon. J. B. Plumb, Senator,
Hon. J. R. Benson, Senator,
J. C. Rykert, M. F.
S. Neelon, M. P. P.
Dr. Ferguson, M. P.,
Col. Moran, M. P. P.,
L. McCallum, M. P.
R. Harcourt, M. P. P.
D. Thompson, M. P.,
J. Baxter, M. P. P.,
T. R. Merritt St. Catharines.
J. P. Merritt, do
Col. Macdonald, do
R. Lawrie, do
Thos. Keyes, do

Jas. Seymour, St. Catharines.
J. A. Woodruff, do
W. Kirby, Niagara,
J. G. Dickson, do
R. Dickson, do
Col. Clench, do
Dr. Anderson, do
Dr. Canniff, Toronto.
C. E. Eyerson, do
Col. G. T. Denison, do
D. B. Reed, do
J. Playter, do
R. B. Miller, do
J. C. Kirby, do
Rev. Dr. Withrow do
G. A. Clement, do
Ven. Archdeacon McMurray, Niagara.

A. Hill, Chief of Mohawks, Bay of Quinte
S. Green, Chief of Mohawks, Bay of Quinte,
H. Paffard, Niagara
J. W. Ball, Niagara Township.
W. A. Thompson, do
J. Cooper, do
Jos. Clement, do
J. Butler, do
R. N. Ball, do
Alex. Servos, do
Peter Whitmore, do
Rev. Dr. Scadding, Toronto.
Dr. Ruttan, Napanee.
D. W. Allison, M. P.
Rev. R. S. Forneri, Adolphustown
Arch Deacon Dixon, Guelph.

Rev. W. S. Ball, Elderton
W. A. Campbell, Chatham
Jas. Ingersoll, Woodstock.
Jas Davis, sr. Hamilton.
E. Servos, Hamilton.
T. Davis, Winona,
John D. Servos, Niagara,
J. B. Secord, Niagara
S. Secord, Louth.
Rev. J. A. Anderson, Penetanguishene,
I. P. Wilson, Welland,
Rev. W. Walsh, Fonthill,
Rich'd Miller, St. Catharines.
P. H. Ball, Thorold.
P. I. Walsh, Simcoe,
G. Whitmore, Niagara Towns'p,
Rev. LeRoy Hooker, Kingston.

THE CELEBRATION WILL BE HELD
ON THE HISTORIC PLAINS OF NIAGARA.
All descendants of the U. E. Loyalists, and all other loyal Canadians are cordially invited to join in this Celebration.

After the Pic-Nic in the adjoining Oak Grove, the business of the day will commence at one o'clock p m., when addresses will be delivered by prominent gentlemen. In case of rain, the addresses will be delivered in the Court House

---

On the following day, Friday 15th, there will be Races and other Athletic Games on the Commons,
A SEPARATE PROGRAMME OF WHICH WILL BE ISSUED

JAS. HISCOTT, Warden.   F. A. B. CLENCH, Chairman.   DAN. SERVOS, Secretary.
GOD SAVE THE QUEEN.

Broadside, 1884 Niagara Loyalist centennial celebration

1784.

1884.

CENTENNIAL
CELEBRATION
—MOHAWK,—
THURSDAY SEPT. 4TH, 1884.

In commemoration of the landing of the MOHAWKS on Tyendinaga Reserve, to be held in the grounds near the Lower Church---one mile from Deseronto. The following gentlemen will be present on the occasion and deliver addresses :---

John White, M. P.; W. Hudson, M. P. P.; Alex. Robertson, M. P. (West Hastings). Dr. Canniff, Toronto; W. Kirby, Esq., Niagara; A. Ford, Esq., Belleville; Dr. Ruttan, Napanee; Rev. G. A. Anderson, Penetanguishene; Rev E H M Baker, Tyendinaga; Rev T G Porter, Rev J C Ash and A L Roberts, Esq., Shannonville; Chief Sampson Green and Ex-Chief W. J. W. Hill, Reserve.

Meals will be furnished on the grounds by the Committee at twenty cents. Admission to the grounds, ten cents.

Platforms will be erected and STRING BANDS furnished.

THE DESERONTO CORNET BAND WILL BE IN ATTENDANCE.

COMMITTEE OF MANAGEMENT:

A. Culbertson, Sampson Green, Cornelius Maricle, Wm. Green, T. Blanchard, D. Smith, Joseph John, John Loft, J. P. Brant, Josiah Brant, Wm. Powles, and Thomas Claus.

SOLOMON LOFT,   F. CLAUS,   W. J. W. HILL,
Chairman.   Treasurer.   Secretary.

GOD SAVE THE QUEEN.

Broadside, 1884 Mohawk centennial celebration, Tyendinaga

Joseph Brant monument, Victoria Park, Brantford

Laura Secord monument at Lundy's Lane

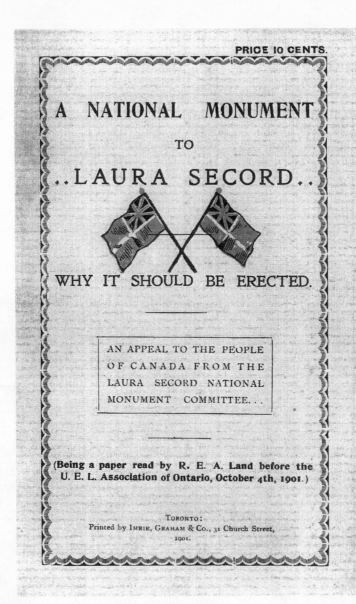

Cover of R.E.A. Land's *A National Monument to Laura Secord: Why It Should Be Erected*

Laura Secord monument at Queenston Heights

Barbara Heck monument, Prescott

George Sterling Ryerson, founding president of the United Empire Loyalist
Association of Ontario

United Empire Loyalist monument, Hamilton

United Empire Loyalist monument, Belleville

United Empire Loyalist Association tree planting at Queen's Park, Toronto,
Empire Day 1902

4

'A sacred trust':
The 1884 Toronto, Niagara, and Six Nations
Loyalist Centennial Celebrations
and the Politics
of Commemoration

On the morning of 3 July 1884 hundreds of Torontonians gathered at the city's horticultural pavilion to commemorate the centennial of the settlement of the province by the Loyalists. Between speeches delivered by William Canniff, Senator George W. Allan, Lieutenant-Colonel George Taylor Denison, and Chief Sampson Green of the Six Nations reserve at Tyendinaga, the crowd joined in singing 'Rule Britannia,' 'Who's for the Queen?' and 'If England to Herself Be True.' Charlotte Morrison recited Rev. LeRoy Hooker's poem 'The United Empire Loyalists' and Etheline Kittson's poem 'Loyalist Days.' The proceedings concluded with a benediction by Rt Rev. T.B. Fuller, Bishop of Niagara, and the singing of 'The Maple Leaf Forever.'

The scene was repeated on 14 August in Niagara-on-the-Lake as a large crowd assembled around a bunting-festooned platform erected on the site of Upper Canada's first parliament. Tablets inscribed with the names of local Loyalists who had fallen during the War of 1812 surrounded the stage. After a few words of welcome from the master of ceremonies, R.N. Ball, and prayers led by the bishop of Niagara, Lieutenant-Governor John Beverley Robinson made a brief address, observing that 'this was the third time had been called upon to greet the descendants of the U.E. Loyalists gathered together to celebrate the deeds of their ancestors.'[1] The principal speakers during the day's proceedings were Senator J.B. Plumb, Lieutenant-Colonel George Taylor Denison, William Kirby, and Chief A.G. Smith of Grand River. The exercise concluded with three cheers for the queen.

Throughout the proceedings at Toronto and Niagara the Loyalists were upheld as a superior class of men and women, who nobly endured untold persecution and privation in order to remain true to the British

Empire and British constitutional principles. 'I have ever admired,' Bishop T.B. Fuller asserted in Niagara, 'the noble body of men who sacrificed their all – their comfortable farms and everything they had accumulated for a principle, that of loyalty to the British Crown.' The 'bravery,' 'endurance,' 'devotion,' 'gallantry,' and 'fidelity' exhibited by the Loyalists were repeatedly cited as evidence of the Loyalists' sterling character. William Kirby asserted that the Loyalists were drawn from the 'best and wealthiest class,' and Colonel George Taylor Denison hailed them as 'the very best of the old colonies.' All of the speakers appealed to the current generation to remain true to the legacy of the Loyalists. 'It must not be forgotten,' Colonel Denison concluded, 'the advantages we have to-day we owe to our ancestors, the U.E. loyalists, and the sacred trusts handed down by them should be passed on intact and unimpaired to our children.'[2]

An explicitly political message lay behind all the praise and honour heaped upon the Loyalists: advocates of Canadian independence must be silenced and the unity of the British Empire preserved and strengthened. Senator Allan concluded his remarks in Toronto by denouncing those who would 'abandon the rich heritage of centuries, and cut ourselves and our children [adrift] from the glorious memories and associations which now belong to us Canadians as members of the one great United Empire.' 'By our gathering here to-day,' Allen proclaimed, 'we desire to show that, as did our fathers in those days of old – so we desire to preserve the unity of the Empire, and shall ever honour the memory of those who cheerfully risked every worldly gain or advantage ... to preserve unbroken the ties which bound them to the Motherland.' During his Niagara speech, Senator J.B. Plumb 'scorned' those 'who urged that there would be certain advantages in dollars and cents' in establishing closer ties with the United States. 'Fealty to the monarch,' Plumb concluded, 'is deeply implanted in Canadian hearts' and 'cannot be weighed, measured or appraised.' In both of his Toronto and Niagara addresses, Colonel Denison characterized the advocates of independence as 'agitators and Bohemians' motivated by 'envy and jealousy.' 'If we were independent tomorrow,' Denison warned, 'we would be more dependent upon the United States than we are to-day upon England.'[3]

Pro-imperialist rhetoric was accompanied by a zealous anti-American jingoism. 'If Canadians know what is good for them,' Colonel Denison remarked in Toronto, 'they will have nothing to do' with the United States or its form of government. 'Are we not better off,' Denison enquired, 'than the people of a country where they carry deadly weapons

with impunity; where lax divorce laws have shaken the sanctity of the marriage tie; where the principal, if not the sole test of respectability is
wealth, and where lynch law spasmodically attempts to remedy the lax
administration of justice by the regular courts?' Denison was even more
condemnatory in his remarks at Niagara. 'The Republican form of government,' he insisted, 'attracts all those who love license rather than liberty.' The result, according to Denison, was that the United States
'attracted the worst classes from the old world' and had become 'the cess-
pool of Europe.'[4]

At first glance, the Toronto and Niagara celebrations convey an impression of consensus and unity. Without exception, the proceedings were
characterized by an anti-American and pro-imperial sentiment that portrayed the Loyalists as men of superior character who sacrificed everything in defence of the Empire and British constitutional principles. The
perception of unity, however, quickly dissolves upon closer examination.
Organizers were in fact sharply divided in their understanding of Loyalist
principles and in opinions about the most appropriate means of observing the centennial. Organizers did share, however, a common conviction
that the past could be used to provide legitimacy for their varying values
and beliefs in the face of the upheaval and disorientation that accompanied industrialization and urbanization. Although the Toronto and Niagara celebrations commemorated individuals and events of the previous
century, contemporary concerns and realities were foremost in the minds
of the organizers.

The origins of the Toronto Loyalist centennial celebrations can be traced
back to an 1876 meeting of the York Pioneers, the province's first local
historical society. At that meeting a Loyalist descendant, Richard H.
Oates, suggested that in the light of the extensive celebrations taking
place in the United States in honour of the centennial of the Declaration
of Independence, it was fitting that a similar celebration should be held
in recognition of the sacrifices endured by the Loyalist founding fathers.
William Canniff contended that since the first wave of Loyalist settlers
had not arrived in the province until 1784, a celebration would more
appropriately take place in 1884.[5] The Upper Canada Association also
proposed a commemoration of the centennial of the Loyalists' arrival.[6] In
The Sense of Power, Carl Berger maintained that 'Canadians of the loyalist
persuasion saw in the American centennial attempts to vilify their ancestors in particular and demonstrations of hostility to British American in
general. They responded with the loyalist centennial celebration in

1884.'[7] As the excitement surrounding the American festivities subsided, however, interest in the upcoming Loyalist centennial rapidly dissipated. The Loyalist centennial was not referred to in the press again until October of 1880, when Canniff Haight, a journalist and author of Loyalist descent, suggested in the *Daily Mail* that 'an Exhibition, or some other demonstration' be held 'in honour of the men, who through privation and toil, laid the foundation of this free and prosperous Province.'[8] Haight's proposal, however, also failed to arouse much interest.

It was not until the establishment of a committee in the fall of 1882 to organize celebrations in commemoration of the semi-centennial of the incorporation of the city of Toronto that any real effort was made to observe the hundredth anniversary of the Loyalists' arrival. The idea of observing Toronto's semi-centennial was conceived by the city's mayor, William McMurrich, after he had attended events commemorating the fiftieth anniversary of Buffalo's incorporation in July of 1882. The celebrations impressed McMurrich as a testimony to the 'rapid strides' and 'commercial progress' of the city. In September of 1882 McMurrich suggested that a representative committee of citizens be struck involving all organizations in the city. The intention of the celebration was to offer 'a display of our institutions and an exhibition of our resources' in such a way as would 'reveal and illustrate the City's growth and progress.' McMurrich envisaged a week-long celebration. Each day would be devoted to a particular interest. The celebrations would commence with a historical parade 'illustrative of the settlement, rise, and progress of the City.' Events on subsequent days would include a civic procession involving members of the military, police force, and fire department, and parades involving trades and industry, and benevolent societies.[9]

On 14 December 1882 William Canniff wrote to his friend McMurrich, congratulating him on the proposed semi-centennial celebrations and suggesting that 'it might be possible, and deemed advisable to widen the basis of the commemoration and celebrate at the same time the centennial of the settlement of the province.'[10] McMurrich responded favourably to Canniff's proposal and suggested that he take the initiative in making whatever arrangements were required. McMurrich and Canniff agreed that the celebration should be non-political and structured to appeal to a broad segment of the population, not just to Loyalist descendants. The Loyalists were to be honoured as the pioneer settlers of Ontario and the bedrock upon which the province's current progress and prosperity rested, not set apart as an elite clique.[11]

After several months of informal discussions with various friends and acquaintances, Canniff organized a preliminary meeting in late October of 1883 to commence arrangements for the upcoming centennial. After several suggestions had been considered, it was decided to hold a public meeting on 23 November 1883 at the Mechanics Institute.[12] In a move designed to arouse greater public interest and add credibility to the movement, Canniff invited Lieutenant-Governor John Beverley Robinson to address the 23 November meeting. Public indifference to the whole affair was evident in the sparse turnout for the November meeting. Undeterred by the poor attendance, Lieutenant-Governor Robinson predicted that 'when the nature of this movement became properly known ... there would be found a living sentiment held by scores and thousands of descendants of these men which only needed the opportunity to make it a grand success.'[13] D.B. Read's assessment of the situation was probably more accurate. Shortly after the November meeting, Read advised Canniff that 'the few of today are too far removed from the men of 1784 to be very enthusiastic about the matter.'[14]

Lieutenant-Governor Robinson commended Canniff for his initiative in calling the meeting and moved that he be appointed chairman of a committee responsible for overseeing the organization of a suitable celebration. Upon assuming the chair, Canniff described the type of event he envisioned. The celebration, Canniff insisted, should be provincial in scope and free of politics. Loyalists and non-loyalists from beyond Toronto should be actively encouraged to take part in the event. The celebration itself should consist of a morning reception given by the mayor and city council in the council chamber at which a few brief addresses would be made, an afternoon demonstration of lacrosse, an evening concert when the songs of 100 years ago might be sung in costume, and an exhibition of pioneer artefacts to remain on view throughout the semi-centennial celebrations. Canniff's proposed program failed to arouse much enthusiasm and the meeting disintegrated into a state of confusion as individuals put forth their own proposals. Lieutenant-Governor Robinson felt a procession would be appropriate. Rev. William Withrow suggested that General Depaster, a celebrated American of Loyalist descent, be asked to address the proceedings. D.B. Read suggested that since the Loyalists were such God-fearing people, a church service, preferably Methodist, ought to be part of the celebration. William Withrow protested that any service should not be of a denominational character. Since the committee was unable to agree on what form the celebrations should take, a committee of management was struck to meet and settle upon a suitable program.[15]

The committee of management eventually numbered forty-six. All of the members of the committee were prominent Toronto residents and with one exception were professionals or businessmen. Only half of the committee members were actually of Loyalist descent. Conservatives outnumbered Liberals, and four of the committee members identified themselves as independents. Almost half of the committee members were Anglicans.[16] Most of the individuals listed as sitting on the committee did not take an active part in the organization and planning of the celebration; their nominal inclusion was designed to add status to the movement in the eyes of the public. The Toronto celebrations were actually organized by a much smaller group consisting of William Canniff, George Taylor Denison, Frederick Denison, Septimus Denison, A. McLean Howard, Canniff Haight, Rev. W.H. Withrow, D.B. Read, Dr George Sterling Ryerson, and Charles Egerton Ryerson.

The organizers of the 1884 celebrations have generally been portrayed as like-minded imperialists with identical agendas. The committee of management was in fact deeply divided. Two factions coalesced around the competing visions of William Canniff and George Taylor Denison. William Canniff has been described as 'the moving force behind the whole idea of the celebration' and 'representative of the others involved in the fete of 1884.'[17] Canniff's views, however, were far more moderate and ambivalent than has often been portrayed. Canniff did not automatically condemn all things American. In his Adolphustown address, he rejoiced in the fact that Canadians and Americans were now good friends and that 'the bitterness of the last century is all buried.'[18] Canniff displayed a similar ambiguity in his attitude towards the imperial connection. Although Canniff celebrated Canada's British inheritance, he also insisted, as he wrote in *Canadian Nationality: Its Growth and Development*, that Canadians 'will be satisfied with nothing less than equality with the people of the United Kingdom' and dismissed as unfounded hysteria fears that the United States seriously coveted Canadian territory.[19] Canniff saw Canadian independence as the natural outcome of Canadian maturation and did not automatically equate the prospect of Canadian independence with either disloyalty to Britain or inevitable American annexation. In *A Patriotic Address*, Canniff asserted that 'nations, like individuals have their period of infancy, of adolescence, maturity, and, judging from the past, inevitable decline.' Canada had 'already emerged from a state of infancy' and was 'fast passing through the adolescence of life.' 'No longer an infant colony, but a country possessing many of the features of an independent nation,' Canniff was confident that this 'healthy development' would continue and that Canada would take her place among the nations of the world.[20]

Canniff's moderate views contrast sharply with the extreme and strident stance of his main nemesis, Lieutenant-Colonel George Taylor Denison III. Known by his contemporaries as 'the watchdog of the Empire' and 'her majesty's most loyal colonial born subject,' Denison inherited a family legacy of antipathy to the United States, service and devotion to the Crown and Empire, and conservative political values.[21] Denison's great-grandfather John Denison, a brewer and farmer from Heydon, Yorkshire, was induced to emigrate to Upper Canada in 1792 by Peter Russell, a family friend and the administrator of the colony. After an unsuccessful brewing venture in Kingston, John Denison moved to York, where he managed Russell's estate. His services were rewarded by a 1,000-acre land grant. The family's respectability was further enhanced in 1806 when Denison's grandfather George Taylor Denison I married Esther Borden Lippincott, the daughter of a prominent landowner and Loyalist. George Taylor Denison I added to the family tradition of service to Crown and Empire by serving with the York Volunteers during the War of 1812. The family's military tradition continued with Denison's father, George Taylor Denison II. During the 1837 rebellions Denison's father served at the battle of Gallows Hill and the siege of Navy Island. In 1838 he was commissioned a lieutenant in the Governor-General's Body Guard and in 1846 took command of the regiment. Denison's father played a prominent role in the reorganization of the Canadian militia in 1855 and in the establishment of the Queen's Own Rifles in 1860. He was also an alderman for St Patrick's ward.[22]

George Taylor Denison III was born in 1839. Although his academic performance was unspectacular, he eventually received a law degree from the University of Toronto. He was called to the bar in 1866 and went into practice with his brother Frederick. That same year, Denison served during the Fenian raids and was made colonel of the 1st York Cavalry. In 1865 Denison succeeded his father as an alderman for St Patrick's Ward. Denison wrote extensively about military matters and in 1877 won a prestigious Russian competition for *A History of Cavalry from the Earliest Times with Lessons for the Future* and was appointed police magistrate for Toronto. Denison's nationalism and anti-Americanism found expression in the Canada First movement and later in the Imperial Federation and British Empire Leagues in Canada.[23]

Denison's rabid anti-Americanism and ultra-imperialism were shared by his brothers Frederick and Septimus and by A. Maclean Howard. Frederick Denison served with the militia during the Fenian Raids of 1866, accompanied Wolseley in 1870 on the Red River Expedition, and in 1872 assumed command of the Governor-General's Body Guard. He sat as an alderman for St Stephen's Ward from 1878 until 1884. In the fall of 1884 Frederick left municipal politics to command a Canadian expedition to the Nile in aid of General Gordon's campaign in Sudan. After his return, Frederick successfully contested the federal riding of West Toronto for the Conservatives in 1887. Septimus Denison followed in his brothers' footsteps. He was commissioned an officer in the Royal Canadian Regiment in 1888, served as aide-de-camp to the governor-general, Lord Aberdeen, from 1893 until 1898, when he volunteered to serve in South Africa during the Boer War. The Denisons found an ally in A. Maclean Howard. Howard's father emigrated to Upper Canada in 1819 and married into the Loyalist family of Col. Allan Maclean, commander of the 84th Highland Regiment. In 1854 Howard was made clerk of the first division court. He later became a director of the Central Bank of Canada and of the Confederation Life Insurance Company.[24]

William Canniff's views were shared by Canniff Haight. Haight was among the first persons to suggest that a celebration should be held in 1884 in honour of the centennial of the settlement of Ontario by the Loyalists. Haight was born in 1825, the son of a Picton area farmer and the grandson of one of the original Loyalist settlers of Adolphustown. In 1850 he established himself as a druggist and bookseller in Picton. Haight served as chairman of the Picton School Board and president of the Mechanics Institute and was instrumental in establishing the first county library. By 1884 Haight had moved to Toronto and established himself as a well-known journalist and author.[25] Haight produced a series of articles for the *Canadian Monthly* and *Canadian Methodist* magazines to further interest in the centennial movement. These articles were consolidated into book form and published in 1885 as *Country Life in Canada Fifty Years Ago: Personal Recollections and Reminiscences of a Sexagenarian.*

Haight's understanding of the significance of the province's Loyalist past differed significantly from that of George Taylor Denison. Unlike Denison, Haight had very little to say about the American Revolution, the War of 1812, or Loyalist principles. According to Haight the Revolution was not a travesty but rather the justifiable result of 'the narrow-minded and unyielding policy of George III.' Although critical of the hypocrisy of the Patriots, who claimed to be defending freedom yet oppressed and persecuted those who differed from them, Haight observed that 'the wounds that were inflicted nearly a century ago have happily cicatrized, and we can now look with admiration on the happy progress of the American people in all that goes to make up a great and prosperous country.' He believed that the Loyalists ought to be remembered and celebrated because they were pioneers. According to Haight, it was 'the muscular arm of the sturdy pioneer' that laid 'the foundation of Canadian prosperity.' 'We can hardly realize,' he concluded, 'that not a century has elapsed since these strong-handed and brave-hearted men pushed their way into the profound wilderness of Upper Canada.'[26]

Similar views were held by the Reverend William Henry Withrow, the editor of the *Canadian Methodist Magazine*, and David Breakenridge Read, a prominent Toronto lawyer and former mayor of the city. Like William Canniff and Canniff Haight, both men had an ardent interest in Canadian history. Withrow's works included *Barbara Heck: A Tale of Early Methodism* and *A History of Canada for the Use of Schools and General Readers*. D.B. Read was one of the founding members of the York Pioneers and the author of *The Life and Times of Sir John Graves Simcoe*. Although both men were proud of Canada's British heritage, neither Withrow nor Read shared Denison's rabid anti-Americanism. While they believed the imperial connection should be maintained for the present, Withrow and Read did not dismiss out of hand the possibility of Canadian independence and both were sceptical about imperial federation.[27] The remaining two members of the committee, Dr George Sterling Ryerson and Charles Egerton Ryerson, proved more malleable and moved between the Canniff and Denison camps. Charles was a son and George a nephew of Egerton Ryerson. The Ryersons traced their Loyalist ancestry back to Colonel Joseph Ryerson, an officer in the Prince of Wales New Jersey volunteers during the American Revolution. Colonel Ryerson emigrated to New Brunswick in 1783 and moved to Upper Canada in 1799. He served with British forces during the War of 1812. George Sterling Ryerson graduated in medicine from Trinity College in 1875 and joined the staff of Toronto General Hospital. He served as surgeon to the Royal Grenadiers and accompanied the regiment to the northwest in 1885. He sat as a Conservative member of the provincial legislature for East Toronto from 1893 to 1898. Charles Egerton Ryerson was born 1847 and educated at Upper Canada College and the University of Toronto. He was called to the Bar in 1874 and later became assistant librarian of the Toronto Public Library.[28]

The inherent divisions within the committee of management were clearly in evidence during the committee's first meeting on 30 November 1883. Canniff began the meeting by stressing that the committee should aspire to 'make the celebration a provincial affair' and of interest to more than Loyalist descendants. The success of the celebrations, Canniff insisted, depended upon securing the support of other municipalities and upon not allowing political or sectarian questions to enter into the celebrations. The committee thus must make every effort to ensure that participants refrain from expressing any feeling they cherished for or against the British connection. Indeed, Canniff could not see any reason why persons who held the opinion that Canada should not always remain a dependency of Great Britain could not conscientiously participate in the proceedings. Although the Loyalist descendants celebrated the arrival of their forefathers and honoured their principles, it 'did not follow that they held the opinion that Canada must forever be a part of the British Empire. It must be useless to ignore the fact that some descendants of the UE Loyalists hold otherwise.'[29] After considerable debate, it was agreed that D.B. Read, W.H. Withrow, Charles Egerton Ryerson, and George Taylor Denison would form a committee of correspondence to draft a circular to be sent to all newspapers and municipalities in the province soliciting support for the Toronto celebrations.

Canniff's remarks appalled George Taylor Denison, who saw the centennial celebrations as an opportunity to further the cause of imperialism. Denison later acknowledged that his interest in the celebrations had been primarily political. In a letter written in 1907 to the governor-general, Lord Grey, he recalled: 'In 1882, 3 and 4 there had been quite a wave of Independence feeling going through our young men and a number of country newspapers took up the idea ... We of the Loyalist side took the opportunity of the 100th anniversary of the arrival of the UE Loyalists in 1784 to make a series of loyalist demonstrations.'[30] For Denison and his supporters, the celebrations were to be an exclusive affair in which only genuine Loyalists who remained true to their forefathers' principles would participate.

Denison was not alone in his outrage at Canniff's suggestions. Senator George Allan advised Canniff that a 'Canadian-Independence-UE Loyalist' was 'a contradiction in terms!!' 'If any sentiments of that kind are to be broached,' Allan proclaimed, 'I would rather have nothing to do with the matter!' Allan regretted that the 'UE Loyalist commemoration should be mixed up with this semi-centennial business' and suggested that a gathering of Loyalist descendants be held separate from the civic affair.[31] G.H. Hale informed Canniff, 'I greatly regret that you throw out a bait to those who would sever the connection of our Dominion with the Empire to join in the UEL Celebrations,' and he warned that if such people were to be included, 'some at least will not wish the movement Godspeed.'[32] In many respects, the Loyalists were secondary figures to these people, of interest only in so far as they could be used to support a political agenda.

The committee of correspondence met throughout the month of December to draft the circular. Despite the objections of George Taylor Denison, the final form of the manifesto clearly reflected Canniff's moderate views. The document stated, 'it is earnestly desired that this Celebration shall not be a local but a Provincial movement' involving 'all patriotic Ontario Canadians, and especially, the descendants of U.E. Loyalists in all parts of the country.' Significantly, the point was made that 'the term U.E. Loyalists' was intended 'to embrace all who came to Upper Canada in consequence of the political troubles attending the Revolutionary War, whether their names were on the Official "U.E. list" or not.' The circular stressed that the celebration was 'designed to be a patriotic tribute to the heroism and fidelity of our U.E. Loyalist Forefathers, without pronouncing judgement on the political issues which divided the British American Colonies a hundred years ago.' It thus was hoped that 'a generous tribute shall be paid to our common ancestry, without reference to party lines or political opinions.' The communique insisted that 'the *pro-tempore* Committee does not presume to make any suggestion as to the mode of the Celebration,' but rather it encouraged the organization of local committees in as many places as possible to discuss the centennial and send delegates to a public meeting to be held in Toronto on 19 February 1884, which would settle the nature of the celebration.[33]

Canniff's success in ensuring the circular's inclusive and moderate tone was largely a product of the committee's desire to secure public support in the face of growing criticism of the centennial movement. W.S. Griffen charged in the *Globe*: 'if a small committee, living in Toronto and apparently self-appointed assumes the responsibility of arranging the whole business it will amount to nothing more than a mere local enterprise, and only one item in the programme of the city's semi-centennial celebration.'[34] Another correspondent queried: 'Are the thousands of descendants of UE's in this province to be quite ignored for the sake of a few who wish to figure in the front, and become famous at the expense of others, whose claims to be recognized are equal to and beyond many that are mentioned in this movement?'[35] Several correspondents feared that the organizers had a hidden political agenda. A writer to the *Globe* wished the centennial organizers well if they 'merely wish[ed] to express their appreciation of what their forefathers did for Canada as pioneer settlers in an unbroken wilderness.' The correspondent warned that 'if the proposed revival of UE Loyalism means that those who take part in it are to be regarded as thereby endorsing any condemnation of the American colonists ... its promoters will find themselves left pretty severely alone.'[36] These views were echoed by a writer to the *News*, who asserted that he was 'heartily for a centennial celebration' that 'venerates the memory of the first settlers, who came to this vast wilderness in 1784' and 'by their toil and hardships laid the foundations of this grand province.' He believed that the centennial should honour all the early settlers, however, not just Loyalists.[37]

The public meeting held on 19 February 1884 failed to attract the widespread participation from across the province Canniff had hoped for. Only twenty-nine people actually attended the meeting. Although participation from outside Toronto was encouraged, just two municipalities sent official representatives. Warden Cyrus Kilbourne and Col. F.A.B. Clench represented the county council of Lincoln and Arthur Craig and P.H. Spohn represented the county council of Simcoe. The Napanee town council sent a letter supporting the celebration but did not send a delegate to the meeting. Several individuals attended the meeting on behalf of Loyalist descendants in their areas, but they were not officially representing their communities.[38]

Canniff began the meeting by reading a letter from Mayor McMurrich, who was unable to attend. McMurrich wished the organizers well in their endeavours to honour the 'fathers of Ontario.' He also responded to the concerns raised in the press. 'No one will deny,' McMurrich confidently asserted, that the Loyalists deserved recognition, since 'the heritage' enjoyed by 'the descendants of all' rested upon 'the hardships of pioneer life' endured 'by the founders of the province.'[39] In his opening remarks, Canniff repeated the call for an inclusive celebration that focused on the Loyalists' contributions as pioneers and avoided potentially divisive political questions. He suggested a program that included an Indian lacrosse match, a display of historical artefacts, and an evening concert of music from 100 years ago. George Taylor Denison immediately took issue with Canniff's proposed agenda; he felt that the centennial should be observed with a procession of Loyalist descendants and a private reception at Government House. Loyalists should also be issued a special badge or medallion for the occasion. The exclusiveness of Denison's proposals disturbed William Withrow, who believed a day in the park would be more appropriate. To ensure that the celebration was truly provincial, Withrow proposed that a permanent committee be appointed to represent all parts of the province.[40] Since there was little consensus about the most appropriate means of observing the centennial, it was decided to submit each suggestion to a committee for further consideration.[41]

The committee responsible for organizing Toronto's semi-centennial celebrations originally set aside Thursday, 19 June, as Loyalist Day. Early in April, however, the Secretary of the city's Semi-Centennial Committee informed the local organizers of the Loyalist celebration that bicycle races were to be held on the 19th and requested that the committee transfer the Loyalist demonstration to Thursday, 3 July. The request was readily agreed to since the committee was far from finalizing any plans.[42] The decision to change the date of the Toronto Loyalist centennial celebrations, however, angered some residents of Niagara, and a meeting was called for 6 May 1884 to discuss the 'arbitrary change of date made by the Toronto Semi-Centennial committee.' At the meeting it was resolved to 'hold a grand centennial celebration of the settlement of this province by the Loyalists' in Niagara-on-the-Lake, 'the true historical and proper place for such a commemoration.'[43] At a subsequent meeting on 17 May 1884 a general committee was appointed to organize 'a mammoth celebration' to be held on 15 August 1884. Col. F.A.B. Clench, the county clerk of Lincoln, was appointed chairman and Daniel Servos secretary. Other members of the committee included William Kirby and the warden of Lincoln county, Capt. James Hiscott. The presence of Col. Clench and Capt. Hiscott on the organizing committee ensured that the celebrations received the official endorsement and financial support of the county of Lincoln. The committee was unsuccessful in its efforts to secure support from the neighbouring counties of Haldimand and Welland.[44]

Much more lay behind the decision to hold a local celebration at Niagara than simply a change in the date of the Toronto celebration. There was considerable resentment in Niagara, and elsewhere, that a handful of men in Toronto had taken over the centennial celebrations. The Welland *Tribune* voiced the widely held belief that the whole affair was 'a mere business scheme and advertising card for the city of Toronto.'[45] Organizers of the Toronto celebrations had insisted, however, that the event was to be provincial in scope and involve representatives from across the province. The fact that members of the general committee outside Toronto had not been informed of the change in date until after the fact confirmed the suspicions of many that the Toronto organizers were not at all interested in the input of others. Others were disturbed by the proposed agenda. William Kirby was outraged by the open, non-political celebration of the Loyalists' pioneer achievements envisioned by William Canniff. Appalled that independentists were apparently welcome to participate in the Toronto centennial celebrations, Kirby wrote to Rev. R.S. Forneri that 'any man' who claimed to be a United Empire Loyalist and advocated independence was 'a traitor to the old loyalists who founded for us under the British flag this noble dominion of Canada.'[46] Moreover, the virtual paralysis of the Toronto committee by factionalism disturbed and disillusioned many.

Unlike the Toronto committee, the organizers of the Niagara celebration were united in their conception of the purpose of the event. The demonstration at Niagara was organized, first, to assert the area's claim to recognition as the heartland of Loyalism and, second, to assert the continuing value of the imperial connection. The Welland *Tribune* hailed the organizers of the Niagara celebrations for recognizing that the Loyalist centennial should rightly be 'held on historic ground' where the 'distinctive merit' of the Loyalists continued to live on.[47] Later, during the observances at Niagara, William Kirby insisted: 'this spot consecrated by so many honourable memories of the fathers and defenders of our country is after all the true historical and proper place for the centennial celebration of the settlement of Upper Canada. Here was the principal landing place of the expatriated loyalists, here came the loyal fighting men of the Revolutionary War, and here they planted their war torn but glorious flag.[48] Organizers of the Niagara celebrations were motivated in the first instance by a desire to bring people and publicity to their communities.

The political objectives of the organizers were made clear in a letter to the Welland *Tribune* from I.P. Wilson. 'Very shortly,' Wilson asserted, 'a great moral battle is to be fought in this country' over the question of Canada's relationship to the Empire. It thus was crucial that preparations for the approaching political battle be made. 'In view of the possibilities and probabilities of the near future,' Wilson continued, it is essential that 'U.E. loyalist families and those in sympathy with them' become 'better acquainted and know where to find each other upon the shortest notice' in order that a 'united effort be made as certain as possible.'[49] The militaristic language evident in the statement make it clear that the organizers of the Niagara celebrations shared the views and objectives of George Taylor Denison. Indeed, Denison was one of the first people invited to speak during Niagara's observation of the Loyalist centennial. Although Denison initially declined the invitation, organizers readily repeated their offer after his Toronto address was widely condemned in the press.[50] Denison's close friend William Kirby was confident that the Niagara celebrations had fulfilled their purpose. 'This meeting is a proof,' Kirby observed, 'that, after the lapse of a hundred years, the spirit which animated the U.E. Loyalists is still alive, slumbering perhaps, in quiet leonine strength in the hearts of our people, but ready to wake up as of old, whenever called upon.'[51]

Preoccupied with their own factional struggles, the organizers of the so-called provincial celebrations at Toronto took little notice of the plans to hold a local demonstration at Niagara. Organizers spent most of the months of April and May debating the merits of establishing a museum of pioneer and Loyalist artefacts. Canniff repeatedly asserted that the museum should be a central feature of the centennial celebrations and a 5 April meeting of the committee of management appeared to support the idea. It soon became apparent, however, that Denison and his allies endorsed the idea only as a ploy to induce the provincial government to support the celebrations financially.[52] When a provincial grant was not forthcoming, Fred Denison moved that the proposed museum be removed from the managing committee's agenda and that the committee established to oversee its development be disbanded.[53] Early in May, however, the managing committee was informed that the government had approved a $400 grant. Canniff at once insisted that the museum project be resurrected. Fred Denison again scuttled the idea by insisting that there was not enough time to bring together any artefacts. Canniff pointed out that he had already received several letters expressing pleasure that a museum was being considered and offering to donate items for display.[54]

Canniff's increasing impotence was most apparent in the selection of individuals asked to speak during the celebrations. Canniff suggested that the former lieutenant-governor of Rupert's Land, William McDougall, address the gathering. McDougall was of Loyalist descent, his grandfather having served with the British commissariat during the American Revolution. Canniff wrote to McDougall on 28 May 1884 requesting that he consent to deliver a brief address on the occasion.[55] McDougall responded that he would be glad to speak, although he noted, 'I am not so enthusiastic as some of the descendants of the UE Loyalists in eulogizing their so called loyalty.' 'The student of history,' McDougall asserted, 'must admit that the dynasty and the system of administration in defence of which they sacrificed their fortunes and many of them their lives were unworthy of their sacrifice.'[56] Such comments were of course heretical to men like Denison, and Canniff was forced to withdraw the invitation. An embarrassed Canniff wrote to McDougall that although he 'personally was not dissatisfied with the tone and spirit of your letter,' others 'took exception' and insisted that the invitation to speak be withdrawn.[57] By June Canniff clearly felt that he had lost control of the entire proceedings. He desperately asserted in a letter to Judge W.W. Dean, one of the approved speakers, that 'the celebration is to honour the memory of the Loyalists who were the founders of the Province. It is not desired that anything offensive be said against the "rebels."' Although Canniff wrote that 'the committee lay great stress' on this point, it was obvious that he no longer spoke for the committee as a whole.[58]

Conflicting visions prevented finalizing of an agenda until 14 June, only three weeks before the actual celebrations. The final program was clearly a victory for George Taylor Denison and his supporters. Little remained of Canniff's vision of an inclusive and non-political celebration of the Loyalists as pioneers of the province. The proceedings were to commence with a 10:30 a.m. concert and speeches at the Horticultural Pavilion followed by a reception at Government House. Admittance to both events was to be restricted to Loyalist descendants, who had to apply in advance for a badge to be admitted or who had a certificate signed by a member of the organizing committee.[59] The main speakers were scheduled to be Denison himself and his close and like-minded friend, Senator G.W. Allan.

It was an embittered Canniff who officially opened the Loyalist centennial celebrations at the Horticultural Pavilion on 3 July. Distraught from the constant infighting and dissatisfaction with his chairmanship, Canniff once again felt compelled to explain how he had come to hold the position. Sensing the political nature of the speeches that were to follow, Canniff declined to speak: 'I have already, on another occasion and at another place, said all I might have wished to say on the subject relating to the U.E. Loyalists.'[60]

Neither the Toronto nor the Niagara celebrations received the positive public response organizers had hoped for. The press was overwhelmingly negative in its assessment. The *Globe* asserted that 'it was probably a mistake to sandwich in between two such "drawing" spectacles as the Trades Unions procession and the parade of the Benevolent societies the comparatively unexciting celebration of the virtues of the UEL.'[61] Even the generally supportive *Mail* acknowledged that 'people did not get excited over the UE Loyalists and the memories of their history.'[62] The *Week* asserted: 'We are getting tired of all this fanfaronade about the UE Loyalists; the people have had enough of it, and it is time the nonsense ceased.'[63] The most offensive aspect of the celebrations was their political and exclusive nature. The *News* commented that 'the paltry spirit of caste and social prescription begotten of U.E. Loyalism' was far more dangerous than the voices of independence attacked by the likes of Denison. 'Fortunately for the future of Canada,' the *News* continued, 'our people are beginning to rate the pretensions of the Denisons, Robinsons, Plumbs and the rest of the loyalist clique.' The *News* dismissed the speeches delivered in Toronto and Niagara as the desperate efforts of an 'insignificant, but very noisy and insolent set of windbags' who do not represent Canadian opinion.[64]

While individuals such as George Taylor Denison and William Kirby insisted on remembering the Loyalists for their devotion to the Empire and British constitutional principles, a considerable proportion of the public preferred to commemorate the Loyalists simply as pioneers. A writer to the *World* commented that the contributions of Loyalist pioneers 'merited honour.' The celebrations, however, had been 'perverted by the spread-eagle tory orators.'[65] The Toronto *News* charged that Denison had violated the terms by which it was agreed to hold the Loyalist celebrations in conjunction with the semi-centennial. It was clearly understood, the *News* insisted, that the organizers were not to exploit the occasion for propaganda purposes, but were rather 'to do honour to their ancestors as the pioneers of civilization and settlement in this province.' 'Those struggles, those hardships, of which we their descendants or successors, reap the benefit in such ample measure,' the *News* concluded, 'should never be forgotten by Canadians.' By turning the celebrations into a political affair, Denison was guilty of 'a wanton, deliberate breach of faith with the public.'[66] Another letter, from a member of the Canadian National Society, also challenged George Taylor Denison's right 'to speak in the name of the UE Loyalists.' The writer observed that the attempt by Denison and others to turn the centennial into an occasion 'for foisting upon the public their old-fogey flapdoodle has already disgusted some of the truest representatives of the same UE Loyalists.'[67] D.B. Read perhaps captured the public mood best when he wrote to the *Globe*: 'The US men have celebrated the evacuation of New York; the UE have had their centenary three times repeated. Let us have rest and cultivate the arts of peace.'[68]

An examination of the events preceding the 1884 Loyalist centennial celebrations in Toronto challenges the view that the event was the product of the efforts of like-minded individuals. Organizers were clearly divided into two factions, one headed by William Canniff, the other by George Taylor Denison. Canniff and his supporters envisioned an inclusive and non-political event that focused primarily upon the pioneer legacy of the Loyalists. Denison and his followers, however, saw the centennial essentially in political terms and as an opportunity to expound their imperialist views. Judging from the reactions to the celebrations, the views of William Canniff were more in tune with popular sentiment than were those of George Taylor Denison.

Colonel George Taylor Denison described the Loyalists' legacy as 'a sacred trust' that 'should be passed on intact and unimpaired to our children.'[69] Although organizers were deeply divided about the type of celebration that should be held and had differing conceptions of the significance of the Loyalists, they all maintained that the memory of the Loyalists must be preserved and perpetuated. Such faith in the past was rooted in the anxieties that accompanied the socio-economic forces that were transforming Ontario into an increasingly urbanized and industrialized society.[70] The emergence of mass industrial society proved particularly problematic for members of the middle class, especially as social mobility and the wide range of wealth and influence within the middle class made clear criteria for social distinction increasingly elusive. The situation was complicated further as the groups and occupations claiming or aspiring to middle-class status increased. According to Eric Hobsbawm, the problem confronting the middle class was how to define and separate itself 'once the relatively firm criteria by which subjective class membership could be determined in stable local communities had been eroded, and descent, kinship, intermarriage, the local networks of business, private sociability and politics no longer provided firm guidance.'[71] One response was to cling to ancestry as a badge of distinction and to the past as a guide for the future. Celebrations and commemorations consequently assumed an important role as a new kind of social and political communication that allowed groups threatened by the emergence of industrial society to defend and reassert their claims to position and influence.[72]

The organizers of the Toronto and Niagara celebrations were drawn primarily from the ranks of middle-class professionals. Encoded in the imperialist and anti-American rhetoric that dominated the celebrations were middle-class fears about class polarization, labour unrest, vice, crime, immigration, racial supremacy and the future of the patriarchal family. In looking to the Loyalist past, the middle-class participants in the celebrations sought refuge from an increasingly complex urban and industrial society and hoped to recapture the symmetry, order, and harmony of the imagined world of their ancestors. Some, such as George Taylor Denison, believed that this world could be preserved and recovered only through a steadfast allegiance to the Empire and British constitution. This belief had more to do with current conditions than abstract notions of Loyalist principles. Imperialists believed that Canada's British institutions and heritage were the only certain means of ensuring that the problems that accompanied urbanization, industrialization, and immigration in the United States did not afflict their nation. Beneath the language of imperialism and Loyalism lay a desire for the serenity of a more stable class order in which the position and authority of the Anglo-Canadian middle class were secure. The social anxiety that underlay imperial sentiment was often concealed, however, by the sense of mission and destiny described by Carl Berger. Men like Denison confidently predicted that as part of the Empire, Canada would surpass the influence and accomplishments of the United States.

Others were less optimistic and focused on the Loyalists' pioneer experience to offer a critique of modern society. Much of Canniff Haight's *Country Life in Canada Fifty Years Ago*, for example, is a lament for the passing of the values and qualities he believed were characteristic of the pioneer. Haight attributed the success of the early settlers to their economy, industry, and concern with the welfare of all. According to Haight, 'there was no ostentatious display, or assumption of superiority by the "first families"'; rather, 'the sufferings or misfortunes of a neighbour, as well as his enjoyments, were participated in by all.' Such virtues however, were in danger of being destroyed by the materialism and class consciousness Haight found endemic in modern society. 'In our haste to become rich,' he complained, 'we have abandoned the old road of honest industry' and 'have been gradually departing from the sterling example set by our progenitors.' Haight advised Canadians 'to step aside from the hustle and bustle which surrounds us, and look back.' The virtues and values of the Loyalist pioneers, he insisted, were 'too sacred a trust to be forgotten, and their lives too worthy of our imitation not to bind us together as a people.' In calling for a return to the virtuous simplicity, rural independence, and class harmony of the Loyalist pioneers, Haight hoped to restore a sense of unity to an increasingly fragmented society. There was a strange ambivalence, however, in Haight's anti-modernism. While he lamented the loss of community before the forces of materialism and social divisions, he none the less celebrated the tremendous progress made by Canada over the century. Haight enthused that no place in the world had witnessed 'such marvellous changes' and experienced 'a more rapid and vigourous growth.'[73] His ambivalent feelings reflected the confusion voiced by many middle-class Anglo-Canadians at the end of the nineteenth century.

Not only were the Loyalist centennial celebrations a product of class anxieties; questions of gender and race also shaped the commemorations. Women were notably absent as either organizers or speakers. This lack of involvement by women underscores the gendered nature of acts of commemoration. As public affairs that often involved important social and political questions, celebrations were controlled and dominated by men. Patriarchal definitions of appropriate female roles and behaviour precluded the active participation of women in such events. As a result, the Loyalist centennial was an overwhelmingly male affair. Speakers repeatedly invoked a masculine past preoccupied with the character and accomplishments of the province's 'founding fathers.' Although the contributions of Loyalist women were overlooked or ignored during the celebrations, many speakers appealed to the current generation of mothers to instil Loyalist principles in their children. Such assertions served to confirm women in their maternal and domestic roles. In the years following the centennial, however, a number of women set out to write their foremothers back into the Loyalist past and thereby to subvert the masculine focus of Loyalist history. The result was a broader Loyalist narrative that could be used to enhance the claims of women to greater status and recognition in Canadian society.

While women did not play a public role in the centennial, representatives from the Six Nations reserves at Grand River and Tyendinaga were invited to speak at each of the 1884 celebrations. Organizers hoped that an appearance by the Natives in their 'paint and feathers' would prove a popular crowd pleaser. By the end of the nineteenth century the widespread conviction that Natives belonged to a dying race doomed to extinction created a romantic and sentimental interest in the North American Indian. The dislocation that accompanied urbanization and industrialization also created a nostalgic idealization of a simpler and nobler Native way of life.[74] Both sentiments found expression in the immensely popular Wild West Show founded by William 'Buffalo Bill' Cody in 1882. While organizers recognized the Natives' value as an attraction, the Six Nations had their own reasons for participating in the centennial celebrations. The chiefs who spoke on these occasions echoed the Loyalist and imperialist rhetoric uttered by non-Native speakers. They stressed, however, that the Six Nations were not subjects of the Crown, but rather were allies entitled to certain rights and privileges and were nations with their own culture and traditions. Native leaders appropriated the rhetoric of Loyalism to further their own political agendas. During the Niagara celebration, for example, Chief A.G. Smith of Grand River asserted that the Six Nations were 'anxious to be identified with the descendants of the U.E. Loyalists of Canada.' He predicted that 'the day is not far distant when the Indians will be able to take their stand among the whites on equal footing.' A necessary step in that direction, Smith insisted, was Native representation in Parliament. He hoped 'that the white population of the Dominion will be forced by their sense of justice to accord the Indian that right which is their just due.'[75]

Although happy to put Natives on display and to praise their loyalty, organizers were unwilling to endorse the Six Nations' political objectives. Instead they hailed the Six Nations' progress in 'civilization.' During the Niagara celebrations, Senator J.B. Plumb asserted that the Six Nations were entitled to 'special greeting and honour' for the 'unwavering fidelity and indomitable courage' shown on behalf of the Crown during the Revolution. Plumb was particularly impressed, however, with the Six Nations' 'achievements in civilized life.' 'Our Iroquois,' Plumb rather patronizingly continued, 'are to be greatly commended for improvement in agriculture, for peaceful conduct, and for the progress of education and growth of Christianity among them.'[76] Plumb and others upheld the Six Nations as a model for all Native peoples to follow. Whereas the chiefs felt that their loyal past entitled them to justice and equality, non-Natives redefined loyalty in terms of assimilation to Anglo-Canadian ways and subjection to Canadian institutions. Such feelings were dramatically represented by several of the tableaux that appeared in the Toronto semi-centennial parade.[77] One tableau portrayed Britannia seated on a Roman throne, her hand outstretched to an Indian maiden. Another depicted Governor Simcoe being warmly welcomed and embraced by a crowd of loyal Natives on the shores of Lake Ontario.[78] Such images highlight the important role that race played in shaping the Loyalist tradition. Convinced of their own racial superiority, the Anglo-Canadian organizers of the 1884 celebrations used the centennial to impose their own racial assumptions and expectations upon the Six Nations.

Disillusioned by the lack of support they received at Adolphustown, Toronto, and Niagara, the Six Nations of the Tyendinaga and Grand River reserves decided to hold celebrations of their own in the fall of 1884. Native speakers used these occasions to assert their identity and to voice their concerns. During the celebrations held at Tyendinaga, Dr Peter Martin, the Mohawk head of the International Order of Foresters, challenged white perceptions of Natives with considerable wit and humour. Despite his considerable achievements, Martin was fully aware of the constraints and limitations placed on Native peoples by the racial assumptions of the day.[79] He began his address by asserting that he was 'proud of being a Mohawk, as they [are] the best people on the face of the earth,' and he proceeded to tell a story about the origins of the Indians, which accounted for their superiority. 'Philologists,' Martin observed, 'had shown that language is the index of character. Indians cannot swear except in English, and further still they had never drunk whisky until the advent of the whites. This was the result of bad company.' He concluded his address by appealing to Parliament to recognize the accomplishments and abilities of the nation's Native peoples by granting them the franchise.[80] During the celebrations held at Grand River, Chief Clench asserted that the Six Nations had sacrificed their 'wealth, happiness and enjoyment' in order to remain 'faithful to the covenant' they had made with the British. Clench complained that while the Six Nations had 'fulfilled their covenant to the letter,' the Canadian government had not respected Native 'rights.'[81] Unwilling to accept the version of the Loyalist past articulated by Anglo-Canadians, the Six Nations invoked an alternative narrative that supported their claims upon the state.

Although the 1884 Toronto and Niagara Loyalist centennial celebrations commemorated individuals and events of the previous century, the celebrations were clearly a product of contemporary concerns and realities. Sharply divided in their understanding of Loyalist principles and in the most appropriate means of observing the centennial, the professional middle-class organizers of the Toronto celebrations shared a common faith in the value and usefulness of the past in confronting the disorientation and upheaval that accompanied urbanization and industrialization. By invoking the Loyalist past, the Toronto organizers hoped to recapture the class stability and harmony of a world without industrial conflict, corporate barons, and urban blight. Just as the reorganization of the economy threatened to concentrate power and influence within the hands of a small corporate elite, it also foreshadowed the ever-increasing importance of metropolitan centres such as Toronto. The Niagara celebrations were essentially an expression of local boosterism and regional rivalry as local residents laid claim to a Loyalist past they felt rightfully belonged to them, not to the provincial capital. The events organized by the Six Nations represented the attempts of a marginalized people to claim and assert their own past.

The controversy surrounding the 1884 Loyalist centennial celebrations reveals a great deal about the politics of commemoration. While there was widespread support for the idea of celebrating the settlement of the province by the Loyalists, there was little consensus about how the Loyalists were to be remembered or what form the celebrations should take. The result was a contest over the meaning of the past and the uses of history as different groups attempted to employ the Loyalist centennial as a vehicle to serve particular causes and interests. The objectives of organizers and the divisions that surrounded the celebrations were deeply rooted in their immediate social context. The religious and political divisions that dominated events in Adolphustown, the fears and anxieties that concerned the middle-class organizers of the Toronto celebrations, and the local boosterism of Niagara's promoters reflected a unique set of social circumstances. The marginalization of women and members of the Six Nations during the celebrations demonstrates the importance of gender and race in shaping the past. Not only did Natives of the Six Nations and women participate in the celebrations in different ways from their male Anglo-Canadian organizers, they constructed their own usable pasts that challenged prevailing gender and racial assumptions.

Widely condemned in the press for their social exclusiveness and self-serving agendas, the 1884 celebrations were not the popular successes that their organizers had hoped to stage. The generally negative reaction challenges the characterization of events of this kind as straightforward exercises in hegemony and social control. The reception given to the centennial celebrations by the press and public highlights the degree to which hegemony is in fact a two-way process in which dominant groups must win the support and consent of the rest of society. Divided among themselves, organizers were unable to develop a unifying view of the Loyalist past that could win wide public acceptance. The 'official' histories that organizers tried to promote were confronted by the alternative pasts of women and members of the Six Nations as well as a popular 'vernacular' past of the pioneer that was both more inclusive and politically neutral. Although the pioneer tradition enjoyed a wide popularity, it did not find support among the filiopietistic descendants, political partisans, status-conscious middle-class professionals, and local boosters who came to dominate the planning and organization of the 1884 celebrations. Seeking to promote their own claims to status and recognition and unwilling to accommodate other views and ideas, the organizers failed to convince the wider public that their particular interests were those of society at large.

Unlike the celebrations surrounding the centennial of the Declaration of American Independence held a few years earlier, the Loyalist centennial did not succeed in creating a common sense of identity rooted in a shared past. The American celebrations centred in Philadelphia were the creation of a broad coalition involving federal, state, and local governments, business, and a large number of historical and patriotic organizations. The many interests involved in the 1876 celebrations shared a common desire to instil a new sense of nationalism based on widely held ideas of progress and achievement.[82] In contrast, the 1884 Loyalist celebrations were largely independent affairs with little government involvement, which focused on controversial political questions and unpopular social and religious pretensions. Had the organizers been less concerned with furthering their own immediate interests and more willing to broaden the Loyalist tradition to include other segments of society, the celebrations might have helped to produce a sense of national consciousness at a time when the country lacked a clear identity.

5

'Fairy tales in the guise of history':
The Loyalists in Ontario Publications,
1884–1918

In the years following the 1884 Loyalist centennial celebrations a plethora of publications dealing with the Loyalists appeared. The large volume of Loyalist publications reflected an unprecedented interest in the Loyalist past, which did not begin to subside until the end of the First World War. Although commemorative celebrations temporarily caught the public's attention and received considerable coverage in the press, it was political pamphlets, textbooks, local histories, and genealogies that were the principal means by which the Loyalist tradition was sustained and disseminated to the public. The wide range of material published during this period provides considerable insight into the different interpretations and uses made of the Loyalist tradition. Polemicists, educators, local historians, and filiopietistic genealogists all appropriated the Loyalist past and infused with it new or altered meanings that served their particular purposes. New elements were added by women and ethnic minorities, who attempted to claim a place in the nation's past. Despite their different interests and agendas, all of these groups drew heavily on the work of contemporary American historians in shaping their versions of Loyalist history.

The unprecedented interest shown in the Loyalist past between 1884 and 1918 developed in response to contemporary needs and closely followed the political, social, and economic development of the nation. The politics of the period were dominated by an emotional debate over the nation's political future. The controversy that surrounded the discussion of imperial federation, independence, annexation, and closer economic ties to the United States stimulated a search for historical antecedents that could be called upon to support different political points of view. The Loyalist past was frequently invoked in the polemics and propaganda of the period by imperialists, protectionists, and feminists as a means of furthering their own political agendas. The bitter sectional and ethno-religious tensions evident in the Jesuit estates dispute, the trial of Louis Riel, and the Manitoba school question highlighted the need for a shared national history that could uphold a common identity, for political stability, and for social order. The Loyalists figured prominently in the search for a unifying past and historical role models. In the history textbooks of the period the Loyalists were upheld as 'the makers of Canada' and exemplars of patriotism and morality. Disillusioned by the country's economic difficulties and its continuing political, racial, and linguistic problems, many Ontarians redirected their historical interests to the local level. The result was a boom in the publication of local histories, sustained to a considerable degree by the efforts of civic boosters. Many promoters sought to increase the status and prestige of their communities by establishing a link with the province's Loyalist origins and by creating a set of local Loyalist worthies. Rooted in popular knowledge and immediate sources, local histories often challenged some of the exclusive claims of the Loyalist tradition. Local historians were more likely to recognize and to acknowledge the contributions made by ethnic and religious minorities than were imperialists and nationalists. The result was a greater sensitivity to the diversity of the province's Loyalist past. Ontario's transformation into an urban and industrial society further stimulated historical interest. The disorientation that accompanied social and economic change generated a nostalgic interest in the past among an anxious middle class concerned about the effects of industrialization, the vices of the city, and the impact of mass immigration. The tremendous popularity of genealogy among middle-class Loyalist descendants reflected a quest for status and security in the new urban and industrial order. In this context, the Loyalist past proved to be a popular, malleable, and useful weapon that could be used to advance political, class, local, and personal interests.

Much of the Loyalist literature published following the 1884 celebrations was blatantly polemical and took the form of political pamphlets and propaganda. The commercial union movement launched in 1887, the Liberal party's endorsement of unrestricted reciprocity, and the heated election campaign of 1891 rekindled the debate over Canada's destiny. The Loyalists' reputed steadfast adherence to the Empire and their constant vigilance against American ambitions added historical legitimacy to the political agenda of imperialists and economic protectionists. Advocates of continental economic integration and those who dared to question the nature of the imperial relationship were denounced as a threat to those historical foundations that were essential to the nation's survival.

In 1892 Rev. Henry Scadding, an avid amateur historian and rector of Toronto's Church of the Holy Trinity, published *The Revived Significance of the Letters U.E.* The pamphlet called upon Loyalist descendants to stand guard against the pernicious influence of continentalism. Scadding predicted that in the face of continentalist sentiment 'the initials UE seem likely ere long to assume a fresh importance in Canadian history,' and 'the unity of the empire, in a grander sense than that which inspired the enthusiasm of our forefathers, will again become a stirring watchword among us.' 'Inheriting as we do so largely a deep respect for the old UE principles,' Scadding continued, 'it will be expected of us, I think, and of our children, when the critical time shall come, that we shall present a very decided front against all who shall be engaged in any movement for the dismemberment of the great British Empire.'[1] Scadding suggested that an effective means of combatting the continentalist threat would be to hold yet another celebration commemorating the establishment of the province by the Loyalists. The centennial of the proclamation of 1791, which created Upper Canada, however, had already passed. It thus was decided to celebrate the centennial of the first meeting of the Upper Canadian Legislative Assembly and the division of the province into electoral districts.[2] Events were planned for 16 July 1892 at the site of the province's first legislature in Niagara-on-the-Lake and for 17 September 1892 on the grounds of the new Parliament buildings in Toronto. Rev. E.J. Fessenden's *Upper Canada: A Centenary Study* was typical of the rash of publications generated during the centenary. Fessenden appealed to Canadians to look to the past for guidance in the current debate over Canada's future course. 'It is most fortunate,' Fessenden asserted, 'the year we commemorate recalls to mind that nothing can give us more light and guidance, as to what we may and ought to make that policy, than to turn to "the rock whence we are hewn."' According to Fessenden, that 'rock' consisted of constitution and patriotism bequeathed a century ago by the United Empire Loyalists. 'The Canadian Loyalists,' he continued, 'were ready at every crisis in their history to imperil life and fortune, personal and national, that they might secure for themselves and their children their home in the United Empire under her [Britain's] constitution.' To be 'tempted by any annexation, "Stanley's handkerchief," however brilliantly dyed in any "Commercial Union,"' Fessenden warned, amounted to 'bartering' away Canada's 'Loyalist inheritance of a United Empire with all its possibilities of material greatness.'[3]

The attempt to appropriate the province's Loyalist past to the imperialist and anti-continentalist causes did not go unchallenged. In a series of tracts drawn from lectures delivered before the Young Men's Liberal Association of Toronto, Goldwin Smith questioned the motives of those who used the Loyalist past as a justification for the current course of the country's policy. 'A Loyalist's virtue,' Smith perceptively observed, 'follows the lines of his own interest.' 'There are not a few cases,' he insisted, 'in which loyalty to the Crown is a fine name for disloyalty to the country, and loyalty to the British connection is a fine name for disloyalty to Canada.' He reminded imperialists that the Loyalists had attempted to preserve the unity of an empire that included the United States. True loyalists should thus direct their efforts towards healing the schism that divided England and the United States rather than engaging in damaging anti-American rhetoric and attempting to reopen the wounds of the past. Smith urged Canadians not to be deceived by the 'unmanly' jingoism represented by the 'hoisting of flags, chanting of martial songs, celebration of battle anniversaries, erection of military monuments, decoration of patriotic graves.' 'Celebrations of victories gained in bygone quarrels over people who are now your friends,' he insisted, 'are perhaps not the sort of things to which the bravest are most prone.'[4]

The earnestness that characterized such early works gradually faded. The economic expansion of the Laurier boom years quelled fears about the future and dissolved most of the earlier annexationist anxieties. The Loyalist tradition, however, continued to be a useful political resource. During the debate surrounding Canada's role in the Boer War, the example of the Loyalist was frequently cited by advocates of full Canadian participation. In an issue of *Acta Victoriana* published in December of 1899, Sir John Bourinot observed, 'at the present time, when England is asserting the principles of equal justice in the Transvaal and fighting for her supremacy in South Africa, we have very eloquent evidence on all sides that the spirit which the Loyalists showed from the beginning to the close of the American Revolution pervades all classes of the British inhabitants of that Dominion of which they were builders more than a century ago.'[5] Similar views were expressed by Nathanael Burwash in two essays published by the United Empire Loyalist Association of Ontario. Burwash maintained that the province's Loyalist settlers possessed those characteristically Anglo-Saxon traits, 'genius for organization,' 'great physical virility, strong will power and a sense of order' upon which all civilization rested.[6] Fortunately, this 'peculiar strength of character' was 'a grandly hereditary trait.' 'The leading names among the sixty thousand of a hundred years ago,' Burwash asserted, 'are still the leading names among the six millions of today,' and 'their names are not wanting in the South African contingents of 1899 and 1900.'[7] As in all of the polemical works, the message was clear: failure to stand by the Empire was nothing less than a betrayal of the inheritance of the nation's founders.

The attempts of partisans and propagandists to politicize the Loyalist past seriously limited its ability to serve as the basis for a unifying national mythology. The appropriation of Loyalism by imperialists immediately tainted the tradition in the eyes of those who held a different view of the nation's destiny. As a result, the Loyalist past proved to be more a source of contention than a force for unity.

The attempt to create a usable past was not limited to the efforts of political partisans. Governments appreciated the importance of history in creating a national identity, political stability, and social order. Control over school curriculum and textbooks provided governments with the most direct means of creating a usable past. Textbooks were designed not simply to inform and instruct but to inculcate social values and attitudes.[8] History textbooks in particular were viewed as important tools of socialization and nation building. Ontario's minister of education, G.W. Ross, readily admitted that the function of the history text was to 'indoctrinate our pupils, so that when a child takes up the history of Canada, he feels ... that he is taking up the history of a great country.'[9] Ross served as minister from 1883 until 1899. During his tenure he made the study of Canadian history compulsory in the elementary grades and ordered history texts to be standardized and rewritten. Patriotic exercises were encouraged in the schools on national and imperial holidays. Ross himself wrote *Patriotic Recitations and Arbour Day Exercises* to be used as a resource on such occasions.[10] The authors of history texts also appreciated the social importance of their works. In the preface to *Public School History of England and Canada*, G. Mercer Adam and W.J. Robertson stressed the importance of history as 'a great teacher of morals.' 'Rightly studied,' Adams and Robertson asserted, 'history teaches us to admire and esteem the brave, the honest, and the self-denying; and to despise and condemn the cowardly, the base, and the selfish. We are led to see that virtue preserves and strengthens a nation, while vice inevitably causes decay and weakness.'[11] The lessons learned from the rise and fall of nations, however, were equally applicable to the individual. The underlying purpose of the history textbook was to create good citizens who lived morally upright lives.

The history textbooks authorized for use in Ontario's schools between 1884 and the First World War hailed the Loyalists as 'the makers of Canada.'[12] In *A History of Canada* Charles G.D. Roberts insisted that the migration of the Loyalists 'changed the course of history' and was no 'less significant and far-reaching in its results than the landing of the Pilgrim Fathers.'[13] David Duncan asserted in *The Story of the Canadian People* that 'the importance to Canada of the arrival of the United Empire Loyalists can hardly be overestimated.'[14] The textbooks also portrayed the Loyalists in heroic terms. Steadfast in character, true to their principles, loyal to the king, the Loyalists sacrificed their homes and property and chose to begin their lives anew in the Upper Canadian wilderness. 'Preferring to live under the old flag,' J. Frith Jeffers observed in his *History of Canada*, these 'true men and women' chose 'rather to lose all than give up their allegiance to and love for the mother country' and 'made for themselves new homes in the Canadian forest.'[15]

The province's textbooks were generally free, however, of the extreme rhetoric that characterized the polemical pamphlets of the period. It was widely accepted that the American Revolution, if not inevitable, was certainly understandable. Most of the history textbooks used in Ontario's schools agreed that the Revolution was a product of an 'unwise policy,' which treated 'the settlements of the New World as colonial possessions to be held solely for the financial benefit of England rather than for their own advancement and material well-being.'[16] In *The Story of the Canadian People* David Duncan maintained that 'the cause of the war must be sought alike in the folly of the British government and in the impatience of the American colonists.'[17] The Revolution thus was an unnatural tragedy. J. Frith Jeffers lamented that the Revolution 'was very sad because it was between people of the same blood and language; even families were divided, fathers and sons fighting against one another.'[18] Although all the textbooks mention the 'unparalleled sufferings and privations' endured by the Loyalists at the hands of the Patriots, it is also acknowledged that the Loyalists were not above committing atrocities themselves. In *The History of the Dominion of Canada* W.H.P. Clement insisted that 'it can serve no good purpose to dwell upon the details of the war – the fiendish outrages committed upon both sides – with a view to striking a balance.'[19] A certain degree of ambivalence and ambiguity thus pervades the treatment of the Loyalists in the history texts of the period.

Although ambivalent in their treatment of the causes and course of the

Revolution, textbook writers were clear in the lessons to be gleaned from the Loyalists' experience and example. The first lesson was political.[20] The Loyalists were to be admired because they were peaceful and law-abiding citizens, who deferred to higher authorities and favoured evolutionary rather than revolutionary change. J. George Hodgins observed in *A History of Canada and of the Other British Provinces in North America* that 'the adherents to the royal cause felt that loyalty to the sovereign was their first and highest duty.' According to Hodgins, such loyalty was required 'by the divine authority of God himself.'[21] In his *Ontario High School History of Canada* W.L. Grant insisted that the Loyalists 'had wished to reform the Empire and the old colonial system as strongly as the rebels, but they had sought reform by peaceful means and not by the rough road of revolution.'[22] The rewards of evolutionary change were evident in Canada's growing place of importance within the Empire. In the preface of *The History of the Dominion of Canada*, W.H.P. Clement announced that he intended to 'convey a fair and inspiring impression of the grandeur and importance of the heritage committed to us as Canadians and as citizens of the British Empire.' In his conclusion, Clement exhorted students 'to look forward to the still wider federation of all the lands which fly the Union Jack.'[23]

Throughout the history textbooks of the period, the Loyalists were upheld as models of the virtues and values espoused by middle-class Victorian Ontarians: patient persistence in the face of adversity, hard work and industry, and faith in God.[24] The pioneer motif figured prominently in the history textbooks. In *A History of Canada and of the Other British Provinces in North America* J. George Hodgins described the Loyalists as 'self-denying, devoted men, who cheerfully submitted to the privations and discomforts incident to a new and thinly settled country.' According to Hodgins, the 'heroic fortitude' displayed by the Loyalists as they endured 'unparalleled suffering and privations' was largely a product of 'their ardent love for the Bible, and for 'the God of their Fathers.'[25] These views were echoed by Charles G.D. Roberts. Roberts hailed the Loyalists as 'the makers of Canada' and praised their 'stubborn energy' in subduing the wilderness. The Loyalists were also 'God-fearing men' who 'held sacred the education of their children.' Consequently, 'as soon as the wilderness began to yield before their axes, they made haste to build the school-house and the church in every district.' Roberts attributed much of the Loyalists' success to their selfless concern with the welfare of the community. 'At the very beginning,' he asserted, 'they had realized the value of co-operation; and instead of each man painfully levelling his own patch of forest, hauling his own logs, building his own meagre cabin, a system of 'frolics' or 'bees' was instituted.'[26] The traits attributed to the Loyalists thus read like a litany of Victorian concerns and preoccupations.

The lesson textbook writers hoped to impress upon young minds was clear: loyalty, industry, perseverance, cooperation, and trust in God were always rewarded. The Upper Canadian wilderness thus was transformed into a productive and prosperous society. W.H.P. Clement observed in *The History of the Dominion of Canada* that the Loyalists 'fought their way through much discouragement to comfort and even affluence.'[27] Similarly, in his *History of Canada*, J. Frith Jeffers concluded that 'by industry their little possessions increased, their stock multiplied, and the lonely families after a time had all things needful for living.'[28] It was upon the efforts of the Loyalists that the province's progress rested. J. George Hodgins asserted that 'by their early labours, their example of thrift and industry, and their sterling loyalty, they have largely contributed to the prosperity and stability of the British American colonies.'[29]

The Victorian concern with respectability pervades the textbooks. It is repeatedly asserted that the Loyalists were 'people of culture and social distinction.' In *A History of Canada* Charles G.D. Roberts insisted that Loyalist ranks were filled with 'the choicest stock the colonies could boast ... the most influential judges, the most distinguished lawyers, the most capable and prominent physicians, the most highly educated of the clergy, the members of the council of the various colonies, the Crown officials.'[30] In *Ontario High School History of Canada* W.L. Grant described the Loyalists as 'the best blood in the United States, well-to-do men and women of the landed gentry or the merchant class.'[31]

W.S. Herrington's *Heroines of Canadian History* has special significance for the messages it conveys about gender. Herrington devoted an entire chapter to the sufferings and travails of Loyalist women. The experience of Mrs Jacob Bowman was presented as typical of the plight endured by Loyalist women during the Revolution. In November of 1775 Bowman was forced to stand by as Rebels stripped her home of nearly all its bedding, clothing, and provisions and arrested her husband and eldest son. She gave birth soon after and was left destitute with six young children and a newborn. 'This brave woman,' Herrington asserted, 'did not despair, nor was her loyalty shaken in the least.' She joined a party of five other women and thirty-one children and made a perilous journey to find protection and assistance under the British at Fort George. 'Hundreds of the United Empire Loyalist mothers,' Herrington insisted, 'suffered the same cruel separation from members of their families.' All displayed the 'same loyal hearts and the same patient endurance.' Life in the wilderness proved to be even more demanding. 'It was no trifling matter,' Herrington asserted, 'to battle with the impediments that nature placed in the way of the early settlers,' and 'many a mother laboured in the forests digging the roots of the wild plants or eagerly gathering the buds from the trees in order to secure some scanty nourishment for her starving children.'[32] Although Herrington believed that the deeds and sacrifices of Canada's Loyalist pioneer women were as deserving of praise and recognition as those made by men, his overall message served to confirm prevailing views of female domesticity and maternalism. 'While we exalt the brave soldier,' Herrington asserted, 'let us not forget the braver wife at home.' It was as loyal wives and dedicated mothers that Loyalist women made their greatest contribution. 'Canada owes much,' Herrington concluded, 'to the men who have fought her battles and borne the burdens of state – but she owes as much, yea, more, to the noble women who instilled the principles of loyalty and devotion in the breasts of their sons.'[33] By invoking the experiences of Loyalist women, Herrington hoped to inspire female students to the same levels of loyalty, industriousness, and perseverance in their future roles as wives and mothers.

The attempt to uphold the Loyalists as icons to be revered and models to be imitated was not without its problems. At the time, Canadian historiography was decidedly Whig in its approach and emphasized the economic, social, and moral progress of the nation, the development of democratic institutions, and the evolution towards nationhood. The Loyalists' place in these developments was ambiguous. The Loyalists could easily be upheld as pioneers who had laid the foundation of the nation's economic progress and had created many of the country's educational and religious institutions. They could also be praised for acting 'as a constant barrier to the designs of the United States,' particularly during the War of 1812. The Loyalists also were associated, however, with reactionary forces that opposed the development of responsible government and labelled as disloyal attempts to reform the colonial relationship. G.W. Ross observed that 'the only shadow cast by the UELS on the history of Canada' was that 'in the maintenance of the prerogatives of the Crown,' Loyalists 'were not susceptible to the growth of those democratic tendencies which always characterize the Anglo-Saxon race under new conditions' and were 'unnecessarily alarmed at the urgent demands of Canadians for all the privileges of self-government.'[34] Although the Loyalists were often praised as 'the best material out of which to build a nation,' they disappear from the textbooks after their initial settlement and the War of 1812 and play virtually no role in the subsequent history of the country.

In his studies of the formation of the educational state in Upper Canada / Ontario, Bruce Curtis explores the means by which government created and employed a system of public education to produce a citizenry. State control over school curriculum and textbooks provided one of the essential tools in this process. Authorized textbooks enabled the state to 'diffuse useful knowledge' and 'sound habits' as well as to preserve social harmony by instilling a common set of social values.[35] The treatment of the Loyalists in the history textbooks authorized for use in Ontario's schools was in keeping with these general objectives. History was viewed as a means to create good citizens with a shared sense of origins and a belief in a common destiny. To achieve this end, history textbooks generally avoided partisan debates or divisive issues and focused on themes of nation building. In their treatment of the Loyalists, writers of Ontario history texts usually spoke in vague and general terms about the Loyalists' role in the American Revolution and focused instead on their contributions as founders of the nation and as pioneers. It was as role models for the values and behaviours that the state hoped to inculcate through education, however, that the Loyalists were chiefly utilized.

The final decade of the nineteenth century witnessed a growing interest in local history across Ontario. The disillusionment that followed the apparent failure of Confederation to create prosperity, the continuing debate over the nation's destiny, and the failure to eliminate sectional, racial, and linguistic tensions redirected historical interest from the national stage towards the provincial and local scenes. This development was reflected in the creation of local historical societies that encouraged and published local historical research.[36] Throughout the period, local researchers and antiquarians set about producing histories that were rooted in their particular families and communities. Although such works were largely descriptive and lacking in analysis, they did not merely represent an interest in history for history's sake. Local boosterism, filiopietism, and the desire to inculcate Victorian values pervade the works of local history published throughout the period.

The appropriation of the Loyalist tradition by Toronto interests during the celebrations of 1884 and 1891 produced considerable resentment in those areas of the province that were actually the original centres of Loyalist settlement. In *Sketches Illustrating the Early Settlement and History of Glengarry in Canada*, J.A. Macdonnell complained that 'there is but little, if any, mention made of the part which the Highlanders of Glengarry took in the American Revolutionary war of 1776–83, and the early settlement of the country at the close of the war, its defence in 1812–14, and the suppression of the rebellion.' 'Others, the York volunteers in particular,' he observed, 'come in for at least their fair share of credit. Their flags are paraded, and their deeds are made to speak again after the lapse of many years, and the inference is given, with painful reiteration, that to them and theirs among the local forces of the country, is the credit chiefly due on these occasions.' Macdonnell insisted that such recognition was often ill founded. 'Individuals who never left their provision shops except to take to the woods,' he charged, 'would appear to have become of late great military commanders of those days – the very saviours of their country, in fact, in the hour of its utmost need.' Glengarry, however, could legitimately boast 'as many loyalist settlers who had fought for the Crown during the first War as any other of the earliest settled counties' and had contributed during the War of 1812 and the Rebellion of 1837 'more fighting men for the preservation of the country, its connection with the Mother Land, and the Maintenance of our Institutions, than any other part of the Province.'[37] Such rivalry and boosterism was typical of the local histories of the period.

Communities with a Loyalist past hoped to shine in the reflected glory of their founders. W.S. Herrington differentiated those areas of the province first inhabited by the Loyalists from those settled at a later date. 'The Loyalists,' Herrington asserted, 'were above the ordinary type of emigrants who, too frequently, having made a failure of life in their native surroundings, seek other fields in which to begin anew their struggle for existence.'[38] Communities in decline placed particular importance on their Loyalist origins. In an address about his home town of Adolphustown, presented to the United Empire Loyalist Association of Ontario, William Canniff reminded his audience that this community was the 'first' Loyalist settlement in the province and had once been 'the centre of Upper Canada.' 'Indeed, this, the smallest of the townships,' Canniff continued, 'took the lead for many years in political, as well as other general matters relating to the country.'[39]

Just as the appropriation of the Loyalist tradition by particular communities created resentment elsewhere, the portrayal of the Loyalists as uniformly English in background and predominantly Anglican in religion produced a similar reaction. In *The Story of Dundas*, J. Smyth Carter insisted that the Loyalists 'were found among all classes, all denominations, and all nationalities represented in the colonies.'[40] J.A. Macdonnell challenged the suggestion that the Scotch were an insignificant element among the Loyalist population. The Scotch, he insisted, played an 'instrumental' role in the development of the province, 'not only in preserving it by their prowess, but developing it from the primeval forest to the fruitful land it is today.'[41] Rev. A.B. Sherk complained that 'It has been common to classify as UE Loyalists only those settlers who were ready to bear arms in defense of the "British cause." But there are others who evidently deserve to be ranked as Loyalists, namely, large numbers of the Mennonites of Pennsylvania and the Quakers also.' Sherk insisted that these sects came to Canada because 'they were in love with British institutions and wished to be under British protection.' Although their religious convictions prevented them from taking up arms, 'they were thoroughly loyal to the British cause and, we think, should be classified as Loyalists.' 'The Mennonites, who settled in Canada in considerable numbers, more than a century ago,' Sherk maintained, 'have been among the sturdiest pioneers of our country. The descendants of this quiet, industrious, high-minded, God-fearing people, have done much to help to give character and stability to our institutions.'[42] The demands of ethnic and religious minorities to have their contributions to the founding and development of the province recognized represented an attempt to legitimize their place within Ontario society.

Most works of local history were decidedly didactic in tone and intent. In the preface to *Pioneer Sketches of Long Point Settlement*, E.A. Owen acknowledged that his purpose in writing the book was 'to instill in younger minds a keener sense of gratitude for the wonderful advantages which have fallen to their lot, and inspire them with renewed courage to battle for the right and overcome the many difficulties which await them in the pathway of life.' 'If future generations of Norfolk's citizenship are to remain as patriotic and loyal as the present and past have been,' Owen insisted, 'we must awaken in the minds of the young an interest in the story of pioneer life. They must study the character of the men and women who lost everything and suffered everything for conscience['s] sake; and they must know of the hardships endured with fortitude, the privations suffered with patient resignation, and the great obstacles surmounted by firm determination and resolute perseverance, which marks the lives of these old pioneers in their struggles for existence in the primeval forest.' Owen worried, however, that 'avarice, pride, egotism, selfishness, hypocrisy and a host of other evils' threatened to replace the honest toil, social equality, and simple faith that were characteristic features of Loyalist pioneer life.[43] The litany of virtues attributed to the Loyalists, however, reveals more about the ideals upheld by Victorian society than it does about the reality of the Loyalist experience.

In *Pioneer Sketches of Long Point Settlement* Owen praised the Loyalist pioneer women of Norfolk as models of true womanhood. He called upon the wives and mothers of the present day to 'hold sacred the remembrance of these grand old pioneer mothers,' who 'toiled under so many disadvantages, and yet by preserving industry, trust in an overruling Providence, and an unflinching fidelity to duty accomplished so much ... and were brave enough to make the best of their surroundings and to be content with the possibilities that confronted them.' 'Purity of motive and action, persevering industry, patient and cheerful resignation to the inevitable, and a firm determination to grapple with the possible,' Owen concluded, 'are the four cardinal principles involved in the development of a true and noble womanhood.'[44] For men like Owen, the Loyalist and pioneer past provided an opportunity to affirm traditional values and role models.

Local histories shared an antiquarian interest in the preservation of the fading realities of pioneer life. Most of the space in such works was taken up in detailed descriptions of the pioneer way of life, with chapters devoted to clearing the land; building a log cabin; clothing; cooking; the making of soap, candles, and maple syrup; and amusements and pastimes. Such knowledge was usually derived second-hand. The material for E.A. Owen's *Pioneer Sketches of Long Point Settlement*, for example, was 'obtained by careful and repeated interviews with the remaining few, who, in their youthful days, sat at the feet of the old pioneers themselves.'[45] Sentimental accounts of rural life reflected a nostalgia for a simpler, stabler past during a period of socio-economic transformation.

Another characteristic of local histories was the inclusion of biographical sketches of the area's original settlers. In part, this format grew out of economic necessity. Local historical writing was frequently published by subscription. Inclusion of particular individuals and families within a volume often ensured advance sales among descendants. Biographical sketches were also popular vehicles in late nineteenth-century Canada for illustrating the progress of the nation and the virtues necessary for success. Works such as Henry James Morgan's *Sketches of Celebrated Canadians*, G. Mercer Adam's *Prominent Men of Canada: a collection of persons distinguished in professional and political life, and in the commerce and industry of Canada*, and John Alexander Cooper's *Men of Canada: a portrait gallery of men whose energy, ability, enterprise, and pubic spirit are responsible for the advancement of Canada* attributed Canada's development to the character, determination, and ingenuity of individuals.[46] Sketches of local Loyalists sought to impress on the current generation the qualities of integrity, industry, love of law and order, piety, and patriotism, which Victorian Ontarians believed were essential to success.

Local histories presented a past that was frequently at odds with that expounded by political partisans and textbook writers. Rooted in local knowledge and experience, local histories tended to be concerned more with the details of everyday life than with questions of ideology or politics. Local histories were often more sensitive to ethnic and religious diversity than were textbooks that overlooked plurality in favour of creating a common identity. Local histories were no less didactic or self-serving, however, than other forms of historical writing. Pride of place or family were the principal motivations of many local historians.

The most popular form of Loyalist historical writing was genealogy. The late nineteenth century witnessed a passion for genealogy throughout North America among an established middle class anxious about the implications of industrialization and mass immigration. Genealogy provided a feeling of rootedness in an increasingly complex urban and industrial society. Ancestor worship aimed more to enhance the prestige of the living than to honour the dead. It also sought to marginalize and exclude less desirable groups. Filiopietism did not develop simply from a desire to affirm and demonstrate higher status, however; it also reflected a widespread belief in the biological implications of bloodlines. Works such as Sir Francis Galton's *Hereditary Genius* found a large audience among an ancestor-conscious public convinced that heredity truly mattered. The search for ancestors reflected common and increasingly urgent preoccupations with class and race.

The growing popularity of genealogy in Ontario at the turn of the century was reflected in the pioneering work of the Toronto lawyer Edward Marion Chadwick. Chadwick's interest in the province's pioneers and passion for genealogy culminated in the publication of *Ontarian Families: Genealogies of United Empire Loyalist and other Pioneer Families of Upper Canada* in 1894. In 1898 Chadwick created the *Ontarian Genealogist and Family Historian*, a magazine designed to further popularize genealogical research. The purpose of the magazine was to collect and publish personal and genealogical information 'regarding the families of UE Loyalists and other pioneer settlers ... for the use of future generations before it passes out of memory.'[47] Although Chadwick could not claim to be of Loyalist descent, his avid interest in genealogy attracted him to the newly formed United Empire Loyalist Association of Ontario. Chadwick served as the association's legal adviser from 1897 until 1912 and was its official genealogist from 1913 to 1921. Under Chadwick's guidance, the association became one of the principal vehicles for genealogical research in the province and a major publisher of such material.[48] Most of the genealogical works published by the Loyalist Association followed a similar formula. After describing the distinguished ancestry, upstanding character, dedication to principle, persecution, struggle, and success of their Loyalist forebears, genealogists traced the accomplishments of the family, always portraying descendants as worthy heirs of their ancestors. Frequently vague and imprecise, the works were long on family folklore and anecdotes and short on reliable and verifiable information.

Loyalist genealogists placed considerable stress on the antiquity of the family name. Canon A.W. MacNab boasted that Clan MacNab 'is a very ancient one and takes rank amongst the noted and time-honoured houses of Scotland.'[49] Similarly, Alexander Fraser claimed the origins of the Shaw family extended back to Shaw MacDuff, a warrior who was created earl of Fife in 1057 for services rendered to Malcolm Canmore, king of Scotland.[50] Catherine Nina Merritt claimed that it had 'been established without a doubt' that the Merritts could trace their ancestry back to the reign of William the Conqueror.[51] One of the more outrageous claims was that of Frederick Gregory Forsyth. Forsyth was born in Portland, Maine, in 1856 and claimed to be of Loyalist descent. An amateur historian and the author of various musical compositions, Forsyth was a genuine eccentric obsessed with proving the authenticity of the family claim to the title Viscount de Fronsac and achieving the restoration of all its historic rights and privileges.[52]

Forsyth went to considerable lengths to uphold the family claim to the title, immersing himself in genealogy and heraldic folklore and publishing *Memorial of the De Forsyths de Fronsac* in 1897. To further his cause he even organized a chapter of the Aryan and Seigniorial Order of the Empire in America, an organization dedicated to the restoration of hereditary titles. Forsyth was also a founding member of the United Empire Loyalist Association of the province of Quebec, and the founder and herald marshal of the College of Arms of Canada. The purpose of all this activity was nothing less than to 'restore royal legitimacy wherever practicable' and to 'maintain the supremacy of Aryan Aristocracy and chivalry against the pretensions of vulgar wealth.'[53] In 1906 in Kingston Forsyth published *Rise of the United Empire Loyalists: A Sketch of American History* to further his cause. Only the last chapter of the work in fact deals with the Loyalists; the remainder consists of an impassioned polemic against republicanism, democracy, and materialism and an equally impassioned defence of the merits of restructuring North American society along the aristocratic and feudal models contained in the colonies' original royal charters. Forsyth appealed to Loyalist descendants to remain true to the legacy of their forefathers and stand by fellow members of the 'class of honour' in their efforts to revive the hereditary titles and privileges to which they were entitled.

Claims of family antiquity were accompanied by declarations of continued loyalty and dedication to principle down through the ages. Canon A.W. MacNab boasted that the MacNabs were characterized by an 'inborn loyalty.' He noted with pride that MacNabs had fought at the Battle of Culloden, stood with Wolfe at Quebec, and joined the Loyalist forces during the American Revolution. Sir Allan MacNab 'was but following clan tradition' in 1837 when he drove the rebel followers of William Lyon Mackenzie out of Toronto and forced them back to their final stronghold and refuge on Navy Island in the Niagara River. Canon A.W. MacNab was particularly proud of James MacNab, who served and died at Waterloo.[54] In similar fashion Alexander Fraser delineated the unceasing dedication of the Shaw family to the Crown and Empire. The patriarch of the family in North America, Alexander Shaw, saw action during the Seven Years' War as an aide-de-camp to General Provost. His brother Aeneas entered the British army at an early age and served in Simcoe's corps during the American Revolution. During the War of 1812, Aeneas Shaw was placed second in command of British forces after the death of Brock at Queenston Heights. His son Alexander joined the British military and participated in the battles of Alexandria, Calabria, and Waterloo. In true family fashion, Alexander's son George came to Upper Canada's defence during the rebellion of 1837. The family tradition lived on in Colonel George A. Shaw, a veteran of the Fenian raids and 'a highly respected citizen of Toronto, proud of his distinguished ancestry, as is his right and duty to be, and jealous of the escutcheon he worthily bears.'[55] The purpose of such exercises was clear: Loyalist descendants had inherited the noble traits of their ancestors and were thus deserving of special recognition. 'Fortunate is he,' Anne Cawthra unabashedly proclaimed, 'who can call himself the descendant of a United Empire Loyalist.'[56]

Such self-serving filiopietism was frequently based on very imprecise and highly anecdotal family folklore. Peregrine Otway-Page's sketch of his family history was typical of much genealogical writing of the time. 'It was about the year 1776, after the loss of all their property because of loyalty to the King and Crown,' Otway-Page asserts, 'that my ancestors on my mother's side were forced to migrate to Canada.' He was uncertain, however, about when the family arrived or from what part of the United States they came. Despite such lack of information, Otway-Page says with confidence that 'they reached Canada after a long, dangerous journey of much suffering and privation.' Otway-Page is obviously simply fitting his family history into the established paradigms of the Loyalist tradition. Family tradition also maintained that his mother had an encounter with Sir Isaac Brock during the battle of Queenston Heights. Otway-Page related that 'it was she who remarked that Gen. Brock had forgotten his sword, a very strange incident, but he refused to return for it and remarked that he had a presentiment that it would be his last battle, which subsequently proved true.'[57] The story is characteristic of the sentimentality and unsubstantiated hearsay frequently found in the genealogical writing of the period.

Genealogical works usually concluded with an appeal to future generations to remain true to the legacy of their forefathers. In his sketch of the Teeple family, W.B. Waterbury expressed the hope that the current generation would 'prove worthy successors of those sturdy "Pilgrim Fathers of Canada."'[58] Similarly, Canniff Haight concluded 'A Genealogical Narrative of the Daniel Haight Family' with the panegyric: 'All honor to the memory of those noble men; they are worthy of the warmest admiration, and the recollection of what they have done should make the heart of every son of this fair Dominion thrill with pride.'[59] Behind such assertions lay concerns of class and race. Many middle-class Anglo-Canadians looked to ancestry as a means of defending their social status and position against the challenges presented by emergent classes and immigrants.

When Lorenzo Sabine published *The American Loyalists* in 1847, he was very much a lone voice in the wilderness. By the turn of the century, however, a new generation of American historians, both amateur and professional, had revised the history of the Revolution. In the process they displayed far more interest in and sympathy towards the Loyalists than had their predecessors. A common feature of the Loyalist literature published in Ontario between the 1884 and the First World War is its heavy reliance on contemporary American sources. Key elements of the Loyalist tradition – the Loyalists' dedication to principle, superior social origins, and persecution – depended almost entirely on references to American works and writers for support.

This decided reorientation in American historiography stemmed from a variety of forces. The prevailing Whig and Nationalist interpretation of American history had been irrevocably damaged by the Civil War. Americans emerged from the Reconstruction period sceptical of the view of the Revolution as a unified effort of a united people. American historians were thus susceptible to the influence of new interpretations during this period.[60] The most important outside influence was W.E.H. Lecky's *History of England in the Eighteenth Century*. Lecky challenged the portrayal of the Revolution as a virtually unanimous uprising of the whole people. He saw the Revolution as the work of an energetic minority 'who succeeded in committing an undecided and fluctuating majority to courses for which they had little love, and leading them step by step to a position from which it was impossible to recede.' Lecky described the Loyalists as 'brave and honest men' who 'were proud of the great and free Empire to which they belonged.' Counting among their ranks 'some of the best and ablest men America has ever produced' the Loyalists 'were contending for an ideal which was at least as worthy as that for which Washington fought.' 'The maintenance of one free, industrial, and pacific empire, comprising the whole English race,' Lecky concluded, 'may have been a dream, but it was at least a noble one, and there were Americans prepared to make any personal sacrifices rather than assist in destroying it.'[61] Lecky's assessment of the course of the Revolution had a significant influence on many American historians. Moses Coit Tyler, for example, recommended Lecky's work as 'the very best means of getting the coming generation of American students out of the old manner of thinking upon and treating American history, which has led to so much chauvinism among our people.'[62]

The revisionist interpretation of the Revolution that emerged during the last two decades of the nineteenth century was also a product of the tumultuous changes that accompanied industrialization, urbanization, and large-scale immigration. Besieged by economic and social forces that threatened fundamentally to transform the nation, some conservative American writers began to question whether the history of the United States was in fact one of continuous improvement and progress and expressed a new-found empathy with the position and plight of the Loyalists.[63] American interest in the Loyalists was aided further by the erosion of the animosities of the past. By the end of the nineteenth century, Britain and the United States increasingly viewed each other as friends and allies rather than rivals and enemies. Calls for Anglo-Saxon unity were heard in the United States as Americans attempted to come to terms with the ethnic pluralization of American society that accompanied immigration.[64] A new perspective on the Revolution was also added as the United States itself began to emerge as an imperial power at the turn of the century.

Among the earliest works to demonstrate this reorientation in American thinking about the Loyalists was George E. Ellis's 'The Loyalists and Their Fortunes' in Justin Winsor's *Narrative and Critical History of America*. The president of the Massachusetts Historical Society, a Unitarian clergymen, the son of a wealthy Boston merchant and grandson of a Loyalist, Ellis portrayed the Loyalists as 'men of the noblest character and of the highest position,' 'eminent in private and public virtue, ardent in their patriotism, and thoroughly sincere in the position to which they committed themselves.' 'They differed from their contemporaries of equal virtue, sincerity, and intelligence on the patriot side,' Ellis insisted, 'in that single quality of loyalty.'[65] He was particularly critical of the Loyalists' persecution and exile and suggested that the United States would have been better equipped to handle the current economic and social forces transforming the nation had the Loyalists and their conservative values not been expelled.

The Loyalists found another advocate in James K. Hosmer, a professor of history, literature, and rhetoric at Washington University. 'History at this late date,' Hosmer asserted in his *Life of Samuel Adams*, 'can certainly afford a compassionate word for the Tories, who, besides having been forced to atone in life for the mistake of taking the wrong side, have received while in their graves little but detestation.' 'There were in fact,' Hosmer maintained, 'no better men or women in America as regards intelligence, substantive good purpose and piety.'[66] A strong advocate of Anglo-Saxon unity, Hosmer contended in *A Short History of Anglo-Saxon Freedom* that the Revolution was a contest 'not of countries but parties,' and he appealed to the English-speaking peoples to recognize their kinship.[67]

The changing nature of history itself promoted revisionism. A new generation of historians, equipped with the teachings of scientific history and its emphasis on objectivity and the critical use of sources, challenged earlier interpretations of the Revolution and the Loyalists. Among the most influential revisionist treatments of the Loyalists was Moses Coit Tyler's essay, 'The Party of the Loyalists in the American Revolution,' which appeared in the first volume of the *American Historical Review*. The essay was both a reassessment of the Loyalists and an appeal for the use of scientific methods in history. 'The truth,' Tyler insisted, 'is to be found only by him who searches for it with an unbiased mind.' Historians must adopt the attitude of 'scientific investigators' if they were to acquire a 'thoroughly discriminating and just acquaintance with that prodigious epoch in our history.' Tyler claimed that examined 'calmly,' 'considerately,' and 'fairly,' the Loyalist side was 'in argument not a weak one, and in motive and sentiment not a base one, and in devotion and self-sacrifice not an unheroic one.' 'By any standard of judgement,' Tyler concluded, 'the Tories of the Revolution seem to have been not a profligate party, nor an unprincipled one, nor a reckless or even a light minded one, but, on the contrary, to have had among them a very considerable portion of the most refined, thoughtful and conscientious people in the colonies.'[68]

Tyler's views were shared by Charles Kendall Adams and Sydney George Fisher. In 'Some Neglected Aspects of the Revolutionary War' Adams denounced the 'partiality and incompleteness' that characterized most treatments of the Revolution. Historians such as Bancroft, Adams maintained, proved to be 'great advocates rather than great judges.'[69] Similarly, in *The True History of the American Revolution* Fisher complained that in the past historians have assumed that 'we want to think of England as having lost the colonies by failure to be conciliatory, and that the Revolution was a one-sided, smooth affair, without any difficulties or terrors of a rebellion or a great upheaval of settled opinion.'[70] Both Adams and Fisher challenged the 'erroneous impression' that the Revolution was the product of the efforts of a united people and that opposition was insignificant and completely misguided. The Revolution was in fact America's first civil war and 'a far more desperate and a far more doubtful struggle than the historians have led us to believe.' The Loyalists constituted a considerable opposition, 'but it is not in numbers only that the Tories were formidable. They were even more formidable in influence, character, and respectability.' 'The ranks of the Tories,' Adams concluded, 'contained a very considerable portion of the most thoughtful, the most intelligent, and the most refined of the colonial people.'[71]

Such sentiments found a warm and enthusiastic reception among Loyalist writers in Ontario. In *History and Historiettes: United Empire Loyalists* Edward Harris rejoiced that 'after the lapse of a century, American historians ... are writing disinterestedly and with historical accuracy, towards those Americans who thought and fought against the Revolution.'[72] The indebtedness of Ontario's writers to American revisionists is perhaps best illustrated by Arthur Johnston's *Myths and Facts of the American Revolution*. Johnston's purpose was to refute the 'flimsy illusions,' 'unsubstantial conceits,' and 'impudent perversions' contained in the American version of the 'so-called history' of the Revolution. 'Surely it is time,' Johnston asserted, 'that the citizens of the great Republic should more closely scan the records of its foundations, and no longer remain complacently content with fairy tales in the guise of history, vicariously flattering to their vanity.' There is more than a little irony in the fact that Johnston modelled the work on Sydney Fisher's *The True History of the American Revolution* and drew heavily upon the writings of American historians such as Hosmer and Tyler. It is even more ironic that Ontarian writers like Johnston seemed oblivious to the fact that they were selectively using the work of the American revisionists to fabricate a mythology of their own. Johnston dedicated the book to 'the memory of the Loyalists,' the 'true "Heroes of the Revolution,"' who sacrificed their lives and their fortunes in an attempt to preserve the integrity of an empire that has forgotten them.' 'Their steadfastness of character, their patience, and courage under the infliction of cruel and undeserved persecution,' Johnston asserted, 'has been transmitted to [Canada's] citizens, and has helped to raise higher its character among the nations of the earth.'[73]

Loyalist writers were very selective in their reading of American historians. The work of figures such as Hosmer, Tyler, and Adams inspired students to re-examine the American Revolution, which resulted in a number of dissertations that examined the Loyalists in greater detail than had hitherto been the case. Although largely descriptive, the dissertations often qualified their mentors' findings. In *Loyalism in New York during the American Revolution* Alexander Flick maintained that the Loyalists of New York exhibited a wide range of motivations from 'the basest material greed to the loftiest sense of religious duty and the highest type of patriotism' and included within their ranks 'persons of all social positions,' 'of all grades of intelligence,' 'of all lines of work,' and 'of all creeds.' The common characteristic of all Loyalists was a conservative tendency that 'clung to the established order of things' and 'shunned association with those that are given to change.'[74] Claude Van Tyne reached a similar conclusion in *The Loyalists in the American Revolution.* According to Van Tyne, the definitive feature of the Loyalist was a 'natural conservatism' that 'strove to keep things as they were.' 'The very conservatism, which made them opponents of the Whigs,' however, 'rendered their opposition weak and ineffectual.'[75] Not surprisingly, the works of Flick and Van Tyne proved less useful to Ontarian writers and were consequently ignored.

All of the Canadian works examined to this point were written by amateur historians: civil servants, politicians, lawyers, clergymen, and housewives with the time and resources to dedicate to writing and research.

Although they lacked formal training in the study of history or the use of documents, their passion for the past often resulted in useful insights and the preservation of many documents. Their interest in the Loyalist past, however, was immediate and rooted in the present. Whether its purpose was to defend imperialist ideology, to inculcate Victorian values, or to worship ancestors, the Loyalist tradition was essentially self-serving. Most Ontarians were in fact 'content with fairy tales in the guise of history, vicariously flattering to their vanity.' By the turn of the century, however, a body of professional historians familiar with the techniques of scientific history and the critical use of sources began to emerge in Canada and to challenge the interpretations of their amateur predecessors.[76] To a great extent, this assault was part of the natural dialectic of historical discourse. It constituted as well an attempt by the rising generation of professional historians 'to secure their own credentials' by calling into question the validity of previous work.[77]

William Stewart Wallace, a professor of history at McMaster University, was a member of this small group of professional historians.[78] Born in 1884, Wallace was educated at the Universities of Toronto and Oxford. He went on to become the chief librarian of the University of Toronto and the first editor of the *Canadian Historical Review*. Wallace's first work, *The United Empire Loyalists: A Chronicle of the Great Migration*, was published in 1914 and marks a turning point in the treatment of the Loyalists in Ontario. Wallace observed that 'the United Empire Loyalists have suffered a strange fate at the hands of historians.' Ignored or vilified by American writers for over a century, 'American historians of a new school have revised the history of the Revolution, and a tardy reparation has been made to the memory of the Tories of that day.' 'Indeed, some of these writers in their anxiety to stand straight,' Wallace exclaimed, 'have leaned backwards; and by no one perhaps will the ultra Tory view of the Revolution be found so clearly expressed.' Wallace was especially sceptical of the 'uncritical veneration' of the Loyalists contained in Canadian works. 'The interest which Canadians have taken in the Loyalists,' Wallace complained, 'has been either patriotic or genealogical; and few attempts have been made to tell their story in the cold light of impartial history, or to estimate the results which have flowed from their migration.'[79]

In *The United Empire Loyalists: A Chronicle of the Great Migration* Wallace attempted to present a balanced assessment of the Loyalist experience based on hard documentary evidence. In the process, he challenged many of the key elements of the Loyalist tradition. 'It is commonly supposed,' Wallace asserted, 'that the Loyalists drew their strength from the upper classes in the colonies, while the revolutionists drew theirs from the proletariate.' While it was true that 'that among the official classes and the large landowners, among the clergymen, lawyers, and physicians, the majority were Loyalists,' it was also true that 'there were no humbler peasants in the revolutionary ranks than some of the Loyalist farmers who migrated to Upper Canada in 1783.' 'While there were members of the oldest and most famous families in British America among the Loyalists of the Thirteen Colonies,' Wallace concluded, 'the majority of those who came to Nova Scotia, New Brunswick, and especially Upper Canada, were people of very humble origin.' He also acknowledged that loyalty was not simply a matter of principle. Factional rivalry, dependence on government for a livelihood, the conviction that England could not be beaten, the excesses of the revolutionary mob, and the failure of certain groups to assimilate into American society determined the 'loyalty' of many. 'All that can be said,' Wallace concluded, 'is that the Loyalists were most numerous among those classes which had most to lose by change.' Nor did the Loyalists play a particularly heroic role during the conflict. According to Wallace, they lacked initiative and were slow to organize and defend themselves. Although the Loyalists were the objects of excessive persecution, atrocities were in fact committed by both sides. Wallace did acknowledge, however, that the Loyalist migration had had a significant influence on the course of Canadian history, laying the foundation of two new provinces and ensuring English ascendancy over the French majority.[80]

Wallace's critical treatment of the Loyalists marked the beginning of a decided falling off in the number of Loyalist publications. The decline in the proliferation of Loyalist materials can be attributed to a number of factors. Wallace's demythologization undermined the cachet associated with the Loyalists. Communities and individuals were no longer quite so certain that their Loyalist past was a badge of unquestioned distinction. Moreover, Canada emerged from the First World War, a significantly changed nation. The war diluted the intense imperialist and anti-American sentiment that had come to characterize the Loyalist tradition. The Empire was in the process of transformation into the Commonwealth, and Canadians were increasingly intent on asserting their independence. Much of the hostility and mistrust of the Americans had been eroded in the face of wartime association as allies and increasing economic, social, cultural, and political contact and exposure.[81] The imperialist and anti-American sentiments that had come to characterize the Loyalist tradition thus became increasingly anachronistic as the political debates in which the Loyalist past had been a useful weapon faded into memory. Unlike the legend of the founding fathers in the United States, the Loyalist tradition contained too many ambiguities to continue as a vital influence during the 1920s and beyond. The Loyalists were portrayed as both humble pioneers clearing the wilderness and as a wealthy and exclusive elite. They were said to have laid the foundations of the province's material development but were frequently associated with the reactionary forces that impeded the province's political progress. The regional nature of the Loyalist experience, moreover, limited the possibility of Loyalist tradition's becoming a genuine national tradition. As the study of history became increasingly dominated by trained professionals whose interests lay in the political and economic evolution of the nation, the history of the Loyalists was increasingly regarded as a pursuit best suited to the antiquarian and filiopietistic genealogist rather than to the professional historian. A product of the conditions of the last half of the nineteenth century, the Loyalist tradition gradually faded from the mainstream of Canadian thought following the First World War.

6

'Object lessons': Loyalist Monuments and the Creation of Usable Pasts

The years between the 1884 centennial celebrations and the First World War saw the erection of a number of public monuments commemorating individuals associated with Ontario's Loyalist past. The significance of these monuments has largely been ignored by historians.[1] Such neglect is surprising given the importance attached to such memorials by their contemporaries. A circular addressed to prospective members of the Ontario Historical Society observed in 1901 that 'there is nothing better [than monuments] to promote patriotism' and 'their educational influence can hardly be overestimated.' Monuments, the circular declared, 'are at once an index to the character of a people and constant object lessons of the civic virtues, of heroism, and public and private gratitude.' The erection of monuments beautified their surroundings and brought 'material benefit' in the form of tourists and travellers.[2] As the circular illustrates, monuments performed a variety of functions. Monuments were most obviously a means to commemorate the past and instil patriotism. Monuments rarely sought to commemorate an objective past, however; they celebrated a version of the past that reflected the values, attitudes, and objectives of their promoters. Aimed at a wide audience, monuments had a didactic role in communicating traditions and beliefs from generation to generation and from one class to another. They reminded people of what to believe and how to behave. Monuments were one of the principal channels through which groups and communities expressed their own aspirations and ideals. Public monuments thus played an important promotional role. By invoking an event or individual, a particular cause or objective was frequently being advanced.[3] Every monument has a social history; careful consideration must thus be given to the individuals and groups responsible for its inception and completion and its intended audience. An examination of the movements to erect monuments honouring Joseph Brant, Laura Secord, and Barbara Heck reveals a great deal about how various groups set out to create usable pasts in late nineteenth- and early twentieth-century Ontario.

On 13 October 1886 a crowd of over 20,000 gathered in Brantford's Victoria Park to witness the unveiling of a monument honouring the Mohawk warrior and leader Joseph Brant. The streets were ablaze with bunting and flags as merchants vied with each other to erect the most elaborate display and cash in on the thousands of visitors who had descended upon the city for the occasion. Shortly after noon, the ringing of church bells and the whistles of industry heralded the day's proceedings and a massive procession began to wind its way towards Victoria Park. As it passed through the crowd-lined streets, loud cheers greeted the Six Nations chiefs dressed in Native costume, the lieutenant-governor, John Beverley Robinson, and his escort of Burford militia, and Major-General Sir Frederick Middleton in full military uniform. Arriving at the site of the unveiling, the lieutenant-governor was saluted by 100 members of the Dufferin Rifles. After inspecting the guard of honour, he joined Brantford's civic, economic, and social leaders on the platform erected beside the flag-draped monument. The proceedings commenced with the singing of the one hundredth psalm by members of the city's Mendelssohn Choir and prayers led by Rev. Dr Cochrane. After a few words of welcome from Allan Cleghorn, the president of the Brant Memorial Association, the lieutenant-governor performed the unveiling. Following the ceremony, the Mendelssohn Choir presented a song specially commissioned for the occasion, W.F. Cockshutt recited a memorial ode composed by local Native poet E. Pauline Johnson, Chief John Buck spoke on behalf of the Six Nations, and the sculptor Percy Wood delivered a brief address. The formal proceedings were brought to a close as Allan Cleghorn formally handed over the memorial to Mayor Heyd, who accepted on behalf of the city.[4]

Two themes dominated the day's speeches: Brant's fidelity to the British Crown and Empire and his efforts to civilize and Christianize the Six Nations. In his opening prayer, Dr Cochrane praised Brant for his 'loyalty, fidelity, sincerity and earnestness of purpose.' Lieutenant-Governor Robinson observed that Brant's 'friendship and fidelity to the British had always remained firm and unshaken.' 'Had it not been for Brant and his men,' Robinson concluded, 'there would not perhaps have been a Canada on the map of this continent today.' In his remarks Chief John Buck

assured the crowd that 'even as their great chieftain was loyal,' the people
of the Six Nations remained 'ever loyal to the British Crown.' In addition
to his 'single hearted devotion' to Crown and Empire, speakers acclaimed
Brant's dedication to the advancement of his people. Allan Cleghorn
commented that Brant did 'everything he could to promote civilizing
influences' among the Six Nations. Lieutenant-Governor Robinson
observed that Brant's 'influence in the advancement' of the Six Nations
had been 'incalculable.'[5] The sentiments expressed on the occasion are
perhaps best summed up by an editorial in the Brantford *Courier*: 'When
his single hearted devotion to the English cause and the heritage he
helped to save for the present generation, and the good he accomplished
amongst his own people, both from a civilizing, Christian and temper-
ance standpoint, are considered, who will say that Joseph Thayendenagea
is not fully worthy of the honor now conferred upon him by Canadians.'[6]

Such a celebration of Brant would have been impossible following his
death in 1807. Brant's reputation among non-Natives declined considerably following the Revolution. His efforts to secure sovereignty for the Six
Nations and to promote Native unity caused consternation among colonial officials who sought to restrict his activities and undermine his influence. Brant's loyalty became a matter a considerable dispute in 1797
when he publicly associated himself with the pro-French party during a
visit to the American capital. Colonial officials feared the Natives were
planning to join a Franco-American attack on British possessions. Attitudes towards Brant among Natives at Grand River also were decidedly
ambivalent. Factionalism ensured that Brant's leadership was frequently
challenged. Many resented Brant's influence and questioned the wisdom
of his policy of selling off land to white settlers and encouraging Natives
to abandon traditional practices. Charges of corruption and mismanage-
ment plagued Brant in his final years.[7] Surrounded by controversy as he
was, few hailed Brant as a hero at the time of his death in 1807. He was
buried in a simple, unmarked plot near his home in Burlington.

The popular image of Brant after his death was to a considerable
extent established in Thomas Campbell's poem, 'Gertrude of Wyoming.'
The poem, first published in 1809, portrayed Brant as a 'monster' who
personally orchestrated the massacre of women and children. In 1819
John Strachan published a brief article, 'The Life of Capt. Brant,' in
The *Christian Recorder*. Primarily drawing on conversations with the Rev.
John Stuart, the author described Brant as a drunkard and called into
question his loyalty to the Crown and the church. Offended by the portrait drawn of his father, John Brant accused Strachan of libel. In 1822

John Brant began a correspondence with the author of 'Gertrude of Wyoming,' Thomas Campbell. John Brant sent Campbell documents proving his father was not present at Wyoming and was not the 'monster' he had depicted. Confronted by the mass of evidence, Campbell admitted that he had done Joseph Brant an injustice. In a letter to John Brant, Campbell wrote: 'I rose from pursuing the papers you submitted to me certainly with an altered impression of his character ... Had I learnt all this of your father when I was writing my poem, he should not have figured in it as the hero of the mischief.' Campbell's apology was published in London in The *New Monthly Magazine* in 1822. 'Gertrude of Wyoming' continued to be reprinted, however, without alteration or explanation.[8]

Despite the efforts of John Brant to restore his father's reputation, Joseph Brant had not yet acquired hero status. Much of the credit for this development is due to the American journalist William Stone. Growing up in the Mohawk valley when the events of the Revolution were still fresh in the recollections of the people, Stone developed an avid interest in the history of the region. In 1838 he published the two-volume biography, *Life of Joseph Brant – Thayendanegea*. When preparing the biography, Stone visited the sites of old fortifications and battlefields and interviewed or corresponded with surviving veterans and their families. In 1836 he visited Brant's children in Upper Canada and acquired much of his personal correspondence and papers.[9] Unable to document a single case of wanton cruelty or treachery, Stone set out to restore Brant's reputation. Stone insisted that Brant, far from being 'savage and cruel,' had conducted himself with 'compassion and humanity.' Stone's stories of Brant's humanitarianism were often as unfounded or exaggerated as those of his cruelty. Stone portrayed Brant as a noble and heroic figure possessing 'high qualities and commanding virtues.' As a warrior, Brant was 'cautious, sagacious and brave.' In business, his conduct was 'prompt, honorable, and expert.' He was amiable in temperament and his house was an 'abode of kindness and hospitality.' Though Brant was charged with duplicity in his affairs with the Six Nations, Stone insisted that 'the purity of his private morals' were beyond reproach.[10] Almost singlehandedly Stone had transformed the 'monster Brant' into a noble and heroic figure worthy of emulation and honour. With the passing of frontier conditions, Natives were no longer seen as a threat in eastern North America, and the fear and dread of earlier years was gradually replaced by a sentimental romanticization of what many believed was a dying race. It was in this context that Stone remade Brant into an archetype of the 'noble savage' engaged in a heroic but futile struggle to save his people.[11]

In 1850 civic and social leaders and representatives from the Six Nations gathered at the Mohawk chapel to reinter the remains of both Joseph and John Brant. Deeming it a 'disgrace' to permit the remains of the 'celebrated Indian chief' to remain 'in a spot so slovenly and obscure,' a group of local civic leaders appealed 'to the public in behalf of erecting a proper tomb to contain the bones and to perpetuate the memory and exploits of the daring Brant.' The memorial movement was among the earliest signs of the incipient nationalism and desire to create a heroic past that had begun to emerge in Upper Canada during the 1850s. The figure of Brant was ideally suited to meet the need for indigenous heroes. As a Native war chief loyal to the British cause during the American Revolution, Brant added an exciting and exotic note to the province's past. During the reinterment ceremony Brant was hailed as the finest example of his race and praised for his services to Britain, the Crown and the church. Rev. Peter Jones asserted that Brant's attachment to the Crown was 'strong and sincere' and that he was 'always read to obey the commands of his King.' Sir Allan MacNab commented that 'none had ever more nobly and faithfully performed their duty than the hero whose remains they were now met to deposit finally in the grave.' In his address, Lewis Burwell suggested that the residents of Brantford erect a monument to commemorate the accomplishments of their namesake.[12] It would be nearly a quarter of a century, however, before the subject of a suitable monument captured public interest.

The proposal was revived in 1874 by Allan Cleghorn, an affluent local businessman. Cleghorn moved from Montreal to Brantford in 1847 and went into the wholesale hardware trade. Shortly after his arrival, Cleghorn came into contact with the Six Nations and developed an avid interest in their history. He was among the principal leaders in the movement to have Brant's remains reinterred. In appreciation of his efforts, the Mohawk of Grand River made Cleghorn an honorary chief in 1850.[13] In the years following the reinterment, Cleghorn attempted to interest the Six Nations council in the erection of a monument commemorating Brant. While Cleghorn found support among the Mohawk, the other tribes were either ambivalent or hostile to the project. It was argued by some that the Six Nations lacked the resources to undertake such a project. The most determined opposition came from traditionalists, who upheld the customs, culture, and religion of the Long House. Traditionalists remembered Brant as the author of an assimilationist policy whereby the Six Nations were to be educated, converted to Christianity, and taught farming.[14]

In 1874 Cleghorn succeeded in convincing the Six Nations council to broach the subject of a monument with Prince Arthur, duke of Connaught, during his visit to the reserve in August. In a memorial, the chiefs requested that the prince sponsor 'their contemplated efforts to raise a fitting monument to, and worthy of, the memory of the distinguished Chief' who 'loyally and gallantly led their fathers, as Allies of the Crown in the defence of it and the Empire, and when all was lost, with them maintained his allegiance, sacrificing and giving up all and finding his way to the then wilds of Canada, where he remained to the end of his eventful career, animating and inspiring them with the same loyalism and attachment to the Crown, and its institutions.'[15] The prince enthusiastically endorsed the project. Many traditionalists among the Six Nations, however, continued to oppose the proposal, but the imposition of a system of elected chiefs by the federal government following Confederation effectively circumvented their power and influence in the council.

Encouraged by Prince Arthur's support, Cleghorn formed a provisional committee to approach local civic and business leaders.[16] On 14 April 1876 the Brant Memorial Committee was struck. Its members included the Speaker of the Senate, David Christie; local member of Parliament William Patterson; the mayor of Brantford, Dr J.W. Digby; the warden of Brant County, William Thompson; and representatives from each of the tribes residing at Grand River. In an effort to increase public interest in the project, the committee called upon prominent figures in government, business, and the press to lend their names to the movement. Having secured the patronage of many of the nation's leaders, the Memorial Committee pledged itself to raising the necessary funds. On 2 August 1877 the committee members attended a special meeting of the Six Nations council at Oshweken. Allan Cleghorn informed the council that the probable cost of the monument would be around $20,000; he hoped the Six Nations would contribute a quarter of that amount. After meeting in closed session, the chiefs agreed to contribute $5,000 towards the project.[17] The Memorial Committee had less success with the Brantford city council. Committee members circulated a petition among ratepayers, requesting that the city council hold a public meeting to discuss the issue. The mayor of Brantford, J.W. Digby, acceded to the request, and a meeting was held at the city hall on 3 September 1877. A motion was passed urging the city council to follow the example of the Six Nations and contribute $5,000 towards the monument.[18] Unimpressed with the poor attendance at the meeting and concerned about the appearance of granting money to such a cause in the midst of a serious recession, the city council tabled the request until a more auspicious moment.

An improved economy helped to revive the project in the early 1880s. A new memorial association was organized and a mass public meeting was held in the Brantford Opera House on 6 March 1883. In appealing for support, promoters praised Brant's 'inculcation of loyalty' and his contributions to the 'welfare and moral elevation of his people.' It was noted that Canadian cities lagged far behind their American counterparts in erecting public monuments to their heroes. Such monuments, it was argued, instiled 'nobler and higher inspirations of patriotism.' Advocates looked upon the monument not merely as a tribute to 'the worth of the man,' but as an investment that 'would pay, and pay well.' If erected, the monument would be the first commemorating a Native anywhere in North America and was thus certain to attract widespread notice. The vice-president of the Brant Memorial Association, industrialist Ignatius Cockshutt, noted that as 'a work of art and an adornment to the city,' the monument would beautify its surroundings and provide a popular 'attraction for pleasure seekers.' Impressed with the force of the Memorial Association's reasoning, the meeting enthusiastically endorsed the project.[19]

Such arguments reflected the civic boosterism and urban reform spirit that appeared towards the end of the nineteenth century. Conscious of Brantford's growth as an industrial centre, promoters like Cleghorn and Cockshutt felt that the monument would bolster the city's prestige and attest to its economic and cultural progress. The movement also reflected prevailing beliefs about the importance of uplifting the quality of urban life. Parks, wide boulevards, playgrounds, and public sculpture were widely regarded as means of improving living standards in cities blighted by industrialization. Historical monuments proved especially popular, since they provided a sense of rootedness and tradition at a time when urban growth and change raised serious questions about future community stability.[20]

In July of 1883 the directors of the Brant Memorial Association invited submissions and announced a $1,000 prize for the best design. Seven artists entered the competition and models were put on public display. The judges eventually decided upon the design submitted by the British sculptor Percy Wood. The judges' selection became a topic of considerable controversy and threatened to scuttle the project. Local Conservatives favoured the model submitted by C.E. Zollicoffer. Zollicoffer had worked extensively on the Parliament buildings in Ottawa and had strong ties with the government of Sir John A. Macdonald. Conservatives charged that the president of the Memorial Association and active Liberal, Allan Cleghorn, had influenced the judges against Zollicoffer.[21] The controversy eventually passed, and by the end of the year pledges totalling over $17,000 had been secured from local, provincial, and federal governments, the Six Nations council, and private subscribers. The cornerstone was laid with much fanfare on 11 August 1886, almost exactly twelve years after the Six Nations had broached the suggestion with the Duke of Connaught.

When it was finally unveiled on 13 October 1886, the Brant monument represented much more than a memorial to a heroic figure; it was a tangible manifestation of the beliefs and aspirations of its promoters. Imperialists believed that the monument would 'inspire loyalty' and 'give our young men to feel that they have a country fit to live for, and if need be, to die for.'[22] Special pride was taken in the fact that the monument was cast in bronze from cannons that had seen action at Waterloo and the Crimea. The monument was universally praised as an impressive piece of art that added considerably to the beauty and prestige of the city. Local newspapers published special editions to mark the occasion. The editions not only focused on the monument but described at great length the city's services, industries, and institutions. The visitors who purchased these editions as souvenirs were informed that Brantford was a 'fully equipped' municipality with 'all the modern improvements' but 'lacking many of the temptations of larger cities.' Readers were also told that the 'quality and quantity of the shrewd and enterprising businessmen with which the city is blessed' ensured that 'the outlook for further development and material progress is of the most hopeful and encouraging kind.'[23] Such sentiments testified to the boosterism that motivated the monument's promoters. The monument was widely hailed as an impressive addition to the city, which directly reflected its progress and potential.

Erected in the wake of the North-West Rebellion, the monument also reflected the ambivalent racial attitudes Anglo-Canadians held towards Natives. It was widely believed at the time that Native peoples belonged to a vanishing race, whose only hope was assimilation. The imminent disappearance of Native societies and the increasing complexity of the modern world, however, also created a romantic nostalgia for what was described as a simpler and nobler way of life.[24] Both sentiments found expression in the Brant monument. On the day of the unveiling, Brant was repeatedly praised for his steadfast loyalty and his efforts to convert and civilize his people. In commemorating Brant as a Native who remained loyal and embraced the benefits of 'civilization,' the monument's Anglo-Canadian promoters upheld Brant as a model Indian whose example should be embraced by all Natives. This point was dramatically reinforced by the presence of six western chiefs invited to attend the unveiling with Major-General Sir Frederick Middleton, the commander of Canadian forces during the North-West Rebellion. During the celebrations speakers acclaimed the 'the spirit of amity which existed between the Six Nations and the whites' and expressed a desire 'to see the same amicable feeling existing as well among the Indians of the Northwest.'[25] The key to achieving such 'amity,' of course, was subjection to Canadian institutions and a willingness to abandon traditional lifestyles and accept the Anglo-Canadian way of life.

Confident in their cultural and racial superiority and the inevitable fate of the Native, Anglo-Canadians also began to show a sentimental interest in the quaint and exotic customs of a dying race. Such sentiments were reflected in the monument itself, which presented Brant in traditional dress, and in the recitation of a special ode composed by the Six Nations poet E. Pauline Johnson. The growing fascination with Native ceremonies was evident in the condolence rite performed by the chiefs of the Six Nations at the unveiling. This interest in traditional Native culture did not reflect, as some have suggested, a sense of guilt at the unjust treatment of Native peoples.[26] The monument's promoters spoke not of guilt or injustice but of the 'happy harmony' that characterized relations with the Six Nations. Their expectation was that other tribes would follow Brant's example and dutifully proclaim their loyalty to the Crown and Canadian institutions and accept the benefits of 'civilization.'

The aims of the Brant monument's Anglo-Canadian promoters differed significantly from the objectives of those among the Six Nations who supported the project. Whereas Anglo-Canadians saw in Brant's loyalty an example of submission and assimilation, many among the Six Nations used that loyalty to demand justice and special recognition. During the unveiling, Mohawk speakers hailed Brant as a devoted and loyal servant 'who fought and bled for the old Union Jack.'[27] They stressed, however, that Brant had been an ally, not a subject, of the Crown and called upon Canadians to recognize and respect the difference. Dissatisfied with the powers and restrictions of the Indian Act, in the years following the unveiling of the Brant memorial the Six Nations increasingly invoked the 'red loyalist' theme to further their case for legal equality and self-government. The remarks made by Chief John W.E. Elliott in an address to the Ontario Historical Society in 1911 were typical of the way in which the Six Nations' past was used to serve political ends. Elliott sought due recognition for the Six Nations as co-founders of the province. He reminded his audience that during the American Revolution and again during the War of 1812, the Six Nations had joined with other loyalists and 'fought valiantly for the British Crown and supremacy of British institutions.' In return for the sacrifices incurred on behalf of the Crown and Empire, Elliott insisted that the Six Nations had been guaranteed 'a perpetual independence and self-government' and the right to use their land 'in the most free and ample manner in accordance with our several customs and usages.' Through the Indian Act, however, the Canadian government had violated the treaties and commitments made by the Crown and had reduced the Six Nations to 'the status of minors.' By virtue of their loyalty, Elliott argued, the Six Nations 'hold an unique position apart and different from any other nation in Canada.' They were thus entitled to special status and treatment. Elliott appealed to those 'descended from the great, true, and loyal United Empire stock' whose 'forefathers fought side by side with ours in defence of this country' to stand by the Six Nations in their fight for the rights and privileges guaranteed to them by the Crown.[28]

The appeals of activists like Elliott were severely undermined by F.O. Loft. A Mohawk from Grand River, Loft had received a secondary education, left the reserve, and found employment at the Toronto Insane Asylum and later the provincial secretary's office. In 1898 he married Affa Northcotte Geary, a cousin of Lord Iddesleigh and a Loyalist descendant. In an address commemorating the centenary of Brant's death, Loft upheld the Mohawk warrior as a model for all Natives. He praised Brant as a great leader whose 'purpose was to live and die a British subject' and as a 'statesman' who 'applied his energies towards hastening the gradual process of transition of the people from barbarism to civilization.' As a result of Brant's efforts, Loft concluded, the Six Nations could now 'occupy a position as citizens not by any means subordinate to the position of a considerable portion of our Anglo-Saxon population.' In his address, Loft criticized those who attempted to use the Six Nations' past for political purposes. He dismissed the belief 'current in the minds of some of our Six Nations of to-day' that the Six Nations' loyalty depended on 'concessions' that 'guaranteed ... their independence and freedom of self-government for all time.' Just as Loyalist descendants maintained that principle alone dictated the actions of their ancestors, Loft insisted that nothing other than fidelity to the British Crown determined the position of the Six Nations. He vigorously denied that the 'pledges' made to the

Six Nations 'have not yet been adequately fulfilled.' 'The Six Nations,' Loft asserted, 'have always enjoyed the same measure of freedom and independence vouchsafed alike to all classes of citizens and subjects of the Crown, irrespective of race, color or creed.' Not even the Indian Act was subject to criticism. 'The Government and the [Indian] Department,' he claimed, 'have aimed to govern the Indians in a manner consistent with the demands of justice and equity. Treaty obligations have been carefully observed; and no attempt has been made to seriously or arbitrarily jeopardize the Indians' rights in a free exercise of their own system of local self-government.'[29]

Most non-Natives found Loft's message much more palatable than that presented by critics like Elliott. Happy to celebrate the Six Nations' loyal history in the familiar terms to which they were accustomed, Anglo-Canadians were not prepared to acknowledge any rights or privileges arising from that past. The very different ways in which Anglo-Canadians and the Six Nations understood Brant and the loyalty of the Six Nations highlight the important role that racial assumptions played in shaping the Loyalist tradition. The Anglo-Canadian promoters of the Brant monument participated in a process of racialization that assumed their own superiority and ascribed certain traits and a particular destiny to Native peoples.[30] Through events like the erection of the Brant monument, Anglo-Canadians in effect attempted to take possession of another people's past. At the same time, the Six Nations appropriated the rhetoric of the Loyalist tradition, but for their own purposes. For reformers, the Six Nations' Loyalist past offered both a means of subverting Anglo-Canadian racial and historical assumptions and an opportunity to promote their own claims to status and recognition.

Civic boosters, imperialists, and Native activists were not alone in using the past to promote their aspirations. Reform-minded women also found in the past a means of advancing the cause of women's rights. Dissatisfaction with the constraints of their prescribed roles and growing awareness of the needs and problems of an emerging industrial society drew many middle-class women outside the confines of their Victorian homes. Hoping to break down the isolation, dependence, and low status associated with their domestic function, women pursued activities that would earn them greater respect and influence. Many of these women turned to the past to find an acceptable rationale for their expanded activities.[31] Through organizations like the Women's Canadian Historical Society of Toronto, middle-class women set out to record the contributions of their foremothers and to claim a place in the nation's history. In a paper presented at the inaugural meeting of the Women's Canadian Historical Society, Mary Fitzgibbon affirmed 'the worth of [woman's] influence' in the nation's history. 'On every page of the history of the U.E. Loyalists, and that of the War of 1812–14,' Fitzgibbon observed, 'the energy, loyalty, bravery, and endurance of the women are written in letters of gold.'[32] In asserting their place in the nation's past, such women challenged the male domination of history and insisted on their right to greater status and recognition in Canadian society. Such sentiments lay behind the efforts to popularize the heroic exploits of Laura Secord during the War of 1812.

For most of her life Laura Secord lived in virtual obscurity. Few knew that she had rescued her wounded husband during the battle of Queenston Heights or that she had made a perilous journey to warn Lieutenant James Fitzgibbon of an impending American attack during the battle of Beaver Dams.[33] The years following the war were difficult ones for the Secords. In their struggle to make ends meet, the Secords repeatedly petitioned the government to obtain both recognition and compensation for their wartime services. The extent and importance of the Secord's services grew with each petition. In 1820 James appealed to Lieutenant-Governor Sir Peregrine Maitland for a licence to occupy part of the Queenston military reserve. He noted in the petition that he had been 'wounded in the battle of Queenston,' 'twice plundered of all his Moveable property' and that his wife had 'embraced an opportunity of rendering some service at the risk of her life, in going through the Enemies' lines to communicate information to a detachment of His Majesty's troops at the Beaver Dam in the month of June 1813.' Attached to the petition was a certificate written by James Fitzgibbon confirming Laura's role in the Battle of Beaver Dams.[34]

Confronted by an increasingly precarious financial situation, in 1827 James again entreated the government for patronage. Impressed by the 'character and claims of Mr Secord and his wife,' Lieutenant-Governor Maitland appointed James registrar of the Niagara Surrogate Court in 1828. He was granted a judgeship in 1833 and in 1835 became collector of customs at Chippewa. Despite the appointments, the Secord's financial situation failed to improve. In 1839 Laura herself petitioned the government for the ferry concession at Queenston. She recounted her dangerous journey through enemy lines and Indian encampments and claimed that the 'important intelligence' she carried to Fitzgibbon resulted in the capture of 550 enemy troops. For this service, she concluded, 'your Excellency's memorialist has never received the smallest compensation.' No response was received from the government. Since she was a non-combatant, government officials undoubtedly felt that Laura was not entitled to compensation and that the matter was not worth pursuing. James Secord died on 22 February 1841, leaving Laura without any means of support. In the years following James's death, Laura repeatedly approached the government for a pension and other concessions, but to little avail.[35]

Laura Secord's story first entered the public domain in 1845. In April of that year, Laura's son Charles sent a letter to the editor of the *Church* describing his mother's exploits during the War of 1812. The letter was prompted by remarks in the House of Assembly questioning James Fitzgibbon's contribution to the success at Beaver Dams. The Assembly was currently considering a bill rewarding Fitzgibbon £1,000 for his many years of military service. Hoping to set the record straight, Charles Secord described how his mother had overheard American plans and warned Fitzgibbon.[36] While the letter helped Fitzgibbon, Laura herself received little benefit. Gilbert Auchinleck made passing reference to Laura's deeds in an 1853 issue of the *Anglo-American Magazine*. An account written by Laura herself was included among the notes but attracted little notice.[37]

Widespread public recognition did not come until late in Laura's life. In 1860 the Prince of Wales visited Canada. Niagara Falls and Queenston were among the stops included on the prince's itinerary. Local organizers intended to present an address to the prince signed by veterans of the War of 1812. On learning of the address, Laura insisted that she be included among the signatories. Unfamiliar with her exploits, organizers initially dismissed Laura's request. Determined that her name be included, Secord prepared a memorial to the prince detailing her services and sacrifices. Laura's name was eventually included on the address presented to the prince at Queenston Heights. Impressed by Secord's story, the prince sent Laura £100 after his return to England.[38] The award brought her considerable public attention for the first time. As the story became known, new elements were added.

Much of the mythology that came to surround Laura Secord originated with W.F. Coffin's *1812: The War and Its Moral* published in 1865. Coffin was a lieutenant-colonel in the militia and the commissioner of ordinance lands. In retelling Secord's story, Coffin invented dialogue, created the infamous cow, added an encounter with an American sentry, and imagined the details of the perilous journey. Throughout the account Coffin incorrectly referred to Laura as Mary. Despite its obvious accretions and errors, Coffin's highly fictionalized account became the standard version of Laura's exploits. The popularity of Coffin's version of events owed a great deal to the fact that he left readers with the impression he had received the information directly from Laura Secord herself. Believing the account authentic, subsequent writers repeated Coffin's imaginings and occasionally added some of their own.[39]

Laura Secord died at the age of ninety-three on 17 October 1868, having finally achieved a degree of recognition and notoriety. Despite her fame, Laura was buried in a simple grave beside her husband at Lundy's Lane. When the neglected state of the graveyard became publicly known a few years later, a movement was launched to erect a monument on the site. Sarah Anne Curzon, a British-born essayist, political activist, and social reformer, was among the first to champion a memorial. Curzon was among the original members of the Toronto Woman's Literary Club, the city's first suffrage organization founded in 1876.[40] That same year, she authored a three-act play, *Laura Secord, the Heroine of 1812*. The two events were not unrelated; Curzon's literary work was an essential part of her political activism. The play's political purpose becomes readily apparent in the first act, when Laura learns of the impending American attack and convinces her crippled husband that she must warn Fitzgibbon. At Laura's departure, James comments: 'I'll try to bear / The dreadful pangs of helplessness and dread / With calm demeanour, if a bursting heart.' Laura replies: 'Then will you taste a woman's common lot / In times of strait, while I essay man's role / Of fierce activity.' For Curzon, Secord's ability to overcome the presumed limits of her sex was symbolic of women's ability to rise above the restrictions placed upon female activity by society in general. The example of Laura Secord proved that women could make a vital contribution to their nation's welfare when given the opportunity. 'To save from the sword,' Curzon insisted, 'is surely as great a deed as to save with the sword; and this Laura Secord did, at an expense of nerve and muscle fully equal to any that are recorded of the warrior.' Curzon insisted that women, having proved their worth in the past, were entitled to a voice in determining the nation's future through the franchise. Unfortunately, few Canadians were aware of Secord's contributions. Curzon thus appealed to Canadians to 'rescue from oblivion the name of [this] brave woman, and set it in its proper place among the heroes of Canadian history.' Failure to 'set her on such a pedestal of equality,' Curzon insisted, amounted to no less than a betrayal of the suffering and sacrifices endured by the Loyalist and pioneer women who helped to found and defend the nation. By invoking the example of

Laura Secord, Curzon was able to articulate arguments for female emancipation in patriotic terms and thereby align the women's movement with the fate of the nation.[41]

Curzon's play was not published until 1887, 'owing to the inertness of Canadian interest in Canadian literature at that date.'[42] That same year, the principal of the Drummondville Grammar School, M.M. Fenwick, called attention, in letters to the Toronto *Mail* and *World*, to the 'neglected state' of the cemetery at Lundy's Lane and appealed for subscriptions to erect a 'national monument' to Laura Secord and those who fell during the War of 1812.[43] In 1891 Curzon published a short biography, *The Story of Laura Secord, 1813*, at the request of the Lundy's Lane Historical Society. The society had started a public subscription list and approached the provincial government for a grant to cover the costs of marking Secord's grave 'with a memorial stone somewhat worthy of her and of us.'[44] A petition with over 1,000 names was presented to the provincial government by the local member of the legislature, but to little effect. In 1892 the Lundy's Lane Historical Society issued a circular to teachers and students in the counties of Lincoln and Welland asking for contributions. By 1893 less than £200 had been collected.[45]

Disheartened by the apparent lack of interest in the past among the population at large, Curzon helped to found the Woman's Canadian Historical Society in 1895. The purpose of the society was to encourage the study of Canadian history, to collect and preserve historical records and relics, and to promote Canadian loyalty and patriotism. The founders of the society believed that a thorough acquaintance with the 'heroic past' would instil 'a unity of national purpose and high ideal of loyalty and patriotism.' It was also Curzon's intent that such societies demonstrate that 'together, men and women built up this noble country by whose name we call ourselves; together they must preserve and develop it; and together they will stand or fall by it.'[46] Curzon's efforts inspired other reform-minded women to take up the cause. Friends and fellow members of the Women's Canadian Historical Society, such as Agnes Maule Machar, Mary Fitzgibbon, and Matilda Edgar, composed works that contributed to Laura Secord's legendary status.[47] Despite these efforts, plans for the Laura Secord memorial remained stalled when Curzon died on 6 November 1898.

Shortly before her death Curzon entrusted the memorial movement to Elizabeth Jane Thompson.[48] An active member of the Women's Canadian Historical Society and the Daughters of the Empire, Thompson shared Curzon's interest in the past and her commitment to women's rights.

Thompson interested the Ontario Historical Society in the project, and a monument committee was struck in February of 1899. The committee urged other historical and patriotic organizations to join the Ontario Historical Society in making the Laura Secord memorial a reality. The monument's promoters directed their fund-raising to schoolchildren and women.[49] A letter written by Mary Dunn of the United Empire Loyalist Association to the Toronto *Globe* was typical of the appeals for support. In the letter Dunn enquired: 'Will the women of Canada, rich and poor, join together in making a common cause to recognize bravery in woman as well as man, and help to raise a monument to the memory of one so long neglected and to whom we owe so much?' Completion of the monument, Dunn asserted, would ensure that 'the women of Canada shall have the satisfaction of knowing women's heroic deeds are recognized as well as those of men, although long neglected.'[50] Dunn's appeal alone raised $300 for the monument. On the basis of such pledges, the Ontario Historical Society commissioned Mildred Peel to produce a small bust of Secord to be erected at her grave site in the Lundy's Lane battlefield cemetery.[51]

The monument was unveiled on 22 June 1901 by Catherine Ross, the wife of the province's premier, before a crowd of 2,000 people. During the ceremonies, Secord was celebrated as 'a woman, wife and mother.'[52] Female speakers noted with pride that the monument was the first in the province to be dedicated to a woman, that the monument itself was the work of a woman, and that women had been instrumental in seeing the project through to its completion. Catherine Ross's remarks were typical of the sentiments of the day. 'Laura Secord,' Ross asserted, 'well merited the great honour, and will ever represent that type of patriotism which speaks noble deeds. Realizing her duty as a Patriotic Canadian wife, a daughter of a United Empire Loyalist refugee, her action was prompt, loyal, courageous and effective.' The monument, Ross concluded, would forever stand as 'an inspiration which would keep the fire of patriotism burning brightly in the breasts of future generations.' The celebratory mood of the occasion was dampened when the dates in the inscription were discovered to be incorrect. The bust had to be taken down, the pedestal returned to England, and the inscription removed and corrected.[53]

Not everyone was satisfied with the design, inscription, and site of the Laura Secord memorial. Members of the United Empire Loyalist Association felt that the monument should be located at Queenston Heights and be of much grander proportions than the modest memorial placed by the Ontario Historical Society at Lundy's Lane.[54] In October of 1901 R.E.A.

Land announced the creation of the Laura Secord National Monument Committee and advised the Ontario Historical Society that the funds collected by the United Empire Loyalist Association would be directed to the erection of a monument 'worthy of the nation' at Queenston Heights, 'the starting-point of her great walk,' 'the scene where our heroine saved her husband's life' and 'the place which identified her and her gallant husband with Sir Isaac Brock.' Land was confident 'that the people, especially the women of Canada, will respond to our call, and thus tend to perpetuate as an object lesson for all future generations the patriotic example of this noble-hearted woman.'[55]

Land's concerns were shared by Emma Currie. Like Sarah Curzon, Currie was a champion of female suffrage and was among the founders of the Woman's Literary Club of St Catharines. In 1900 she had published *The Story of Laura Secord and Canadian Reminiscences*. The book was dedicated to Curzon, 'whose highest aim was to inspire Canadian women to take their place in the history of our country.'[56] Based on original documents and interviews with relatives, the biography was less melodramatic than Curzon's earlier effort. Currie none the less felt that Secord merited a grander tribute than the modest bust that the Ontario Historical Society intended to place in the cemetery at Lundy's Lane. Currie donated all of the proceeds from the book towards the erection of a national monument at Queenston Heights. Currie eventually secured a grant from the federal government and a second, more imposing monument was unveiled on Queenston Heights in July of 1911 before a crowd of 3,000. Once again, Secord was hailed for her 'self-sacrificing courage, devotion and heroism.' Appropriately, representatives of the Canadian Women's Historical Society laid flowers and the Women's Literary Club of St Catharines placed a wreath on the monument.[57]

Women were not alone in their efforts to honour Laura Secord. Loyalists, nationalists, and imperialists found much in the example of Laura Secord that was appealing. Reform-minded women, however, were instrumental in popularizing and romanticizing Laura Secord and provided much of the energy and commitment behind the movement to erect monuments dedicated to her memory. Such women found in the example of Laura Secord an inspiring illustration of female courage, foresight, and endurance that could be used to promote their demands for greater status and recognition by demonstrating the vital role played by women in the development of the nation. Their call for recognition of women's heroism challenged the male domination of the nation's past and furthered their demands for inclusion in Canadian society. In contesting

their exclusion from the past, early feminists did not offer a new understanding of the nation's history, but rather, they appropriated the existing rhetoric of Loyalism to justify their own political objectives.

Laura Secord was not the only woman honoured with a monument in the
years between the 1884 celebrations and the First World War. In August
of 1909 Methodists from across Ontario and the northeastern United
States gathered in a tiny churchyard near Prescott, Ontario, to witness the
unveiling of a monument dedicated to Barbara Heck, 'the foundress of
American Methodism.' Unlike Joseph Brant or Laura Secord, Barbara
Heck left no documents of her own. She was an ideal subject for myth
making. Unencumbered by masses of historical documentation, the basic
elements of the Heck story could be appropriated and highlighted to
serve a variety of causes. The absence of evidence, however, ensured that
Barbara Heck also became a figure of controversy.

The principal speaker during the unveiling ceremonies was Rev. John
W. Hamilton. Hamilton used the occasion to trace the 'simple story' of
Barbara Heck's life. Hamilton explained that Barbara was the daughter
of German refugees who had sought the protection of Britain when Louis
XIV's Catholic armies invaded the Protestant Palatinate. The British government settled the refugees in Ireland, where they were converted to
Methodism. Rising rents forced many of the Palatines to emigrate to New
York City in 1760. Surrounded by 'worldliness,' the immigrants quickly
fell into a state of 'spiritual apathy.' Coming upon a game of cards one
day, Barbara 'hastily seized the cards, and, throwing them into the fire,
administered a scathing rebuke to all concerned.' 'Moved by an inward
flame,' she hurried to the home of Philip Embury and beseeched him:
'Philip, you must preach to us or we shall all go to hell together, and God
will require our blood at your hands.' To Embury's protests that he had
neither church nor congregation, Barbara replied: 'Preach in your own
house and to your own company.' A 'great revival' followed and the class
quickly outgrew its accommodations. Divinely inspired, Barbara herself
drew up the plans for the first Methodist chapel erected in America. After
the arrival of two Methodist missionaries from England in 1769, the
Hecks and Emburys left New York City and moved upstate to Camden
township, where they planted another Methodist congregation. 'Resolute' in their loyalty to Britain and the Empire, many of the Palatines
abandoned 'their fertile farms and comfortable homes' at the outbreak
of the Revolution and fled to Lower Canada. Following the war, the
Hecks received a Loyalist grant and resettled in Augusta township near

Kingston, where Barbara laid the foundations for 'another Methodist empire.'[58]

Hamilton admitted in his address that there were 'many variations' and 'misstatements' in the various published accounts of her life and that for a time the honour due Barbara Heck was conferred upon another woman. He also acknowledged that Barbara was denied a place in history because she was 'a humble housewife' drawn from the ranks of 'plain people.' 'History, at best, as the world has written most of it until now,' Hamilton observed, 'would make little mention of a good woman, however remarkable her career.' 'After a hundred years of obscurity,' however, providence 'let down the name of Barbara Heck from heaven to go into the books of church history, on the walls and into the windows of churches and theological seminaries and monuments of enduring stone.'[59] Divine providence was not alone in perpetuating Barbara Heck's memory. Filiopietism, the women's movement, and a denomination's desire for a heroic past all contributed to her glorification.

The earliest American histories of the Methodist church confused Barbara Heck with a Mrs Hick buried in the graveyard of New York's Trinity Methodist Episcopal church. The error originated in Nathan Bangs's *A History of the Methodist Episcopal Church* first published in 1838. Bangs, an early circuit rider on the Kingston circuit, knew Barbara Heck's son Samuel and learned of his mother's role in the origins of the church in New York. Bangs later claimed that he accepted the account until he moved to New York in 1810 and became acquainted with Paul Hick. Hick informed Bangs that it was his mother who had in fact laid the foundations of Methodism in New York.[60] Bangs's error was repeated two decades later in J.B. Wakeley's *Lost Chapters Recovered from the Early History of American Methodism.*

Wakeley's book was brought to the attention of members of the Heck family. Appalled by the injustice to his grandmother, George Heck appealed to his brother-in-law, John Carroll, to set the record straight. In a letter to the *Christian Advocate* Carroll insisted that it was an 'incontrovertible' fact that 'the Christian heroine' who induced Philip Embury to commence preaching was named not Hick but Heck and that the family had removed to Canada at the onset of the Revolution. Carroll's letter outraged descendants of the Hick family of New York. 'Whatever John Carroll or Canada may claim,' J.P. Hick wrote to Wakeley, 'we have the gratification to know from our grandparents' that Paul and Barbara Hick of New York are 'the only ones who have claim to the facts as recorded by different Methodist historians.' Such indignant remarks convinced Abel

Stevens that the disputed claims were essentially a product of family egotism and filiopietism. 'This controversy,' Stevens observed, 'is chiefly of
interest to the personal friends of the family concerned.'[61]

Writing in the *Christian Advocate* of 12 August 1858, J.B. Wakely
responded to the 'gross injustice' that 'has been done to the name and
character' of the Hick family. Wakely maintained that Nathan Bangs had
received the story of Barbara Hick's conspicuous contributions to the origins of American Methodism from her son Paul, a highly respected Methodist class leader and church trustee in New York. J.P. Hick, Paul Hick's
grandson, confirmed this version of events. Noting that it was thirty-five
years since Nathan Bangs first had published his account, Wakeley found
it strange that Carroll should suddenly take such a 'deep interest' in the
subject. Carroll responded that Bangs's history was not widely available in
Canada and that the Hecks were 'not given to writing.' Bangs and Wakely,
Carroll suggested, had conspired to cover up the truth. He produced dis-
positions signed by Barbara Heck's granddaughters Catherine Heck and
Elizabeth Howard and the descendants of fellow Palatine emigrants that
confirmed the Canadian version of events.[62]

The continuing controversy resulted in the creation of a committee by
the Wesleyan Methodist conference to 'collect all the evidence of Paul
and Barbara Heck to favour their claim, and if justified, to erect a suitable
monument to them where they are buried.' The committee, which consisted of John Carroll, Barbara Heck's grandsons John and George, J.B.
Wakely, Abel Stevens, and J.P. Hick, sifted through the available evidence
and eventually verified the Canadian version of events.[63] Although the
committee confirmed Carroll's account, no action was taken to erect a
monument in honour of Barbara Heck. Uncomfortable with her Loyalist
status, American writers simply omitted any reference to her Loyalism or
chose to downplay her role altogether and focus, on the contributions of
Philip Embury, who, fortuitously for them, died before the outbreak of
the Revolution.

Disturbed by American reluctance to honour Barbara Heck with a suitable monument, John Carroll appealed to Canadian Methodists to raise
'a worthy memorial.' 'Canada,' Carroll asserted in the *Christian Guardian*
of 2 April 1862, 'is highly honoured in having the guardianship of the
precious dust of persons who were instrumental in kindling that fire
which has broke forth into such a glorious conflagration on this continent.' It was to the 'shame of Canadian Methodists,' however, that a simple tombstone was all that marked the grave site of Barbara Heck.[64] The
suggestion failed to ignite much enthusiasm beyond descendants of the

Heck family. George Playter's *The History of Methodism in Canada* published in that same year made only passing reference to Barbara Heck.

American Methodists celebrated the centenary of their church in 1866. The centennial witnessed the publication of a number of histories outlining the origins of the American church. Among the works to appear during the celebrations was Abel Stevens's *The Women of Methodism.* Stevens devoted a entire chapter to Barbara Heck. 'The progress of Methodism in the United States,' he observed, 'has now indisputably placed the humble name of Barbara Heck first on the list of women in the ecclesiastical history of the New World.' He acknowledged, however, that the available sources made it virtually impossible to construct 'any adequate or satisfactory sketch of her life and character.'[65]

The Women of Methodism was commissioned by the American Methodist Ladies' Centennial Committee to popularize the important role played by women in the history of Methodism and to raise funds to complete their centennial project. The committee planned to raise over $100,000 to build a residence for theological students at the Garrett Bible Institute in Evenston, Illinois, and to establish a fund to provide assistance for female students. The project was viewed as 'a golden opportunity' for the women of Methodism to write their 'names and influence upon the institutions and Christian agencies of an incoming century.' Significantly, it was resolved to dedicate the residence to Barbara Heck, 'the foundress of American Methodism.' The committee appealed to church women 'to build on a foundation laid by one of their own sex.'[66] Organizers found in the figure of Barbara Heck a model for their own activism and an inspirational figure upon whom they could project their own desires. Not content to be passive figures in the pews, many Methodist women championed social and moral reform and called for conversion to render the world a better place.[67] In calling the first minister, convening the first class and congregation, and planning the first church building, Heck had demonstrated the decisive role that women could play in the church and society.

The attention devoted to Heck during the American centennial celebrations produced a renewed interest in her in Canada. Lacking a literature on Heck's Canadian years, Canadian Methodists set about filling the void. The most enthusiastic chronicler of Heck's Canadian experience was Rev. William Withrow, the editor of the *Canadian Methodist Magazine* and *Pleasant Hours*, a magazine for youth. Of Loyalist descent, Withrow was particularly disturbed by the fact that American historians had virtually ignored Heck's Loyalism. Withrow produced a serialized account of

Heck's life for the *Canadian Methodist Magazine* in 1880. The story was published in book form in 1895 as *Barbara Heck: A Tale of Early Methodism.* Withrow drew heavily upon American works in relating Heck's experience in New York. In the absence of any documentary evidence, Withrow resorted to invented dialogue and fictional characters to tell the story of Heck's flight to Canada during the American Revolution.

According to Withrow, the Palatines were resolute in their loyalty to Britain and the Empire. At the outbreak of hostilities, the loyal Palatines abandoned their fertile farms and comfortable homes and fled to Montreal, where they could safely maintain their allegiance to the Crown. To a neighbour's suggestion: 'cast in your lot with us and fight for rights and liberty,' the 'brave hearted Barbara' responds: 'The service that we love is no bondage but truest liberty; and we have under the dear old flag beneath which we were born, all the rights we want – the right to worship God according to the dictates of our conscience, none daring to molest us or make us afraid.' 'If we must fight,' added her loyal husband, Paul, 'we will fight for the old flag under which we have enjoyed peace and prosperity' and under which 'our fathers sought refuge.' Withrow added that had Philip Embury not died on the eve of the hostilities, he too would have remained steadfast in his loyalty. As the 'little band of loyal subjects' left their homes, the ever faithful Barbara offered comfort: 'we are in the hollow of God's hands, and shall be kept as the apple of His eye. Naught can harm us while He is on our side.' Inspired by her 'faith and courage,' the 'pioneer explorers' completed the long and perilous journey to Montreal with 'gladhearts.' 'True to their providential mission,' Withrow concluded, the Hecks 'became the founders and pioneers of Methodism in Upper Canada, as they had been in the United States. Withrow's book did much to popularize the Heck legend in Canada.[68]

The Heck myth served a number of functions in the Canadian context. In 1884 Methodists celebrated both the centennial of Methodism in Canada and the union of the various Methodist sects into a single national denomination. The past proved particularly useful as Methodists attempted to forge a common identity out of the disparate groups that came together to form a unified church.[69] Barbara Heck provided the new denomination with indigenous origins, a sense of continuity, and a heroic history. Charges that the church had been a bastion of Americanism and Republicanism were refuted by references to its loyal origins.[70] As was the case in the United States, Barbara Heck became an icon for many women within the church in Canada. In 1897 a number of prominent church women formed the Barbara Heck Memorial Association. The purpose of the association was to raise funds to build a women's residence at Toronto's Victoria College. In providing for 'the advancement of Christian women,' the future guardians of the nation's homes, Heck Hall would be both a lasting and a suitable 'memorial to the mother of Methodism in Canada and the United States.'[71] Such sentiments were typical of the maternal feminism that characterized many women's organizations at the end of the nineteenth century. Men frequently picked up the maternal metaphors and upheld Heck as model of true motherhood. Heck was praised for her humility, service, and faithfulness. In his address at the unveiling of the Heck memorial, Rev. John W. Hamilton described Heck as a 'humble housewife' and a 'plain woman.'[72] Methodist women were more likely to refer to Heck's initiative, stamina, and courage and often cited her example in their campaign for ecclesiastical suffrage.[73]

The movement to mark Barbara Heck's grave with an appropriate monument originated with Rev. John Scanlon. Scanlon visited the cemetery shortly after he was posted to a congregation in nearby Prescott. He found the grave 'uncared for and overgrown with thistles and weeds.' Appalled by the 'wretchedly bad condition' of the site, in August of 1904 Scanlon organized a memorial service to commemorate the centenary of Heck's death. The service would provide an incentive to tidy the graveyard and, Scanlon hoped, furnish an opportunity to raise funds to add a memorial hall to his own church. Representatives from several Canadian and American conferences attended the service, and the condition of the site became a topic of discussion among Methodists on both sides of the border. In the United States, Ana Onstott initiated a movement within the New York and Vermont conferences to replace the simple headstone with an appropriately inscribed monument. The proposal was endorsed by the Montreal conference and a committee was appointed to correspond with other conferences. Supportive resolutions were passed throughout the province and beyond and a campaign was launched to raise the estimated $3,000 that would be necessary to erect a suitable monument.[74]

Although interest in the Loyalist past markedly declined following the First World War, the movement to erect monuments in their memory did not abate entirely. On 8 September 1924 the people of Belleville gathered in Victoria Park to witness the unveiling of a monument commemorating the 140th anniversary of the settlement of Ontario by the United Empire Loyalists. The monument consisted of a simple, scaled-down log cabin cast in bronze and mounted on a granite pedestal. 'The monument is plain, simple, inexpensive, and enduring,' explained the mayor of

Belleville, W.C. Mikel, 'to typify the conditions of the early pioneer.' 'The
representation of the log cabin,' Mikel continued, 'reminds of us their
first home and suggests the sacrifices made, the services rendered and the
hardships endured.'[75] Five years later, a crowd of several hundred gathered in front of the Wentworth County courthouse in Hamilton to celebrate the unveiling of a much grander monument honouring the
Loyalists. The imposing monument, donated to the city by a prominent
local family of Loyalist descent, depicted a well-dressed family of Loyalist
refugees setting out to begin their lives anew in Upper Canada after having drawn their lot number from the government surveyor. The story of
the Loyalists was told in a series of bronze panels affixed to each side of
the base of the monument. 'Neither confiscation of their property, the
pitiless persecution of their kinsmen in revolt, nor the galling chains of
imprisonment,' proclaimed the front panel, 'could break their spirits or
divorce them from a Loyalty almost without parallel.'[76]

Both the Belleville and the Hamilton monuments honoured the Loyalists, but they did so very differently. The Belleville monument portrayed
the Loyalists as humble, sturdy, and hard-working pioneers, who laid the
foundations for the nation's future progress and prosperity. The Hamilton monument presented the Loyalists as a principled elite persecuted for
their unwavering dedication to the Crown and Empire. These two images
of the Loyalists underscores one of the central arguments of this study: the
commemoration of the past is contested and often involves a struggle
between champions of varying ideologies, sentiments and interests. In the
cases of Brant and Heck, family pride and filiopietism played an important role in initiating the myth-making process. Self-promotion performed a similar function for Laura Secord. It was only when these figures
were found to be useful in furthering one or more causes, however, that
the movement to commemorate them gathered momentum. Although
there were elements within the experience and example of each figure
that appealed to the historical imagination, Brant, Secord, and Heck
assumed heroic status not so much for their own intrinsic accomplishments and contributions, but rather because of their ability to carry and
convey the political, social, or cultural values of their promoters.

7

'A further and more enduring mark of honour': The Middle Class and the United Empire Loyalist Association of Ontario, 1896–1914

'This is an age of societies and combinations,' observed William Hamilton Merritt, the secretary-treasurer of the newly formed United Empire Loyalist Association of Ontario, in 1896.[1] As North America evolved into an urban and industrial society in the final decades of the nineteenth century, numerous historical, patriotic, and hereditary organizations were created. Economic growth produced a level of prosperity sufficient to facilitate associational activity on a broad scale. At the same time the wide scope of the social and economic changes created both a sense of anxiety about the present and a nostalgia for a simpler, more stable past. Confronted with the class polarization and social problems of an increasingly industrialized and urbanized society and a rising tide of foreign immigration, many middle-class North Americans of older stock turned to the stabilizing influences of patriotism and the past and joined together to form hereditary and historical organizations dedicated to demonstrating their genealogical and patriotic superiority.[2]

On 28 February 1896 a group of thirty-one men and women gathered at the Canadian Institute in Toronto to discuss the formation of an organization of Loyalist descendants. Three months later, the United Empire Loyalist Association of Ontario held its first general meeting. By 1914 the association had grown to 560 members and was the largest hereditary and patriotic organization in the province. Its purpose was not simply to celebrate the contributions of the Loyalists to the founding of the province but to ensure that the Loyalist tradition remained a vital characteristic of Ontario society. From the beginning, the ethos of the association was exclusive, conservative, and defensive. Its middle-class founders and members sought to bestow upon themselves 'a further and more enduring mark of honour' that would protect and legitimize their status, values, and beliefs during a period of profound social and economic change.

Ontario's Loyalist descendants were relatively late in forming an association. A Loyalist society was organized in New Brunswick as early as 1889. A second association was founded in Quebec in 1895.[3] An attempt to found a permanent association of Loyalist descendants in Ontario immediately following the 1884 centennial celebrations had failed. Deterred by the generally negative reaction to the celebrations, many Loyalist descendants decided that quite enough had been made of their past for the time being.[4] The idea was revived in October of 1894 by Dr George Sterling Ryerson. Ryerson proposed that a society, 'The Sons of the Loyalists,' be formed 'to perpetuate the memory of the United Empire Loyalists.' The aims of the society would be 'the perpetuation of the British connection, the dissemination of patriotic literature and observance of Canadian historical events, the collection and preservation of facts relating to the United Empire Loyalist migration, and the formation of a museum of objects of historic interest.'[5] Ryerson's plans to form an association of Loyalist descendants did not generate much interest initially. Undeterred by the lack of enthusiasm that greeted his proposal, Ryerson approached William Hamilton Merritt with the idea. Merritt responded positively and agreed to finance the publication of a circular and to put together a mailing list.[6] A preliminary meeting was held on 28 February 1896 and a provisional committee was appointed to draft a constitution.

The first general meeting of the United Empire Loyalist Association of Ontario was held on 11 May 1896. The main business of the meeting was the adoption of a constitution and the election of officers. The stated objects of the new association were 'to unite together, irrespective of creed or political party' all Loyalist descendants in order 'to perpetuate the spirit of loyalty to the Empire.' The association was also mandated 'to preserve the history and traditions of that important epoch in Canadian history, by rescuing from oblivion the history and traditions of the Loyalist families before it is too late' and 'to collect together in a suitable place the portraits, relics and documents relating to the United Empire Loyalists.'[7] Membership in the association was to be open to residents of Ontario who could trace their descent, by either male or female line, from the United Empire Loyalists. The constitution did not define Loyalist, however – a fact which would soon cause considerable debate within the association.

After approving a constitution, the meeting turned to the election of officers. The lieutenant-governor of Ontario, John Beverley Robinson, was unanimously elected president. It was hoped that 'the prominence of his official and social position' and 'his long experience of public life' would give the fledgling organization immediate status and prestige.[8] The association suffered a serious set-back when Robinson died shortly after he became president. He was succeeded by George Sterling Ryerson. A. Maclean Howard was elected vice-president. William Hamilton Merritt became secretary-treasurer, and Margaret Isabella Maule Clarkson filled the position of assistant secretary. Herman Henry Cook, A.H.F. LeFroy, Stephen Jarvis, Charles Egerton Ryerson, Col. George Alexander Shaw, and Rev. C.E. Thompson were elected to the executive committee.

The association's first officers were largely professionals drawn from the ranks of established Toronto families. Dr George Sterling Ryerson was a nephew of Egerton Ryerson and the Conservative member of the provincial legislature for East Toronto. The association's secretary-treasurer, William Hamilton Merritt, was the grandson of William Hamilton Merritt of Welland Canal fame and a mining engineer. A. Maclean Howard, the association's first vice-president, was a lawyer and active in the affairs of the Anglican church. Stephen Jarvis was the son of Frederick Starr Jarvis, Gentleman Usher of the Black Rod in the Legislative Assembly of Upper Canada. Educated at Upper Canada College, Jarvis was called to the bar in 1843.[9] A.H.F. LeFroy was the son of General Sir J.H. LeFroy and Sir John Beverley Robinson's daughter Emily. LeFroy was educated at Oxford and became a partner in the Toronto law firm, LeFroy, Boulton, and LeFroy.[10] George Alexander Shaw was a lawyer by training and had entered the federal civil service in 1867. He served with the Royal Grenadiers during the Fenian raids of 1860.[11] The Reverend C.E. Thomson was rector of St Mark's Anglican church in Toronto. Thomson was born in 1832 and educated at Upper Canada College and Trinity University. He was among the founders of the York Pioneer and Historical Society and was president of the organization from 1898 until 1903.[12] The lone woman among the association's original office-holders, Margaret Isabella Maude Clarkson, was the daughter of Stephen Jarvis and the wife of the Toronto shipping merchant Benjamen Read Clarkson.[13] The average age of the officers was fifty-seven. All but one of the officers were Anglican in religion and Conservative in politics. The one exception was the Liberal Methodist, Herman Henry Cook. Cook, a wealthy lumber baron from Penetanguishene, was also the lone businessmen in the group. Cook was elected to the House of Commons in 1872 and represented North Simcoe until 1878. From 1879 to 1882 he was the member of the provincial Parliament for East Simcoe. He returned to federal politics in 1882 and represented East Simcoe in the House of Commons from 1882 to 1891.[14]

Despite the similar backgrounds of its founders, the association was plagued by dissent and internal divisions during its first year. Much of the conflict focused on the president, George Sterling Ryerson, and the secretary-treasurer, William Hamilton Merritt. Underlying the personal rivalry between these two strong-willed individuals were serious questions about the purpose of the association. As the founding father and president, Ryerson assumed he possessed the right to manage the organization's agenda and affairs. Merritt, on the other hand, had provided the financial resources necessary to get the association started. From the beginning, Ryerson viewed Merritt as a potential rival.[15]

The tension between the two men first erupted at the 12 November 1896 meeting, when Ryerson introduced the first of a series of motions to amend the constitution. Although the amendments themselves were not particularly controversial, the arbitrary and autocratic manner in which Ryerson attempted to control the process upset some of the association's members.[16] In an attempt to prevent similar incidents from arising in the future, Merritt moved that four weeks' notice must be given before motions to amend the constitution could be introduced and voted upon. Ryerson interpreted the motion as a personal insult to his leadership and ruled it out of order.[17]

The degree of dissatisfaction with Ryerson's leadership became evident at the association's annual meeting in March of 1898. One discontented member charged that Ryerson had been 'dictatorial and overbearing in the performance of his duties' and that 'it was time for a change.' When nominations were opened for the position of president, Ryerson's critics put forward Herman Henry Cook. The meeting immediately became embroiled in a heated debate over how the vote was to be taken. Stephen Jarvis proposed voting by secret ballot. Ryerson rejected the suggestion, maintaining that voting by ballot was not provided for in the constitution. Jarvis demanded that the question be put to a vote. Although Ryerson declared the motion defeated, an official recount revealed twenty-six in favour of the motion and only nine opposed. Col. Alexander Dunn complicated matters further by moving that associate members be permitted to vote. Again citing the association's constitution, Ryerson ruled the motion out of order. An enraged Dunn compared the position of associate members within the Association to that of the American colonists who were taxed without representation in Parliament. 'The Americans,' Dunn concluded, 'rebelled because they were taxed when they had no vote and no representation and if they rebelled because they were thus treated, upon my soul I don't blame them.' The legality of the constitution was brought into question by the association's assistant secretary, Margaret Clarkson. Clarkson maintained that notice of the amendments to the constitution had not been circulated and that the revised constitution was thus of questionable legality. The association's legal adviser, E.A. MacLaurin, insisted that the constitution was 'carefully prepared and perfectly legal in every respect' and to claim otherwise was 'to impugn the honour of himself and his fellow members of the Executive Committee.'[18]

When the vote was finally taken, Cook and Ryerson finished in a tie, forcing the president to cast the deciding vote. Ryerson voted for himself, setting off another round of angry accusations. Despite charges of impropriety, Ryerson refused to call another ballot and insisted that the elections proceed to fill the remaining offices. William Hamilton Merritt was nominated for the position of vice-president. Merritt denounced Ryerson's handling of the meeting, however, and refused to let his name stand. Since no other names were put forward, Ryerson declared Merritt elected, igniting yet another storm of protest. The meeting came to a dramatic end when Ryerson resigned as president and stormed out of the hall. 'No consideration under heaven,' he declared, 'would permit me to occupy the position.' Ryerson accused Merritt of a 'deliberate attempt to wreck the association' and charged that he had repeatedly overstepped his authority as secretary. E.A. MacLaurin repeated Ryerson's charges and accused Merritt of not 'being present at meetings of the association and not attending to his duties.' An infuriated Merritt responded that he 'did not seek the office and never desired it' before he too stalked out of the meeting. A. MacLean Howard took the chair and wisely adjourned the meeting.[19]

Peace and concord did not ensue with Ryerson's departure. Disaffected members began to question the right of other members to belong to the association. Article four of the constitution stated simply that 'all persons of either sex resident in Ontario who can trace their lineal descent, by either male or female line, from the United Empire Loyalists shall be eligible for ordinary membership.'[20] The constitution did not attempt to define Loyalist and did not specify a date of arrival. It was thus not clear whether the so-called late Loyalists or the descendants of Loyalists from other provinces were entitled to membership in the association. Controversy also centred on the question of whether the descendants of regular British military forces active during the Revolution who settled in Upper Canada could be designated Loyalists.

The association's executive committee attempted to resolve the membership issue in 1901. In a ruling upon article four the executive committee resolved that 'no person coming to Canada from the United States after the year 1796 shall be considered as a UE Loyalist ancestor, unless it can be clearly demonstrated that he or she was entitled to be so considered.'[21] The committee further ruled that the disbanded officers and soldiers of the British army who settled in Canada following the Revolution were also eligible for membership. Settlement prior to 1796 was the key factor in determining eligibility. The association's standards were certainly more liberal than the criteria used by the Loyalist Claims Commission. To be considered a Loyalist by the Claims Commission one had to be resident in the American colonies before the outbreak of the Revolution, to have rendered substantial service to the royal cause in the course of the war, and to have left the old colonies during the war or shortly thereafter. The claims of refugees who had not rendered a demonstrable service, of those who had never left the United States, and of those who returned to their former homes were not accepted by the commission. Disbanded British regulars and German mercenaries did not fall within the commission's definition of a Loyalist. The more stringent rules of the Loyalist Claims Commission would certainly have excluded many of the association's members, including those of one its co-founders, William Hamilton Merritt.[22]

Loyalist descent was only one factor in defining suitability for membership in the association. Officials claimed that the association was 'non-political.'[23] The fact of the matter was that members frequently found themselves discussing political issues and that only those committed to the preservation of the Empire need apply for admission. The association publicly criticized the federal government's handling of the question of Canadian participation in the Boer War. Herman Henry Cook, a former Liberal member of Parliament and president of the association, took the extraordinary step of urging members to vote against the Laurier government. 'When a Prime Minister has to be forced into such an action as the sending of the contingents,' Cook charged, 'I believe he should be removed.'[24] The association became actively involved in the debates over tariff and defence policy that dominated Canadian politics in the first decade of the new century and openly endorsed the activities of political organizations such as the Canadian Preference League and the Canadian Patriotic League.[25]

Officials also claimed that the association differed 'from the principal hereditary or historical associations elsewhere, in that it makes no requirement of social status as a condition of membership.'[26] Although not as explicit as similar organizations in the United States, the association's rules on membership ensured that only respectable persons would be admitted to its ranks. 'Proper qualifications of good repute and of desirability for admission to membership' were to be required of all prospective members. Any member who failed to continue to live up to the association's standards could be expelled by a vote of three-quarters of those present at special meeting.[27] Not surprisingly, the ranks were dominated by respectable members of the middle class with proven imperialist credentials. Loyalist descendants of working-class and rural backgrounds were simply not to be found on the membership rolls. This was not an accident. Initiation and membership fees effectively prevented people of humble station from joining. Admitting such people would undermine the exclusive pretensions that drew middle-class descendants to the association in the first place.

The association was particularly anxious to attract people of distinction. Any person, 'well and publicly known, being or having been the holder of any public office or position, and being of good repute in all respects' could therefore be elected without the usual formalities if such election was unanimously agreed to by members of the association at any regular meeting, provided not less than twenty-five members were present.[28] The association eagerly sought out celebrated Loyalist descendants from the ranks of the British aristocracy and invited them to become honorary vice-presidents. It was hoped that affiliation with the likes of the Earl of Carnwath, Lady Dilke, and Sir Roderick Cameron would increase the prestige of the association and its members. Viewing themselves as an indigenous Canadian aristocracy, members bathed in the reflected glory of the British aristocrats who lent their names and titles to the association. Close ties were also cultivated with the Crown's Canadian representatives. The governor-general and the lieutenant-governor of Ontario were deluged with petitions of loyalty and requests to address the association or to attend its social functions. It was believed that such public affiliation with the official leaders of Canadian society attested to the status of the members and to their superior loyalty and patriotism.

The debate about membership was in part a product of the conflicting aims of the association. Some saw its purpose as essentially political, to perpetuate the British connection and inculcate conservative political values. Supporters of this view tended to welcome anyone who shared their imperialist views. Thomas Chisholm, the member of Parliament for Huron, suggested that all defenders of imperial connection should be organized throughout the country with the honoured name *United Empire Loyalists*. Chisholm's proposal appealed to the governor-general, Lord Grey, and Colonel George Taylor Denison. 'If you and your friends were to consent to the adoption, by those who wish to consolidate the Empire,' Grey wrote to Denison, 'no few men would put their backs into a determined effort.' Denison saw merit in the proposal and promised to pursue the suggestion with the association. He cautioned, however, that 'the UEL's whose name is embedded in the history of Canada might be sensitive as to its use by others.'[29] Denison's observations were correct. Many members viewed the association as an exclusive club and insisted that only lineal descendants should be permitted to join. Still others viewed it as a historical and genealogical society, whose chief function was to collect records and artefacts and preserve family histories.

In 1898 R.E.A. Land, a prominent Toronto lawyer and Conservative party organizer, approached Colonel George Taylor Denison with the idea of establishing branches of the association throughout the province. Land saw the establishment of local branches as an ideal way of increasing the association's membership and furthering its influence and ideals. 'Each local organization,' Land wrote to Colonel Denison, would 'become a local centre of patriotism and would aid in teaching loyalty to the people.'[30] An unofficial branch was organized at Virgil in 1898 by members of the Servos family, but little immediately came of Land's proposal. In 1901 Land was elected president of the association on an expansionist platform. 'If this association is to exercise an influence in the state commensurate with its importance,' Land asserted in his inaugural address as president, 'it will be necessary for us to increase its membership.' The creation of local branches, Land advised, would awaken 'memories of the great past' in the breasts of Loyalist descendants and result 'in our receiving their hearty and active co-operation on behalf of the ideals we cherish.'[31]

Attempts to organize local branches of the association met with limited success. In February of 1902 James Edwin O'Reilly and H.H. Robertson organized the Head-of-the-Lake branch in Hamilton. O'Reilly was a lawyer and former mayor of the city. Robertson was also a lawyer and a son of John R. Robertson, the proprietor of the *Spectator*. By the end of the year the Hamilton branch had sixty-one members. Membership climbed to seventy-seven by 1904 and remained at about that level until 1914, when financial difficulties forced the branch to close.[32] In 1907 W.E. Tisdale, the son of the Honourable David Tisdale, attempted to establish a branch in Simcoe. Tisdale presented the idea to the Norfolk Historical Society. He reported to the Loyalist association's secretary, Margaret Clarkson, that the matter was discussed at some length but that it was finally decided that it would not be wise to proceed, since 'the historical society had in view many of the objects of the UEL association while its membership is not limited *in any way*.'[33] Significantly, no attempt was made to organize branches in likely eastern Ontario locales such as Adolphustown, Kingston, Brockville, or Cornwall. Herman Henry Cook attributed the lack of interest shown in the association in eastern Ontario to ignorance. 'There were many who were eastern descendants of the UE Loyalists,' Cook complained, 'who were not aware of it, and they should be sought out.'[34] The more likely explanation is that many Loyalist descendants preferred to pursue their historical interests through the local historical society rather than submit to the control of the central association in Toronto.

In 1898 the United Empire Loyalist Association resolved to make Chiefs Jacob Salem Johnson and Sampson Green honorary vice-presidents of the association and to admit to associate membership the whole of the Six Nations of the Grand River and Tyendinaga reserves. It was further resolved to present Chiefs Johnson and Green with commemorative silver medals to be worn by them and their successors.[35] The idea originated with E.M. Chadwick, the association's legal adviser and genealogist. A long-time advocate of fair treatment for Native peoples, Chadwick felt that such recognition was long overdue. In an address to the Canadian Institute, Chadwick observed that 'while the Indian has been plentifully abused, vilified, and misrepresented, he has had comparatively few apologists.' According to Chadwick, the Six Nations had distinguished themselves by their loyalty and were by nature honest, hospitable, faithful, brave, contemplative, moral, courteous, and intelligent. Chadwick was disturbed that the Native was treated like 'a pupil or a dependent' rather than as 'a friend and equal' and that 'in the process of bringing the Indian into civilization, there has been an effort to make him forget his past history and customs.'[36]

Not all members of the association shared Chadwick's views and many questioned the decision to make Chiefs Johnson and Green honorary vice-presidents and to confer associate membership upon the Six Nations of Grand River and Tyendinaga. A few members objected that Chiefs Johnson and Green did not meet the association's membership criteria and thus were not qualified to become honorary vice-presidents. Others questioned the loyalty of the Six Nations during the Revolution. The popular American literary and historical image of the Six Nations as treacherous and bloodthirsty 'savages' who were unreliable allies during the revolutionary war lingered, despite the tributes bestowed on the Six Nations during the unveiling of the Brant memorial in 1886. Moreover, family folklore, often portrayed Natives as menaces who, like the wilderness, had had to be confronted and overcome by the Loyalist refugees.[37] Added to these literary and folklore traditions, of course, was the contemporary negative stereotype of the drunken, lazy, and backward Indian. Dissatisfaction with the decision to confer associate status upon the Six Nations forced E.M. Chadwick to 'place on record some explanation of the action of the association in this matter.' 'The Mohawks, together with the greater number of the other five nations,' Chadwick reminded members, 'remained steadfastly loyal to the crown; and not only that, but time and again they took the field to defend the crown against the revolutionists.'[38] Such steadfast devotion to the preservation of the Empire, Chadwick concluded, deserved recognition.

For their part, Chiefs Johnson and Green welcomed membership in the association as an opportunity to further their people's struggle against the terms and conditions of the Indian Act. In accepting his medal, Chief Johnson assured the association of the Six Nations' continued loyalty to Britain and spoke of the advancement they had made during recent years. Because of their loyalty and 'superior intelligence,' Johnson insisted that the Six Nations 'should not be governed by the same Indian Act as others.'[39] The call for assistance was repeated by Green in June when members of the association visited the Six Nations reserve at Tyendinaga. Just as 'their ancestors fought side by side with yours to defend their homes and to uphold the Government which they believed to be right,' Green called upon members to stand by the Six Nations in the struggle to have their historic claims recognized by the Canadian government.[40]

Such appeals did not go entirely unheeded. The president of the Head-of-the-Lake branch, Judge Colin Snider, described the Six Nations as 'true United Empire Loyalists' who '[gave] up their homes in the beautiful valleys and mountains of the central and northern states to suffer with their wives and children terrible hardships, to starve and fight and die for England and England's King.' 'The ancestors through whom we trace our right to be members of this association,' Snider asserted, 'knew them well, shared their hardships and many of them at times owed their lives to the timely and sudden appearance of these savage braves.' 'Their descendants now living on the Grand River,' he concluded, 'have no ordinary claim on our good will [and] our kindly feelings.'[41] Frank Keeker expressed similar sentiments in letters to the president and secretary of the United Empire Loyalist Association. 'These Indians by their loyalty, by their intelligence,' Keefer insisted, 'are on an entirely different plane from some of our other tribal Indians, and it seems to me that Canada would make no mistake in granting them the franchise (but not to the other Indians) merely as an encouragement to the other Indians to arise to the high plane that they have arisen.'[42] Most members of the association, however, remained aloof. Support for the Six Nations, they argued, violated the constitution, which prohibited involvement in political questions. Disillusioned by the United Empire Loyalist Association's indifference, the Six Nations of Grand River and Tyendinaga did not act on the invitation to establish branches on the reserves.

The Six Nations were not alone in attempting to use the United Empire Loyalist Association to further their political aspirations. Women accounted for 51 per cent of the association's membership. The female ranks of the association included such notable early feminists as Matilda Edgar, Mary Dignam, and Minnie Caroline Forsyth Grant. All three women held senior positions in the National Council of Women of Canada and the Women's Canadian Historical association. Reform-minded female members of the association believed they could use their Loyalist past to advance the cause of women's rights. In their addresses to the association, women attempted to restore the experience of their Loyalist foremothers to the centre of the Loyalist saga. Men, they stressed, had not been the only ones required to make sacrifices and endure hardships and privations on account of their loyalty. While their husbands, fathers, and brothers were away fighting, Loyalist women were left alone to run the farms and care for their families. Charlotte Bruce Carey, for instance, asserted that her great-grandmother, Margaret Bruce, was 'a woman of great energy and ability, and although left a widow in those times of hardship and trouble, she managed her affairs so well that she not only kept her family in comfort, but she was able to render assistance to many of her less fortunate compatriots.'[43] The women of the association also noted that Loyalist women had played an important role during the Revolution, harbouring spies, hiding escaped prisoners of war, and passing on information.[44] Although the voice of women was muted by the male-dominated power structure of the United Empire Loyalist Association, reform-minded women found in the experience and example of their

Loyalist foremothers a useful vehicle to express their own aspirations for status and recognition.

Despite continuing division and discontent and the failure to establish branches throughout the province, membership in the United Empire Loyalist Association of Ontario expanded rapidly. By 1898 it had grown from its original twenty-five members to 166. Membership doubled to 332 in the following year and peaked at 560 in 1913.[45] Between 1896 and 1913 the association drew most of its members from the ranks of the province's urban middle class. During these years, more than half of the members resided in the province's largest city, Toronto. Most of the remaining members were drawn from smaller urban centres such as Ottawa, Hamilton, Kingston, and St Catharines. Less than 15 per cent of the total membership came from small-town and rural Ontario. Professionals accounted for 48 per cent of the membership, among them thirty-eight lawyers, twenty-two physicians, and twelve clergymen. White-collar workers accounted for another 36 per cent of the membership. Significantly, only 9 per cent of the association's members were entrepreneurs or businessmen engaged in commerce, finance, or industry. Working-class Loyalist descendants were entirely absent from the association's membership rolls.[46]

Why were middle-class professionals and white-collar workers drawn to the association? And why were businessmen so notably absent? In his influential work, *The Age of Reform*, the American historian Richard Hofstadter maintained that industrialization and urbanization revolutionized the distribution of power and prestige in American society at the end of the nineteenth century. This 'status revolution' created a new class of industrialists, nouveaux riches who surpassed the wealth and influence of the old gentry of the northeast. Alarmed by the rise of the industrial plutocracy, the growth of the working class, large-scale immigration, and the social ills afflicting the cities and fearing the loss of their own status and influence, old-stock Anglo-American families took refuge in a vanishing and largely imaginary past. Hofstadter interpreted the avid interest in history and genealogy displayed by the traditional middle class as an attempt to shore up their own declining prominence and prestige by claiming a superior patriotism as descendants of the nation's founders and as guardians of America's culture and traditions.[47] In *The Sense of Power*, Carl Berger perceived a similar pattern 'in the assumption of social superiority based on ancestry and patriotism' articulated by Loyalist descendants in Ontario during the final decades of the nineteenth century.[48]

Members of the United Empire Loyalist Association certainly displayed the same fear of concentrated corporate power and class polarization identified by Hofstadter. In his inaugural address as president of the association, George Sterling Ryerson expressed concern about the course of industrialization in the United States. 'Huge trusts, combines and monopolies,' he asserted, 'are making a mockery of republican institutions. Men may be born equal in the United States, but they don't stay so.' Ryerson was particularly disturbed by the level of labour unrest. 'A painful feature of the strikes and lockouts,' he observed, 'is the resort to force, attended in many instances by a serious loss of life and destruction of property.'[49] Ryerson attributed America's problems to its revolutionary past and warned that similar afflictions could be avoided in this country only if Canadians remained true to their history. Ryerson's remarks were not unusual. Speakers at the association's meetings often railed against the complexities and dangers of modern life and harked back to a simpler past. Such concerns were not, as Hofstadter and Berger suggest, entirely the product of a besieged middle class reacting to the external threat posed to its status and influence by the new industrial elite and the restless masses of the cities. The association's appeal to professionals and white-collar workers can also be understood in the light of developments within the middle class itself.

For much of the nineteenth century, society's natural leaders had been a handful of office-holders, professional gentlemen, and wealthy merchants, whose status and influence depended largely on the ownership of land, education, family connections, and patronage. By century's end, the old assumptions and certainties about the proper ordering of society had been eroded by the forces of commercialization and industrialization and the appearance of a new business middle class made up of entrepreneurs, promoters, and manufacturers.[50] The rise of business challenged the position of the traditional professions and split the middle class in new ways. According to the British historian Harold Perkins, the professional ideal of expertise and merit increasingly found itself in conflict with the entrepreneurial ideal of capital and competition.[51] Perkin's observations apply equally well to Canada. As Michael Bliss has demonstrated, the late nineteenth-century Canadian business community was highly critical of the professions as an 'unenterprising' and 'nonproducing class.'[52] The professions responded to such criticisms by asserting the superiority of their own skills and learning. The position of the traditional professions was further challenged by what R.D. Gidney and W.P.J. Millar have termed *parvenu occupations* which aspired to the status enjoyed by the law, medicine, and theology. It was feared that the claims of land surveyors, engineers, pharmacists, and many others to professional prerogatives would obscure the meaning of what it meant to be a professional. Public education, moreover, increased the number of candidates qualified for professional training. As a result, the economic well-being of many professionals was threatened by overcrowding in their ranks. Forced to engage in the same sort of unseemly competition that characterized business, many professionals feared a breakdown in the standards of conduct that had traditionally defined their occupations.[53]

A pervasive sense of insecurity afflicted the professions as traditional assumptions about status and the social order were subverted by the unsettling forces fragmenting the middle class. These developments produced a concerted search on the part of professionals for new strategies to uphold their position and prestige. Many turned to history and to genealogy to defend their position in society. The professionals who filled the ranks of the United Empire Loyalist Association found in their Loyalist roots a badge of distinction that set them apart from the rest of society. Faced with an unsettled present and an uncertain future, the professionals who joined the association looked to the past to defend their values and to uphold their status.

Professionals were not the only sector of the middle class attracted to the United Empire Loyalist Association. The expansion of capitalist enterprise, the introduction of new technologies, and changes in the organization of production created a new class of managers and significantly increased the size of the white-collar workforce engaged in clerical and service-oriented occupations. The expansion of the managerial and white-collar sectors extended the ranks of the middle class and introduced an unprecedented degree of hierarchy and differentiation into the non-manual workforce as jobs became more distinct and the distance between incomes increased.[54] The end result was the creation of large white-collar workforce that identified itself as middle class but felt increasingly insecure about its position. Membership in organizations like the United Empire Loyalist Association enabled this beleaguered group to assert claims to status and recognition based on ancestry and to associate with other more socially prominent individuals.

Few businessmen joined the United Empire Loyalist Association. Unlike the professionals and white-collar workers attracted to the association, businessmen were full participants in the new world of commerce and entrepreneurship created by industrialization and urbanization. Relatively satisfied with the present state of affairs, firm believers in the idea of progress, and preoccupied with the task of making money, business had little need or desire to look to the past for guidance or reassurance. In contrast, the middle-class professionals and white-collar workers who filled the association's ranks felt increasingly estranged from the emerging urban and industrial world and took refuge in an unrecapturable and largely invented past.

Not surprisingly, most of the United Empire Loyalist Association's time and energy was channelled into efforts to have the status of the organization and its members publicly confirmed and acknowledged. Among Ryerson's first initiatives as president was the attempt to secure official authorization for a special badge and insignia. Such a badge, he believed, would provide a tangible testimonial to the superior status and patriotism of the members. In 1897 the association sent a petition to the queen requesting royal sanction. Pointing out that 'it was the intention of Her Majesty's Royal Predecessor, George III, that the Petitioners' Ancestors and their descendants should be accorded a special mark of honour of a permanent and enduring character whereby they should at all times be distinguished from other settlers in Canada,' the association suggested that the queen's diamond jubilee 'should be the occasion of the more complete carrying out of His late Majesty's intention and be marked by the conferring upon the Petitioners and those whom they represent ... a further and more enduring mark of honour.'[55] While in England to observe Victoria's diamond jubilee, Ryerson attempted to meet with the British prime minister, Joseph Chamberlain, to discuss the proposed insignia. Ryerson recalled that he was able to secure a meeting only with the prime minister's under-secretary 'who had never heard of the Loyalists and could not see any reason why the state should acknowledge our existence.'[56] The Colonial Office contacted the governor-general, Lord Aberdeen, to determine Prime Minister Wilfrid Laurier's views on the subject. Sensitive to anti-imperialist sentiment in his native Quebec, Laurier felt that any action on the matter would have to wait until 'a more propitious season.'[57] The colonial secretary, Lewis Harcourt, informed Ryerson that it would be 'impolitic' to revive a colonial order-in-council that had lain dormant for more than a century.[58] On 10 May 1898 Herman Henry Cook and William Hamilton Merritt discussed the issue with the governor-general. Again, it was made clear that the Colonial Office would not authorize the association's badge without the prior approval of the Canadian government. Cook had few doubts about who was behind the government's reluctance to approve the insignia. The chief culprit, according to Cook, was the minister of public works, J.I. Tarte. 'Mr Tarte,' Cook insisted, 'was at the present time exploiting the race and religious cry in Quebec for all it was worth, and he was one of the parties who objected to the United Empire Loyalists having a badge.'[59] In 1901 the association resolved to proceed with the project without official authorization and a badge and insignia were distributed to members.[60] The amount of time and energy devoted to securing official recognition reveals much about the pretensions and status anxieties of the association's members.

The middle-class members of the United Empire Loyalist Association were also concerned with the preservation of Canada's integrity as 'a British nation.' In his inaugural address as president of the United Empire Loyalist Association in 1901, R.E.A. Land maintained that loyal and patriotic societies had a vital role to play in the war against 'cosmopolitanism.' The mission of the United Empire Loyalist Association was to 'educate those within the sphere of our influence, in the British way of looking at things, and be ever ready to check foreign intrusion in our politics, business, or social affairs.' It was the duty of Loyalists to stand guard against any foreign influence 'whether in speech, thought, dress, or conventional usage, especially those which hail from the south,' and to 'discountenance the use in Canada of alien emblems, especially foreign flags.' 'The burden of our labours,' Land concluded, 'must be directed towards the support of British nationalism' and the 'preservation of the British Empire' against the forces that conspired to subvert the country's heritage.[61]

The first test of the association's self-proclaimed status as guardian of the nation's British heritage and historical integrity occurred in 1898. Rumours circulated that an American organization, the Sons of the Revolution, planned to place a bronze plaque in Quebec in honour of General Richard Montgomery. The association immediately objected and sent a petition to the governor-general, a memorial to the city of Quebec and a letter to various historical and patriotic societies asking for cooperation in the matter.[62] To permit the erection of a monument to an invader, the association protested, would 'be at once an insult to the memory of the men who defended it [Quebec] and to the feelings of their loyal descendants.' More important, the association believed that such a monument 'would also in the future confuse the minds of the children as to the duty they owe to their country.'[63] The depth of opposition to the Montgomery monument arose in large part from the prevalent belief that monuments were powerful expressions of a nation's identity and useful tools of education. To permit a monument to a foreign hero on Canadian soil thus constituted a major assault upon Canadian values and beliefs.

In 1901 the Sons of the Revolution renewed their efforts to honour Montgomery. Again, the association petitioned and protested. R.E.A. Land complained in the *Globe* that the Sons of the Revolution desired to erect such a monument 'in order to insult the national sentiment of this country and to glorify the United States.' 'If erected,' Land warned, 'excursions from the hot-bed of revolution – Boston – will periodically take place.'[64] In a letter to the Sons of the Revolution, he explained that 'the proposition is one which is entirely contrary to international custom and courtesy' and would serve only to 'revive and foster animosities which in the course of a century and a quarter had naturally almost disappeared.'[65] The Sons of the Revolution ignored Land's advice and announced early in 1902 that they intended to place in Quebec not a simple tablet, but rather a twenty-foot cairn costing over nine thousand dollars. For Land, the matter had clearly gone too far, and pressure had to be put on the federal government to resolve the issue once and for all. Land encouraged all patriotic Canadians to write to the prime minister and asked E.F. Clarke, the member of Parliament for West Toronto, to raise the issue in the House of Commons. Prime Minister Wilfrid Laurier enraged opponents of the proposed monument when he responded that he was not aware of any renewed efforts to erect a memorial to Montgomery or of any petitions protesting the action. The government eventually heeded the protests and promised that no such monument would be permitted on public land.[66]

The association reacted with similar indignation to a rumoured plan to erect a memorial to George Washington in St Paul's Cathedral. A cablegram was immediately sent to the archdeacon of London, protesting that the erection of a monument to General Washington would be a grave insult to Canadians.[67] In 1905 A.E. Kemp sought the assistance of the association in thwarting the plans of Clarence M. Burton of Detroit to raise and remove two British gunboats sunk in the Thames River near Chatham during the War of 1812. Burton, a well-known local historian, claimed the right to 'seize and remove' the gunboats as 'spoils of war' and apparently hoped to put them on display in the United States as a tourist attraction. The association was predictably appalled by Burton's proposal. 'We might with equal reason,' E.M. Chadwick wrote to Kemp, 'call upon the Americans to dismantle the White House at Washington and send us parts of it to exhibit all over Canada.'[68] The association's petitions to the governor-general, Earl Grey, and the minister of militia, Sir Frederick Borden, succeeded in creating a public furore and dissuaded the intrepid American from taking further action.[69]

No incident was too small to arouse the wrath of the association. In October of 1906 the association complained to the officers of the Canadian National Exhibition that the Stars and Stripes had been raised to a position of prominence during the exhibition.[70] In January of 1912 the association protested the naming of two townships in Northern Ontario after the American geologists Leith and Vanhise. The minister of lands, mines and forests, William Hearst, assured the association that the townships were not 'named after the gentlemen whose names they bear because they were American' but were so named 'because Mr Leith and Mr Vanhise are geologists whose fame and reputation is world wide and men that any country which takes an interest in geology would be glad to honour.'[71] Although these acts appear trivial and amusing from today's perspective, it should be remembered that the United Empire Loyalist Association was not alone in expressing such views. The Ontario Historical Society, local historical groups, patriotic organizations, and imperialist leagues were just as vocal in their vigilance against such perceived insults and incursions.[72]

Members of the association were also troubled by the Laurier government's open-door immigration policy and the arrival of large numbers of non-Anglo-Saxons. Such immigrants, it was believed, threatened to erode the nation's British heritage and identity with their alien culture and ideas. In an address to the association, John Stewart Carstairs equated the current surge of immigrants into the country and the federal government's liberal land policy with the arrival of the late Loyalists and the generous terms offered by Simcoe. 'We must never forget,' Carstairs insisted, 'that there were U.E. Loyalist and "late loyalists."' Prior to the arrival of the 'late loyalists,' 'Upper Canada consisted almost wholly of men and women whose devotion to the interests of the United Empire had been again and again proved by privation and self-sacrifice during the long struggle.' Simcoe's 'unwise invitation' and 'mistaken land policy' had resulted in the arrival of hordes of American settlers interested only in 'bettering their conditions.' The dangers of admitting so many settlers of questionable loyalty became all too apparent during the War of 1812 and the Rebellion of 1837. 'What shall be the attitude of their descendants toward the land policy of the day when an alien population is flocking to our shores?' Carstairs enquired. The lessons of history provided a clear answer. 'Can we believe in the light of the past not only of our own country but of the older countries,' Carstairs continued, 'that the Galicans, the Doukhobours and the polyglot colonies of the northwest are a stable foundation on which to establish a sound Canadian spirit throughout this portion of Greater Britain?'[73] Just as the Loyalists had opposed the arrival of the so-called Late Loyalists, it was the duty of their descendants to preserve and defend a loyal, Anglo-Saxon country.

The fear that immigrants posed a threat to the British connection and Canada's British nationality prompted President Land and the association's legal adviser, E.M. Chadwick, to draft an act that would regulate the acquisition of land by immigrants. They proposed that 'no person should be allowed to locate or settle upon Crown lands, or to take a transfer of Crown Lands unless he is a British subject, and deposits in the Crown Lands Office a statutory declaration stating that he is a British subject.' Aliens would be permitted to lease or to acquire title to Crown land only if they intended to become a British subject, took an oath 'to render due allegiance to the King,' and committed themselves to 'not directly or indirectly do or suffer any act whatsoever contrary to the King's dignity or authority, or contrary to the lawful authority of any of the King's Ministers, Magistrates, or other public Officers.' Land and Chadwick suggested that persons who did not become citizens within three years of the eligible date for naturalization should be required to sell and dispose of any property they may have acquired. They clearly hoped 'to put the alien to a disadvantage' and thereby discourage the immigration of non-British subjects.[74] Although such nativist sentiment was common, Land and Chadwick were not able to convince either the federal or the provincial government to give their draft legislation serious consideration.

Unable to persuade the federal government to restrict and control the flow, the association advocated a number of measures to ensure the immigrants' assimilation. For members of the association, the vital component in the whole Canadianization process was education. As early as 1897 George Sterling Ryerson called for an increase in the level of 'practical instruction of Patriotism in the Public Schools' through appropriate recitations, readings, and exercises.[75] In conjunction with Loyalist societies in New Brunswick, Nova Scotia, and Quebec, the United Empire Loyalist Association of Ontario campaigned to have 18 May celebrated as United Empire Loyalist Day in the nation's schools. Over 3,000 Loyalists had met together at King's Landing, New Brunswick, on that day in 1783 to give thanks for their safe arrival from the separated American colonies. On 9 April 1898 a deputation waited upon the minister of education, George Ross, to request that schools mark the occasion with appropriate recitations and readings and that classes be dismissed an hour early. The minister shared the deputation's assessment of the utility of such exercises and agreed to the association's requests.[76] The official observance of

United Empire Loyalist Day by the province's schools was short lived. Despite the efforts of the association, United Empire Loyalist Day failed to attract much public interest or support. Part of the problem was that 18 May had no historical resonance in Ontario. Another less exclusive holiday initiated in 1898, Empire Day, proved far more popular.[77] Through the observance of such holidays and daily rituals like flag exercises and oaths of allegiance, the educational system was to be transformed into a machine for political socialization.

It was widely believed that the study of history was an essential ingredient in the process of assimilation and the creation of good citizens generally. In 1905 the association advised the minister of education that 'greater attention should be paid to the study of history' in the public schools. The association called for 'more accurate and interestingly written textbooks,' a high school admission examination in the field of Canadian history, and the establishment of a chair in Canadian history at the University of Toronto.[78] Confronted with a rising tide of immigration, members began to despair that the nation's British heritage was endangered. In looking to the education system, and the study of history in particular, they sought to create social order and political allegiance based upon a knowledge of a past they had helped to invent.

In his inaugural address as president, R.E.A. Land insisted that the association had a responsibility to cultivate 'imperial patriotism' and 'a distinctively national character' and to those ends he suggested a number of practical measures that could be pursued. 'In the manner and matter of celebrations,' Land complained, 'Canadians have much to learn.' He proposed that special observances be held on the anniversary of the landing of the Loyalists at Adolphustown (16 June), Laura Secord's walk (23 June), the battle of Lundy's Lane (25 July), and the victory at Queenston Heights (23 October). Land also suggested that the association lobby to have a national day set aside for 'decorating the graves of our heroic dead.' He was particularly concerned that the association make a concerted effort to erect monuments to the country's heroes. Monuments were 'an object lesson in patriotism to future generations,' Land insisted, and 'we should not be behindhand in the erection of stone and bronze memorials of the heroic age of Canadian history.'[79]

The Loyalist Association heeded Land's advice and became actively involved in efforts to erect a monument to Colonel John Butler and his Rangers at Niagara-on-the-Lake. The dilapidated state of the site known locally as Butler's burying ground had long been a subject of concern. As early as 1890 local dissatisfaction with the site's condition had prompted the Canadian Institute to attempt to exhume Colonel John Butler's remains and relocate them at St Mark's churchyard. The project was halted when a relative objected that the vault assumed to be Butler's resting place in fact belonged to the Claus family.[80] It was not simply the run-down condition of the cemetery that concerned the association. Butler's Rangers were often portrayed in American historical writing as a band of rogues and vigilantes guilty of the most treacherous and cruel guerilla tactics. Members descended from Butler's Rangers had a strong personal interest in changing the corps's negative historical reputation. A suitable monument would serve as a visible testament to the Rangers' heroic status.

In May of 1900 E.M. Chadwick was appointed to investigate the prospects of erecting a monument on the site. Chadwick soon found himself lost in a maze of local folklore and legal questions. There was considerable debate over the actual location of Butler's grave. The president of the Lundy's Lane Historical Society, George Bull, informed Chadwick that Butler and his wife were buried in St Mark's churchyard.[81] Janet Carnochan, however, insisted that 'there is no doubt that Col. Butler was buried in the Butler graveyard' but dismissed as 'erroneous' the commonly held idea that other members of the Rangers were also buried there.[82] Chadwick also discovered that the site had been divided and that the ownership of the cemetery was unclear. Given the legal questions about the site's ownership, the registrar for the county of Lincoln, J.G. Currie, advised Chadwick that 'it would be a great mistake to put the monument in the old grave yard.'[83] Despite the confusion over Butler's actual burial place and the obvious legal difficulties, Chadwick recommended that immediate steps be taken to enclose and restore the site and erect a monument.

Before it proceeded with the project, the association had to raise funds to cover the costs of the monument and secure access to the site. Significantly, E.M. Chadwick advised the association that it was doubtful the project would attract much public support. 'It is not likely,' Chadwick warned, 'that a large subscription could be obtained to the erection of a monument by the public because Col. Butler's services though valuable and important and of a most interesting character were nevertheless not such as would appeal to the sentiment at the present day more than that of any other gallant officers who served in the same period.'[84] Unable to raise enough funds through public subscriptions, the association sent a petition to the minister of militia requesting a grant of $1,000 towards 'the preservation of the Butlers' Rangers graveyard at Niagara and the perpetuation of the memory of that brave company by the erection a suitable mark on the spot.'[85] Fearing a flood of similar petitions, the minister rejected the association's appeal for funds. The project suffered another setback in December when the farmers upon whose land the burying ground was located steadfastly refused to sell any of their land to provide access to the site. The Association's legal adviser, E.M. Chadwick, recommended expropriation and submitted a draft act to the Ontario government.[86] Chadwick's efforts had little impact on the provincial government, which refused to introduce his expropriation legislation.

In 1907 a deputation from the association met with the minister of public works, Dr Joseph O. Reaume, and the chairman of the Niagara Parks Commission, J.W. Langmuir. The deputation suggested that the Niagara Parks Commission be empowered to take over and maintain the site.[87] The proposal was received positively and an act was introduced into the legislature. 'I hope,' Chadwick wrote to Langmuir, 'we have at last reached a point where we may hope to have something done to preserve this spot from further desecration and maintain it as a historic locality.'[88] Yet again Chadwick's expectations proved ill founded. In June of 1909 members of the association organized a pilgrimage to the site. To their horror, they discovered that a path or roadway had not been constructed and that the site was overrun with cattle and 'otherwise in the same disgraceful condition in which it has been for so long.'[89] Nine years of effort had failed to produce a monument to Colonel Butler and his Rangers.

Subsequent attempts to erect monuments honouring Colonel John A. Macdonald and William Hamilton Merritt met with a similar fate. The proliferation of historical and patriotic societies throughout the province meant that the Loyalist association had to compete with other organizations for scarce funds. The ability of the association to raise money among the general public for such projects was further hindered by its exclusiveness and the self-serving filiopietism of its members. Its efforts to create a heroic past were confounded further by the fact that few Loyalists stood out as particularly outstanding individuals. The association thus found itself increasingly turning to the War of 1812 and figures such as Sir Isaac Brock, Laura Secord, and Tecumseh. Although Loyalists accounted for less than one-sixth of the population of Upper Canada at the time of the war, it was repeatedly claimed that they had provided the backbone of the country's defence. Consequently, the traditions surrounding the War of 1812 and the Loyalists became practically synonymous in the public imagination.

The centenary of the death of the Sir Isaac Brock offered the United

Empire Loyalist Association of Ontario an ideal opportunity to promote its particular brand of patriotism. At a meeting held on 11 April 1912, the association committed itself to organizing 'a national demonstration' worthy of the 'hero of Upper Canada.'[90] Although other historical societies, patriotic clubs, and militia regiments were invited to participate in planning the event, the United Empire Loyalist Association exercised careful control over the proceedings. The general committee charged with organizing the celebrations suggested that commemorative exercises be held in all the nation's schools on Friday, 11 October, that salutes be fired on 12 October across the country, that the churches be requested to hold memorial services on Sunday, 13 October, and that the dominion government place a wreath on Brock's monument in St Paul's Cathedral in London.[91] The main event was to take place at Brock's monument on Queenston Heights.

An estimated two thousand people gathered at Queenston Heights on 12 October 1913. George Sterling Ryerson presided over the day's events and delivered the opening address on behalf of the United Empire Loyalist Association. It was not Brock, but the Loyalists, to whom Ryerson first paid tribute. 'The United Empire Loyalists,' he maintained, 'came to this country not as those who desired to better their condition in life, nor were they possessed by land hunger, nor by ideas of political and social aggrandizement. They came solely because of their devotion to the British Crown and the Constitution, and because they preferred to live in peace and poverty under a monarchical Government rather than in wealth and discord under republican institutions.' 'It was to these men,' Ryerson asserted, 'that Brock appealed' during the War of 1812. Canada was today 'a daughter nation within the great galaxy of the nations known as the British Empire,' Ryerson concluded, because of 'the spirit of resistance and Imperialism' displayed by the Loyalists and men like Brock. As frequently happened on such occasions, topics of current political debate found their way into the proceedings. Ryerson was particularly concerned about Canada's contributions to imperial defence: 'Is it not our bounden duty to contribute directly to the support of the British navy? Are we to lag behind the other self-governing nations of the Empire in this essential duty?'[92] Ryerson pledged the support of the United Empire Loyalist Association to any government that would act decisively on the issue.

The formation of the United Empire Loyalist Association was not a unique event. Dozens of similar organizations appeared throughout Canada and the United States at the end of the nineteenth century. Underlying the creation of such associations was a determination to affirm and defend the status, social values, and political beliefs of the professional middle class. The emergence of mass industrial society proved problematic for its members: class polarization, the wide range of wealth and influence within its ranks, and the growing number of groups and occupations claiming or aspiring to middle-class status made clear criteria for social distinction increasingly elusive. Confronted by this problem of definition and disturbed by the social and economic consequences of urbanization, industrialization, and mass immigration, members of the middle class turned to ancestry and the past to affirm their status and to legitimize their social and political values and beliefs.

Part of this larger phenomenon, the United Empire Loyalist Association of Ontario provided a forum in which its predominantly urban, professional, middle-class members could declare their patriotic and genealogical superiority and assert their claims to influence. Exclusive membership criteria, fraternization with distinguished social and political leaders, and officially sanctioned insignia all were part of a strategy to confer status and recognition upon the association and its members. As self-proclaimed guardians of the nation's heritage, members of the association vigorously protested against anything that appeared to threaten their understanding of the nation's history and identity. The association actively attempted to inculcate the social and political values of its members through the erection of public monuments, the commemoration of important anniversaries, and the initiation of patriotic exercises in the schools. At a time when social change raised serious questions about the future position of the middle class, organizations like the United Empire Loyalist Association of Ontario sought to create a sense of continuity and stability.

Conclusion

The Loyalist tradition occupied a prominent place in the social and political discourse of Upper Canada and Ontario in the nineteenth and early twentieth centuries. Most studies characterize the Loyalist tradition as a static body of beliefs and assumptions carried by the Loyalist pioneers and passed on to succeeding generations. The Loyalist tradition was in fact much more fluid. Shaped and reshaped by the political, social, and economic currents affecting successive generations, the Loyalist tradition evolved with changing concerns and conditions. This study has demonstrated the ways in which the Loyalist past was constructed and remade by various groups interested in the creation of usable pasts that spoke to present anxieties and interests. The multivocal nature of the Loyalist tradition challenges interpretations that portray the commemoration of the past as either an expression of popular consensus or an exercise in political and social hegemony. The evidence presented in this study illustrates the need for a pluralistic understanding of the invention of tradition as a process in which different groups and interests compete with each other for control over the content, meaning, and uses of the past. An attempt has been made to go beyond the rhetoric and ideology usually associated with the Loyalist tradition and examine the activity of cultural construction to see how, when, and by whom the Loyalist past was created. Careful attention has been given to the social context in which the Loyalist tradition appeared, the varied and often conflicting intentions of its many creators, and the popular responses that greeted their efforts. By recognizing that different interests and generations reinterpret the past and create their own history, the Loyalist tradition becomes a multidimensional and dynamic phenomenon rooted in changing social contexts and historical circumstances.

The Loyalist tradition was invented not inherited. The original Loyalist settlers of Ontario lacked a well-defined ideology or identity. Mixed motives, ethnic and religious diversity, preoccupation with the everyday work of surviving in the wilderness, frequent relocation, marriage into non-Loyalist families, and the influx of large numbers of American settlers combined to prevent the Loyalists from articulating a unified and distinctive message. All Loyalists, however, shared a common interest in land. It was land that attracted the Loyalists to Upper Canada in the first place or induced them to stay once they had arrived, and it was the right to acquire land that initially set the Loyalists apart as a distinct group. It was during the course of debates over government land policy and American immigration that the Loyalist tradition began to take shape. To defend their claims to such grants, Loyalists greatly exaggerated their losses, social status, and dedication to the Empire. The prolonged debate over the status of American settlers in the province divided the Loyalist population. Many Loyalists welcomed the Americans because of the speculative value they added to Loyalist land grants. Those within the governing elite, however, saw the Americans as a threat to their own power and privilege. The debate over the Alien Question witnessed the first attempt by members of the establishment to portray the province as an exclusive Loyalist preserve. The 'unquestioning' loyalty of the Loyalists became a useful weapon against their political opponents. As the demographic significance of the Loyalist population declined and the controversies surrounding U.E. Rights and the Alien Question resolved themselves, the province's Loyalist origins became increasingly irrelevant to the political discourse of the day. By the 1840s the Loyalists were a distant memory.

A renewed interest in the Loyalist past emerged at mid-century. Economic growth, expansionist ambitions, and sectional tensions combined to produce a growing national sentiment and a desire for a celebratory history of origins that would sanction future aspirations. At the same time, the growth of the state and the need to construct a public out of the province's diverse population contributed to official interest in the production of a unifying and future-oriented past. The anxiety produced by the passing of the last of the Loyalist pioneers, the vilifying treatment of Upper Canada's founders presented in contemporary American histories, and the filiopietism of Loyalist descendants ensured that much of this emergent historical consciousness was focused on the province's Loyalist origins. In 1859 the provincial legislature financially backed the first efforts to collect and preserve historical materials connected with the province's Loyalist founders. The memoirs and reminiscences collected at the time were distinguished by a focus on pioneer conditions, a profound sense of loss and degeneration, an idealization of the past, and repeated injunctions to the present generation to remain true to the legacy of their forefathers. State support for Loyalist history was withdrawn when it became evident that the nostalgic and idiosyncratic vernacular past contained in the reminiscences and memoirs of surviving Loyalists did not meet the needs of official history. A sense of filial obligation compelled Loyalist descendants such as William Canniff and Egerton Ryerson to persevere in their work. Heavily influenced by the conventions of romance and the works of the American historian Lorenzo Sabine, Canniff and Ryerson produced an idealized version of the Loyalist past that greatly influenced the way in which the Loyalists were portrayed by publicists and promoters in later years.

Interest in the Loyalist past peaked with the celebration of the centennial of Loyalist settlement in 1884 and continued unabated until the First World War. Much of the attention shown in the Loyalist past during this period can be attributed to the search for a unifying national past that could surmount the regional, racial, and linguistic tensions that engulfed the country. Many of Ontario's politicians and educators looked to the past to provide a common Anglo-Canadian heritage. In the history textbooks authorized for use in the province's schools, the Loyalists were portrayed as the heroic founders and defenders of English Canada and the carriers of a distinctive set of institutions and values that distinguished Canada from the United States. The desire to create a cohesive national history was often circumscribed by narrower political considerations.

As the debate over Canada's political and economic destiny intensified in the 1890s, imperialists and protectionists found in the Loyalist tradition a convenient historical weapon that could be used against their opponents. Commemorative celebrations and the erection of monuments often turned into political events designed to further the imperialist cause and to discredit alternative visions of the nation's political destiny. The 'independence flurry' was certainly foremost in the minds of organizers of the 1884 Toronto Loyalist Centennial Celebrations such as George Taylor Denison. The imperialist interpretation of the Loyalist past did not go unchallenged. Critics such as Goldwin Smith charged that men like Denison were deliberately distorting history to further their own political and economic interests.

Politicians and propagandists were not alone in manipulating the past to serve their own agendas. Dissatisfied with the constraints of their prescribed roles and the isolation and dependence of their domestic function, many early feminists looked to history to advance the cause of women's rights. Through organizations such as the Women's Canadian Historical Society and the United Empire Loyalist Association, middle-class women set out to record the contributions of their foremothers and to claim a place in the nation's history. In a similar fashion, groups within the Six Nations of Grand River and Tyendinaga employed their association with the Loyalist past to further the cause of Native rights. The efforts of early feminists and Native activists to appropriate the Loyalist past to their own ends highlight the important role played by gender and race in the construction of public memory. Both groups challenged the domination of the province's history by Anglo-Canadian males and created, to varying degrees, alternative narratives that subverted prevailing assumptions about gender and race.

The popularity of the Loyalist tradition was not simply a product of its political utility. The unsettling change that accompanied urbanization and industrialization stimulated a nostalgic interest in the preservation of a simpler past among an anxious middle class. Concerned about their status and influence in the emerging industrial order, many professionals and white-collar workers turned to history and genealogy to affirm and defend their status, values, and beliefs. Some published filiopietistic family histories. Others joined exclusive hereditary and patriotic organizations such as the United Empire Loyalist Association. Still others sought to erect permanent memorials that attested to the enduring value of history and its lessons and provided a sense of rootedness and tradition at a time when urban growth, the collapse of old virtues, and the appearance of new vices raised serious questions about social order and community in the future.

Local boosterism and commercial considerations further contributed to the interest shown in the Loyalist past. Staging commemorative celebrations, erecting monuments, and publishing local histories became a popular means for communities to express local pride and to assert their place in the nation and its history. The use of history in this fashion often resulted in considerable competition and rivalry as communities promoted their historical pretensions. Much of the controversy surrounding the 1884 centennial celebrations centred on the appropriation of the Loyalist tradition by Toronto interests and the competing claims of centres such as Niagara-on-the-Lake. The past could also be profitable. Celebrations and monuments attracted visitors and tourists, who left money in the tills of local businesses. The proliferation of local and family histories at the end of the nineteenth century owed a great deal to the financial interest of enterprising publishers. As history became increasingly commercialized, the Loyalist past became a commodity marketed by promoters.

Most studies discuss the Loyalist tradition in terms of a single, coherent set of ideas. Although there was widespread consensus about the importance of the Loyalist past, there was little agreement about how the Loyalists should be remembered. The various official histories constructed by different interests to further a particular cause frequently were in conflict with each other and with a popular vernacular past of the pioneer. The controversy that surrounded the 1884 celebrations and the erection of Loyalist monuments and the divisions within the United Empire Loyalist Association highlight the degree to which the meaning of the past was contested throughout this period. The attempts by women and Natives to construct their own histories added to the difficulty of creating a unifying discourse. The very pluralism of the Ontario Loyalist tradition[s] demonstrates that the politics of commemoration are neither monolithic nor mechanistic but rather the product of the complex interaction of a wide range of social forces and conditions. Interests of class, gender, and race combined with local conditions and popular culture to create multiple understandings and uses of the Loyalist past. It is through understanding the power and influence of these 'limited identities' that the social and cultural significance of the Loyalist tradition becomes fully evident.

The Loyalist tradition experienced a significant decline following the First World War. The years after the war witnessed a substantial reduction in the publication of Loyalist history. Commemorative celebrations continued to be held and the occasional monument was still erected, but the events attracted much less attention than they had previously done. Membership in the United Empire Loyalist Association stagnated and its activities became increasingly social. Canada's wartime experience effectively marginalized the Loyalist tradition. The First World War diluted the intense imperialist and anti-American sentiment that had come to dominate the Loyalist tradition. The horrors of war cooled Canadian enthusiasm for the Empire, increased nationalist sentiment, and resulted in demands for greater autonomy. At the same time, much of the hostility and mistrust of the Americans was eroded in the face of wartime association as allies and increasing economic, social, cultural, and political contact and exposure. Imperialist and anti-American sentiments became increasingly anachronistic as the political debates in which the Loyalist past had been a useful weapon faded into memory.[1]

By the 1920s the Loyalist tradition had lost much of its appeal to the

middle class that had been at the forefront of the movements to commemorate the Loyalist centennial and erect monuments and that filled
the ranks of the United Empire Loyalist Association. As their initial fears
about the consequences of industrialization and urbanization were molli-
fied, members of the middle class turned away from the past and
embraced a faith in progress and materialism. Moreover, the utility of the
Loyalist tradition as a badge of distinction had been seriously eroded.
The transformation of history into a science practised by professionals
trained in the critical use of sources undermined many of the assumptions about the Loyalists that had been invented over the past half-
century. As the study of history became increasingly dominated by
trained professionals preoccupied with the political and economic evolution of the nation, the history of the Loyalists came to be regarded as a
peripheral pursuit best left to the antiquarian or filiopietistic genealogist.[2] Although the interest of professional historians in the Loyalist past
declined, amateurs continued to do valuable research through local
historical societies.

Unlike the legend of the founding fathers in the United States, the
Loyalist tradition contained too many ambiguities to continue as a vital
influence during the 1920s and beyond. Although the Loyalists were said
to have laid the foundations of the province's material development, they
were also associated with the reactionary forces that impeded the province's political progress. Moreover, the regional nature of the Loyalist
past limited its ability to become the basis of a unifying national tradition.
The exclusiveness of the tradition and the portrayal of the Loyalists as a
superior, cultured, and an elevated elite further limited its appeal in an
age of progressive reform and agrarian populism. The Anglophilia and
racial assumptions of many Loyalist promoters alienated large elements
within Canada's increasingly diverse and multi-ethnic population.
Encumbered by social and racial pretensions, the Loyalist tradition
became an embarrassing part of the nation's past for many Canadians.

Interest in the Loyalists revived briefly in 1934, the 150th anniversary of
the Loyalist migration to Upper Canada. The events of 1934 were largely
free of the controversy, partisan rhetoric, and exclusive social claims that
had characterized earlier celebrations. In May the United Empire Loyalist Association staged a historical exhibition at Toronto's Eaton Audito-
rium that focused on the Loyalists' pioneer experience. This shift in
emphasis reflected several important developments. The cynicism that
developed during the Depression years resulted in a desire for histories
that were 'true' and historical objects that were 'authentic.'[3] The result

was the 'debunking' of many previously unchallenged assumptions about the past. In this context, historians such as A.L. Burt, George Wrong, and R.O. MacFarlane re-examined the Loyalist contribution. Although Burt and Wrong credited the Loyalists with laying the foundations of English-speaking Canada and bequeathing an anti-American bias that preserved British North America from being drawn into the neighbouring republic, neither historian found much evidence to support the exaggerated social claims of an earlier generation. Most Loyalists, they argued, were in fact backwoods farmers of modest means.[4] The revisionism of R.O. MacFarlane went even further. MacFarlane saw the Loyalist migration as a product of land hunger and simply another stage in the unrolling of the frontier. 'To argue that patriotism and the love of British institutions was the sole, or even dominant motive behind the migration,' MacFarlane concluded, 'is obviously an act of faith.'[5]

The exclusive claims of the Loyalist past were further eroded by the new communications technology of the interwar years and the growth of mass culture. With these developments, it became increasingly necessary to depoliticize the past in order to appeal to a broad audience. This trend was reinforced by the growing popularity of automobile tourism and the increasing use of the past for pleasure and profit.[6] Beginning in the 1930s, historical plaques and markers were erected on highways across Ontario to satisfy the needs of tourists. As a result, many sites associated with the province's Loyalist origins were recognized and local movements arose to preserve others that were threatened by decay or demolition. The principle motivation, however, was not to use the Loyalists and their principles to legitimize social or political agendas, as in the past, but rather to attract the new consumers of history. During the 1930s there was also a growing interest in Upper Canadian antiques and in traditional handicrafts. Displays of Loyalist artefacts and pioneer crafts became a regular feature at meetings of the United Empire Loyalist Association and local historical societies.[7] The collection of antiques and the popularity of traditional handicrafts throughout North America reflected a desire for stability and rootedness at a time of tremendous social upheaval and dislocation.[8]

Although the Loyalist past was no longer the subject of intense public interest or debate, it continued to play an important role in many families and localities during the interwar years. Loyalist descendants and amateur historians carried on their research in genealogy and local history. For many, the Loyalist tradition continued to be an important source of family pride and community identification. The genealogists of the United Empire Loyalist Association were kept busy researching the background of new applicants who sought respect and recognition through membership. The association's activities were a regular feature of the society pages of many newspapers. At the local level, the arrival of the Loyalists was celebrated annually in communities such as Picton and Adolphustown with church services and picnics. Pride of place resulted in movements to erect historical plaques and to preserve Loyalist landmarks such as the Hay Bay church.[9] Despite its decline as a source of national or provincial identity, the Loyalist tradition remained a vital part of the popular culture of many communities and families.

The years following the Second World War witnessed a resurgence of national sentiment in much of English Canada. Concerns with the growing economic and cultural influence of the United States resulted in a renewed effort to define and to defend Canada's cultural identity. In 1949 the federal government appointed Vincent Massey to chair the Royal Commission on National Development in the Arts, Letters and Sciences. Included in the commission's terms of reference was a statement of the desirability that 'the Canadian people should know as much as possible about their country, its history and traditions.' Recognizing the need for a unifying national history, the Massey commission recommended that more resources be committed to commemoration and the restoration and preservation of historic sites.[10] In the wake of the Massey report, federal, provincial, and local governments significantly increased their involvement in the heritage field. The celebration of the 100th anniversary of Confederation in 1967, continuing concerns about American domination, growth in the tourist industry, and the sense of discontinuity that accompanied rapid social change sustained interest in the nation's past throughout the 1960s. As a result, the decades following the Second World War saw an unprecedented increase in the number of historic sites, monuments, local museums, and restoration projects. As Ontario's first pioneers, the Loyalists were well represented in the postwar heritage boom: parks and highways were dedicated to the Loyalists, local museums and plaques commemorated Loyalist settlement, and the homes of prominent Loyalists were restored and designated as historic sites. It needs to be stressed that the proliferation of Loyalist history did not represent a revival of the Loyalist tradition for its own sake but was a part of the larger heritage movement. The search for the elusive Canadian identity, the quest for stability and security during a period of social change and upheaval, and the commodification of the past by the tourist industry combined to maintain an active interest in Ontario's history by the state and the public during the postwar period.

In 1984 the province of Ontario officially celebrated its bicentennial. The 1984 celebrations, like those of a century before, were the subject of considerable controversy. It was argued by some that the whole affair was politically motivated – a costly ploy designed by the government of the day to spread generous grants around the province in a pre-election year.[11] Others questioned the date, insisting that 1791, the year the province was separated from Quebec, or 1867, the year the province entered Confederation, were more appropriate points from which to date the founding of the province. Franco-Ontarians and Natives pointed out that they had been present in the province long before the arrival of the Loyalists two hundred years ago.[12]

The bicentennial witnessed the appearance of a host of new publications hoping to cash in on the renewed interest in the Loyalists. The works were as much a product of their time as the publications of a century before had been. The imperialist rhetoric and preoccupation with social status that characterized the 1884 centennial were replaced by a celebration of the Loyalists' 'multi-ethnic heritage.' In the pluralistic Ontario of the late twentieth century, the Loyalists were reinvented as the nation's first refugees and the founders of multiculturalism. 'In their diversity and heterogeneity,' one writer asserted, 'we can find one origin of our "tossed salad" society with its stress on pluralism and tolerance, as opposed to the American melting pot.'[13] Significantly, such comparisons with American society were one of the few similarities between the 1884 and 1984 celebrations. The 1984 bicentennial confirmed the dynamic nature of the Loyalist tradition. The tradition continues to evolve as the past is reconstructed in the light of the conceptual needs of the present.

APPENDICES

APPENDIX I

The Adolphustown Loyalist Centennial Committee, 1884

Name	Religion	Politics
Allen, Parker	Anglican	Conservative
Allison, D.W.	Methodist	Liberal
Allison, H.H.	Methodist	Liberal
Bogart, L.L.	Methodist	Liberal
Canniff, Wm	Methodist	Independent
Clapp, R.	Methodist	Liberal
Diamond, J.A.	Methodist	–
Davis, A.C.	Anglican	Conservative
Davis, P.D.	Anglican	Conservative
Dorland, R.	Methodist	–
German, G.M.	Methodist	–
Green, Sampson	Anglican	Conservative
Huff, Henry	Methodist	–
McQuaig, J.S.	Methodist	Liberal
Outwater, S.M.	Anglican	Conservative
Pearson, M.L.	Methodist	Liberal
Roblin, C.A.	Methodist	–
Roblin, Jacob H.	Methodist	–
Roblin, John H.	Anglican	–
Ruttan, Elisha	Anglican	–
Ruttan, S.W.	Methodist	–
Ruttan, Dr	Anglican	–
Sills, Elisha	–	–
Trumpour, P.	Quaker	–
Trumpour, Thomas	Anglican	Conservative
Trumpour, S.W.	Anglican	Conservative
Watson, J.J.	Anglican	Conservative

APPENDIX II

The Committee of Management of the 1884 Toronto Loyalist Centennial Celebrations

Name	Religion	Politics	Profession
Allan, G.W.	Anglican	Conservative	Senator
Baldwin, J.	Anglican	Conservative	M.D.
Boswell, A.	Anglican	Conservative	Lawyer
Byam, J.F.	Methodist	Liberal	Merchant
Canniff, Wm	Methodist	Independent	M.D.
Caven, Wm	Presbyterian	Liberal	Clergy
Clendennan, D.	–	–	Lawyer
Denison, F.	Anglican	Conservative	Lawyer
Denison, G.T.	Anglican	Conservative	Magistrate
Denison, S.	Anglican	Conservative	Lawyer
Dent, J.C.	Methodist	Liberal	Author
Dewart, E.H.	Methodist	Liberal	Clergy
Foster, Wm	Methodist	Independent	Lawyer
Gamble, N.	Anglican	Conservative	Lawyer
Gregg, G.	Presbyterian	Liberal	Clergy
Hagel, S.D.	–	Conservative	M.D.
Haight, C.	Quaker	Independent	Merchant
Howard, A.	Anglican	Independent	Business
Johnston, H.	Methodist		Clergy
Jones, S.	Anglican	Conservative	Clergy
King, J.S.	Presbyterian	Liberal	M.D.
Macdonald, C.	Anglican	–	Engineer
Macdonnell, D.	Presbyterian	Liberal	Clergy
Macdougall, Wm	Anglican	Conservative	Judge
McCarthy, D.	Anglican	Conservative	Lawyer
Merritt, W.	Anglican	Conservative	Engineer
Moore, R.	Methodist	Liberal	Printer
Morris, A.	Presbyterian	Conservative	Politician
Morris, J.	Presbyterian	Conservative	Lawyer

Name	Religion	Politics	Profession
Playter, J.	Methodist	Liberal	Farmer
Read, D.B.	Methodist	Conservative	Merchant
Rice, S.	Presbyterian	Liberal	Clergy
Richardson, J.	Methodist	Conservative	M.D.
Roaf, J.R.	Anglican	Independent	Lawyer
Roaf, Wm	Anglican		Lawyer
Robinson, J.B.	Anglican	Conservative	Lt. Governor
Rose, J.E.	Methodist	–	Judge
Rose, Rev.	Methodist	–	Clergy
Ryerson, C.E.	Anglican	Conservative	Lawyer
Ryerson, G.S.	Methodist	Conservative	M.D.
Scadding, H.	Anglican	Independent	Clergy
Vankoughnet, S.J.	Anglican	Conservative	Lawyer
Wilson, D.	Anglican	–	Professor
Withrow, J.	Methodist	Liberal	Business
Withrow, Wm	Methodist	Liberal	Clergy
Wood, S.C.	–	Liberal	Business

APPENDIX III

General Membership,* United Empire Loyalist Association of Ontario, 1896–1913

A. Sex

Sex	Adults	Children	Total
Male	185	36	221
Female	156	74	230
Total	341	110	451

B. Religious Affiliation

Denomination	Number	Percentage
Anglican	160	36
Methodist	37	8
Presbyterian	19	4
Other†	9	2
Unknown	226	50

C. Political Affiliation (males)

Party	Number	Percentage
Conservative	44	24
Liberal	20	11
Independent	3	1
Unknown	118	64

D. Occupation (adult males)

I. Professional		II. Finance Industry		III. White Collar	
Architect	1	Banker	1	Accountant	2
Clergy	12	Businessman	2	Artist	1
Com. officer	5	Contractor	2	Author	1
Dentist	1	Commissioner	1	Bank teller	1
Engineer	4	Merchant	5	Bookkeeper	2
Judge	3	Manufacturer	2	Civil servant	2
Lawyer	38	Stockbroker	2	Clerk	17
Pharmacist	1	Publisher	1	Inspector	3
Physician	22			Insurance agent	4
Professor	1			Journalist	3
				Librarian	1
				Manager	3
				Police officer	1
				Real estate agent	3
				Sales	2
				Teacher	13
				Treasurer	2
				Sheriff	1
				Superintendent	1
				Surveyor	1
				Traveller	2
Total	88		16		66
Percentage	48%		9%		36%

Note: The figures given in this table are cumulative totals calculated from individual memberships issued between 1896 and 1913.

* Does not include non-resident, associate, and honorary members, or members of branch associations.

† Includes four Roman Catholics, three Unitarians, one Quaker, one Christian Church.

APPENDIX IV

Officers*: United Empire Loyalist Association of Ontario, 1896–1913

A. Sex

Sex	Number	Percentage
Male	46	58
Female	34	42

B. Religious Affiliation

Denomination	Number	Percentage
Anglican	39	49
Methodist	5	6
Presbyterian	2	3
Other†	3	4
Unknown	31	39

C. Political Affiliation (male officers)

Party	Number	Percentage
Conservative	20	44
Liberal	2	4
Unknown	24	52

D. Occupation (male officers)

I. Professional		II. Finance Industry		III. White Collar	
Clergy	2	Businessman	1	Clerk	4
Engineer	3	Contractor	1	Civil servant	3
Lawyer	14	Manufacturer	1	Commissioner	1
Judge	1			Drawing master	1
Pharmacist	1			Inspector	1
Physician	4			Librarian	1
Professor	1			Real estate agent	1
				Treasurer	2
				Teacher	1
Total	26		3		15
Percentage	57%		7%		33%

*Includes presidents, vice-presidents, and members of the executive, investigating, and ladies committees.

†Includes two Roman Catholics and one Unitarian.

APPENDIX V

Membership: United Empire Loyalist Association of Ontario, 1896–1916

Year	Resident*	Non-Resident†	Associate Member‡	Hamilton Branch	Total
1896	25	–	–	–	25
1898	160	6	–	–	166
1899	232	82	18	–	332
1900	231	125	24	–	380
1902	242	154	29	61	486
1904	236	171	28	77	512
1913	290	240	30	–	560
1916	260	133	–	–	393

* Members residing in Toronto
† Members residing elsewhere in the province
‡ Spouses of Loyalist descendants not of Loyalist descent themselves

Notes

Abbreviations

AO Archives of Ontario

CPUC *Centennial of the Province of Upper Canada, 1792–1892: Proceedings at the Gathering at Niagara-on-the-Lake, July 16, 1892 and also the Proceedings at the Meeting Held in Front of the New Parliament Buildings in Toronto, September 17, 1892.* Toronto: Arbuthnot and Adamson, 1893.

CSUC *The Centennial of the Settlement of Upper Canada by the United Empire Loyalists: The Celebrations in Toronto, Adolphustown and Niagara.* 1885; rpt. Boston: Gregg Press, 1972

DCB *Dictionary of Canadian Biography*

DOA Diocese of Ontario Archives

HPL Hamilton Public Library

LACM Lennox and Addington County Museum

MTRL Metropolitan Toronto Reference Library

NAC National Archives of Canada

UCC United Church of Canada Archives

UELO United Empire Loyalist Association of Ontario

UELATB United Empire Loyalist Association of Canada, Toronto Branch Archives

Introduction

1 Arthur R.M. Lower, *Colony to Nation: A History of Canada,* 5th edition (Toronto 1977) 118, 123

2 J.M.S. Careless, *Canada: A Story of Challenge* (Toronto 1953), 113

3 On Hartz's fragment thesis see his *The Founding of New Societies* (New York

1964) and *The Liberal Tradition in America* (New York 1955). On Lipset's theory of formative events see his *The First New Nation* (New York 1963) and *Revolution and Counter Revolution* (New York 1970).

4 Kenneth D. McRae, 'The Structure of Canadian History,' in *The Founding of New Societies*, ed. Hartz; Gad Horowitz, 'Conservatism, Liberalism and Socialism in Canada: An Interpretation,' *Canadian Journal of Economic and Political Science*, 32 (1966), 147–71; David V.J. Bell, 'The Loyalist Tradition in Canada,' *Journal of Canadian Studies*, 5 (1970), 22–33

5 S.F. Wise, 'The Origins of Anti-Americanism in Canada,' *Fourth Seminar on Canadian-American Relations* (Windsor 1962), 300–1; 'Upper Canada and the Conservative Tradition' in *Profiles of a Province: Studies in the History of Ontario*, ed. Edith Frith (Toronto 1967), 20, 31. Also see Wise's 'The Annexation Movement and Its Effect on Canadian Opinion, 1837–67' in *Canada Views the United States: Nineteenth Century Political Attitudes*, ed. S.F. Wise and R.C. Brown (Seattle 1967) and 'God's Peculiar People,' in *The Shield of Achilles*, ed. W.L. Morton (Toronto 1968), 36–61.

6 Carl Berger, *The Sense of Power: Studies in the Ideas of Canadian Imperialism, 1867–1914* (Toronto 1970) 109

7 David Mills, *The Idea of Loyalty in Upper Canada, 1784–1850* (Montreal and Kingston 1988), 132–9

8 The term 'limited identities' first appeared in a review article by Ramsay Cook, 'Canadian Centennial Celebrations,' *International Journal*, 22 (1967), 663. The term was later used by J.M.S. Careless in an influential article, 'Limited Identities in Canada,' *Canadian Historical Review* 50 (1969), 1–10.

9 Edward Shils, *Tradition* (Chicago 1981), 14. Similar definitions and descriptions of tradition are used by S.N. Eisenstadt, *Tradition, Change and Modernity* (New York 1973) and Clifford Geertz, 'Ideology as a Cultural System,' in Geertz, *The Interpretation of Cultures* (New York 1973), 193–233.

10 On commemorative celebrations see Peter Aykroyd, *The Anniversary Compulsion: Canada's Centennial Celebrations: A Model Mega-Anniversary* (Toronto 1992); Reid Badger, *The Great American Fair: The World's Columbian Exposition and American Culture* (Chicago 1979); W.H. Cohn, 'A National Celebration: The Fourth of July in American History,' *Cultures*, 3 (1976), 141–56; Wesley Frank Craven, *The Legend of the Founding Fathers* (Ithaca 1965); Elizabeth Hammerton and David Cannadine, 'Conflict and Consensus on a Ceremonial Occasion: The Diamond Jubilee in Cambridge in 1897,' *Historical Journal*, 24 (1981), 111–46; Warner W. Lloyd, *The Living and the Dead: A Study of the Symbolic Life of Americans* (New Haven 1959); Charles Rearick, 'Festivals and Politics: The Michelet Centennial of 1898,' in *Historians in Politics*, ed. Walter Laquer and George L. Mosse (London 1974) and 'Festivals in Mod-

ern France: The Experience of the Third Republic,' *Journal of Contemporary History,* 12 (1977), 435–60.

11 On the formation of patriotic and genealogical associations see Wallace Evan Davies, *Patriotism on Parade: The Story of Veterans and Hereditary Organizations in America, 1783–1900* (Cambridge 1955) and Barbara Miller Solomon, *Ancestors and Immigrants: A Changing New England Tradition* (Chicago 1956).

12 On the monument craze see M. Agulhon, *Marianne into Battle: Republican Imagery and Symbolism in France, 1789–1880* (Cambridge 1981); Hebert Bruno, *Monuments et patrie: Une réflexion philosophique sur un fait historique: La célébration commémorative au Québec de 1881 à 1929* (Quebec 1980); George L. Mosse, 'Caesarism, Circuses, and Monuments,' *Contemporary History,* 6:2 (1971), 167–83; Marvin Trachtenberg, *The Statue of Liberty* (New York 1976); Joseph F. Trimmer, 'Monuments and Myths: Three American Arches,' in *Material Culture Studies in America,* ed. Thomas J. Schlereth (Nashville 1976), 269–77.

13 Eric Hobsbawm, 'Inventing Traditions,' *The Invention of Tradition,* ed. Eric Hobsbawm and Terence Ranger (Cambridge 1983), 1–14

14 David Lowenthal, *The Past Is a Foreign Country* (Cambridge 1985), xvi

15 Michael Kammen, *Mystic Chords of Memory: The Transformation of Tradition in American Culture* (New York 1991), 14. Also see Kammen's earlier studies, *A Season of Youth: The American Revolution and the Historical Imagination* (New York 1978), *Selvages and Biases: The Fabric of History in American Culture* (New York 1987), and *A Machine That Would Go of Itself: The Constitution in American Culture* (New York 1986).

16 John Bodnar, *Remaking America: Public Memory, Commemoration and Patriotism in the Twentieth Century* (Princeton 1992), 13–20

17 Kammen, *Mystic Chords of Memory,* 13–14

18 See Geertz, *The Interpretation of Cultures.*

19 Berger, *The Sense of Power,* 81–2

20 In 'The Loyalist Tradition in New Brunswick: A Study of the Evolution of an Historical Myth, 1825–1914,' (M.A. thesis, Queen's University, 1971) Murray Barkley found that the New Brunswick Loyalist tradition had little in common with the tradition described by Berger. In New Brunswick, the struggle against nature, not the Americans, was central to the Loyalist tradition. The emphasis was not on the Loyalists' role in preserving the vital British link, but rather, on their role as pioneers and the founders of the province's progress and prosperity. Nor were New Brunswick Loyalists the principal champions of Canadian imperialism. In New Brunswick, the Loyalist tradition tended towards nostalgia and was not a 'future oriented ideology with a sense of imperial mission and destiny.' In 'Nova Scotian Perceptions of the Loyalists, 1820–1911,' (M.A. thesis, Queen's University, 1989) Eldred MacIntyre discovered that the

Loyalists were either ignored or treated in negative terms by Nova Scotia historians. The province's Loyalists may have 'sought remembrance for past deeds and sacrifices, but, in 19th century Nova Scotia at least, they would best be remembered for their mistakes and vices' (47).

1: The Loyalist Reality

1 William Canniff, *History of the Settlement of Upper Canada with Special Reference to the Bay of Quinté* (Toronto 1869), 616, 617, 625, 634
2 The Loyalist migration to Upper Canada is discussed in Robert Allan, ed., *The Loyal Americans: The Military Role of the Loyalist Provincial Corps and Their Settlement in British North America* (Ottawa 1983); A.L. Burt, *The Old Province of Quebec*, vol. II (Toronto 1968), chap. 15; Gerald M. Craig, *Upper Canada: The Formative Years, 1784–1841* (Toronto 1963), chap. 1; Bruce Wilson, *As She Began: An Illustrated Introduction to Loyalist Ontario* (Toronto 1981).
3 On the settlement of the Six Nations see C.M. Johnston, *The Valley of the Six Nations* (Toronto 1964).
4 The best discussion of Loyalist ideology is Janice Potter, *The Liberty We Seek: Loyalist Ideology in Colonial New York and Massachusetts* (Cambridge 1983). Potter maintains that the Loyalists presented a 'comprehensive, logical, and consistent alternative to Patriot proposals' based on the political thought of Blackstone, Bollingbroke, and Burke (viii). Potter's study is particularly relevant to Upper Canada, since the majority of Loyalists who settled there came from New York. Very few of the vocal elite studied by Potter, however, actually settled in the province. See also Ann Gorman Condon, 'Marching to a Different Drummer: The Political Philosophy of the American Loyalists,' in *Red, White and True Blue: The Loyalists in the Revolution*, ed. Esmund Wright (New York 1976) and John E. Ferling, *The Loyalist Mind and the American Revolution* (University Park and London 1977).
5 For a discussion of the Loyalists' mixed motives see Wallace Brown, *The King's Friends: The Composition and Motives of the American Loyalist Claimants* (Providence 1965); Robert McCluer Calhoon, *The Loyalists in Revolutionary America, 1760–1781* (New York 1973); William Nelson, *The American Tory* (Boston 1964).
6 Major Robert Mathews to Stephen DeLancey, 15 April 1784 in *The Settlement of the United Empire Loyalists on the Upper St Lawrence and Bay of Quinte in 1784: A Documentary Record*, ed. Ernest Cruikshank (Toronto 1934), 67
7 On Native involvement in the American Revolution see Barbara Graymount, *The Iroquois in the American Revolution* (Syracuse 1972) and Francis Jennings, 'Tribal Loyalty and Tribal Independence,' in *Red, White and True Blue*, ed. Wright.

8 Quoted in Burt, *The Old Province of Quebec*, vol. II, 79

9 Wilson, *As She Began*, 13–18, 120

10 Larry Turner, *Voyage of a Different Kind: The Associated Loyalists of Kingston and Adolphustown* (Belleville 1984), 141–4

11 'Major Mathews to Major Ross, 29 March 1784' and 'Memorial of the Associated Loyalists, January 1784' in Cruikshank, ed., *Settlement of Loyalists*, 41–2

12 'Major Mathews to Sir John Johnson, 19 July 1784' in Cruikshank, ed., *Settlement of Loyalists*, 138

13 On the settlement process see Craig, *Upper Canada*, chap. 1, and Wilson, *As She Began*, chaps 3 and 4.

14 'Major Ross to Major Mathews, 7 July 1784,' in Cruikshank, ed., *Settlement of Loyalists*, 132

15 Donald Akenson, *The Irish in Ontario: A Study in Rural History* (Montreal and Kingston 1984), chap. 2

16 'Memorial of the Associated Loyalists, January 1784,' in Cruikshank, ed., *Settlement of Loyalists*, 41–2

17 Robert Gourlay, *Statistical Account of Upper Canada* (1822; Rpt. Toronto: S.R. Publishers, 1966), 115. For a discussion of the Loyalists' decidedly ambivalent attitudes towards Britain and the United States see Jane Errington, *The Lion, the Eagle and Upper Canada: A Developing Colonial Ideology* (Montreal and Kingston 1987).

18 Errington, *The Lion, the Eagle, and Upper Canada*, 30–2

19 J.K. Johnson has calculated that 36 per cent of Conservative members of the House of Assembly between 1791 and 1841 were of Loyalist stock compared with 25 per cent of Reformers. During the same period, the main centres of Loyalist settlement in eastern Ontario returned forty-five Reformers and only forty-two Conservatives; *Becoming Prominent: Regional Leadership in Upper Canada, 1791–1941* (Montreal and Kingston 1989), 140–9.

20 For a discussion of the diffusion of Loyalist power and influence see ibid., chap. 5; H.V. Nelles, 'Loyalism and Local Power: The District of Niagara, 1792–1837,' *Ontario History*, 58 (1966), 99–114; Bruce G. Wilson, *The Enterprises of Robert Hamilton: A Study of Wealth and Influence in Early Upper Canada, 1776–1812* (Ottawa 1983), chap. 3.

21 Quoted in Craig, *Upper Canada*, 89. For a detailed discussion of the rather half-hearted and lacklustre Loyalist contribution to the war effort in Leeds and Landsdowne townships see Akenson, *The Irish in Ontario*, chap. 3.

22 On the controversies that followed the War of 1812 in Upper Canada see George Sheppard, *Plunder, Profit and Paroles: A Social History of the War of 1812 in Upper Canada* (Montreal and Kingston 1994).

23 R.A. Bowler, 'Propaganda in Upper Canada,' M.A. thesis, Queen's University,

1964, 37–40. For a discussion of the evolution of the militia legend see Keith Walden, 'Isaac Brock: Man and Myth. A Study of the Militia Myth of the War of 1812 in Upper Canada, 1812–1912,' M.A. thesis, Queen's University, 1971.

24 S.F. Wise, 'The War of 1812 in Popular History,' in *God's Peculiar Peoples: Essays on Political Culture in Nineteenth-Century Canada*, ed. A.B. McKillop and Paul Romney (Ottawa 1993), 149–68

25 For an analysis of the frequent relocation of Loyalist settlers see Darrell A. Norris, 'Household and Transiency in a Loyalist Township: The People of Adolphustown, 1784–1822,' *Histoire Sociale – Social History*, 13 (1980), 399–415.

26 Lillian F. Gates, *Land Policies of Upper Canada* (Toronto 1968), 15–21

27 *Fourth Report of the Ontario Bureau of Archives, 1906* (Toronto 1907), 184–5

28 Gates, *Land Policies of Upper Canada*, 20–1

29 For a detailed description of the controversy surrounding U.E. Rights between Dorchester's order-in-council of 1787 and their abolition in 1835 see Gates, *Land Policies of Upper Canada*, chaps 5 and 9.

30 Ibid., 132–3

31 'Address to His Majesty on the Subject of U.E. Loyalist Rights,' *Journal of the Legislative Assembly of Upper Canada*, 4th session, 11th Parliament, 1834, Appendix, 51–2

32 Murray Barkley, 'The Loyalist Tradition in New Brunswick: The Growth and Evolution of an Historical Myth, 1825–1914,' *Acadiensis*, 4 (1975), 10

33 R.C. Harris and John Warkentin, *Canada before Confederation* (Toronto 1974), 116–7

34 Gates, *Land Policies of Upper Canada*, 99–100

35 Cited in Mills, *Idea of Loyalty*, 47.

36 Kingston *Chronicle*, 1 Feb. 1822

37 Cited in Mills, *Idea of Loyalty*, 76

38 Ibid., 99–104

39 This transformation in the understanding of political allegiance is admirably described in ibid.

40 Barkley, 'Loyalist Tradition in New Brunswick,' 18–20

2: The Shaping of the Loyalist Tradition at Mid-Century

1 Toronto *Globe*, 30 Oct. 1856

2 Bodnar, *Remaking America*

3 The most valuable general study of the political, economic, and social maturing of Upper Canada remains J.M.S. Careless, *The Union of the Canadas: The Growth of Canadian Institutions, 1841–1857* (Toronto 1967), 149–58. On the disappearance of the agricultural frontier see David Gagan, *Hopeful Travellers:*

Families, Land, and Social Change in Mid-Victorian Peel County, Canada West (Toronto 1981). On the transportation revolution see Peter Baskerville, 'Transportation, Social Change and State Formation: Upper Canada, 1841–1864,' in *Colonial Leviathan: State Formation in Mid-Nineteenth-Century Canada*, ed. Allan Greer and Ian Radforth (Toronto 1992). On the growth of the professions and banking see R.D. Gidney and W.P.J. Millar, *Professional Gentlemen: The Professions in Nineteenth-Century Ontario* (Toronto 1994) and Peter Baskerville, *The Bank of Upper Canada* (Ottawa 1987).

4 On the process of state formation see Greer and Radforth, eds, *Colonial Leviathan* and J.E. Hodgetts, *Pioneer Public Service: An Administrative History of the United Canadas* (Toronto 1955).

5 On the growth of national sentiment and Upper Canadian expansionism see Doug Owram, *Promise of Eden: The Canadian Expansionist Movement and the Idea of the West, 1856–1900* (Toronto 1980), chap. 2; Allan Smith, 'Old Ontario and the Emergence of a National Frame of Mind,' in *Aspects of Nineteenth-Century Ontario*, ed. F.H. Armstrong, H.A. Stevenson, and J.D. Wilson (Toronto 1974), 194–217; M. Brook Taylor, *Promoters, Patriots and Partisans: Historiography in Nineteenth-Century English Canada* (Toronto 1989), chap. 5.

6 Benedict Anderson, *Imagined Communities: Reflections on the Origins and Spread of Nationalism* (London and New York 1983)

7 *Journals of the Legislative Assembly of the Province of Canada*, (8 October 1842), 117

8 *Journals of the Legislative Assembly of the Province of Canada* (18 August 1851), 292–4

9 J.M. McMullen, *The History of Canada from its Discovery to the Present Time* (Brockville 1855), preface

10 See Taylor, *Promoters, Patriots and Partisans*, 165–7.

11 On the use of the public school system to create a public see Bruce Curtis, *Building the Educational State: Canada West, 1836–1871* (London, Ontario 1988). Alison Prentice uses a more traditional social control model in *The School Promoters: Education and Social Class in Mid-Nineteenth Century Upper Canada* (Toronto 1977).

12 UCA, Egerton Ryerson Papers, Address, 1841. Ryerson's conviction that it was the function of public education to promote local and imperial patriotism, social harmony, and loyalty to properly constituted authority are most clearly expressed in his *Report on a System of Public Elementary Education for Upper Canada*, published in 1847.

13 On the debate over textbooks see Susan E. Houston and Alison Prentice, *Schooling and Scholars in Nineteenth-Century Ontario* (Toronto 1988), chap. 8.

14 Cited in Smith, 'Old Ontario and the Emergence of a National Frame of Mind,' 195.

15 J. George Hodgins, *The Geography and History of British America and of the Other Colonies of the Empire* (Toronto 1857), iii–iv

16 *Journals of the Legislative Assembly of the Province of Canada*, XVIII (31 Jan. 1869), Appendix I, 1–7

17 Nathanael Burwash, 'U.E. Loyalists, Founders of Our Institutions,' UELO, *Transactions* (1901–2), 35

18 *Globe*, 30 Oct. 1856

19 Craven, *Legend of the Founding Fathers*, chaps 3 and 4

20 Cobourg *Star*, 20 Nov. 1861

21 Loyalist obituaries published in the *Journal of Education for Upper Canada* by Ryerson included those of Nicholas Brouse, 12 (April 1859), 58; D. Burritt. 12 (May 1859), 75; Hon. George Crookshank, 12 (Aug. 1859), 121; George Brouse, 13 (31 March 1860), 44; John Willson, 13 (June 1860), 94; William Woodruff, 13 (July 1860), 108.

22 The Literary and Historical Society of Quebec was founded in 1824 and enjoyed the patronage of the governor-general, Lord Dalhousie.

23 J.P. Merritt, *Biography of the Hon. W.H. Merritt, M.P.* (St Catharines 1875), 424

24 J.J. Talman, 'William Hamilton Merritt,' *DCB*, vol. 9, 544–8

25 Merritt, *Biography of the Hon. W.H. Merritt*, 215, 406–7

26 George Coventry quoted in Gerald Killan, *Preserving Ontario's Heritage: A History of the Ontario Historical Society* (Ottawa 1976), 7.

27 Merritt, *Biography of the Hon. W.H. Merritt*, preface

28 *Journals of the Legislative Assembly of the Province of Canada*, 1859, XVII (10 Feb. 1859) 38, (2 March 1859) 137, (7 March 1859) 156

29 *Journals of the Legislative Assembly of the Province of Canada*, XVII (April 1859) 525–6, 928; XX (1862) 246

30 J.J. Talman, 'George Coventry,' *DCB*, vol. 9, 163–4

31 AO, George Coventry Correspondence, Merritt Papers, MU 4374, Series D, Envelope 1, 'Prospectus for the Formation of an Upper Canadian Historical Society'

32 AO, Historical Society of Upper Canada, Merritt Papers, MU 4374, Series E, Envelope 1

33 *Globe*, 15 Nov. 1861

34 UCA, Egerton Ryerson Papers, 'History of the British United Empire Loyalists of America,' Box 13, File 365

35 Egerton Ryerson, *The Loyalists of America and Their Times from 1620–1816*, vol. I (Toronto 1880), v

36 'Reminiscences of Captain James Dittrick,' in J.J. Talman, *Loyalist Narratives from Upper Canada* (Toronto 1946) 63. The original transcripts of many of the

reminiscences can be found in the George Coventry Papers at the National Archives of Canada.

37 'Reminiscences of the Hon. Henry Ruttan of Cobourg,' *Loyalist Narratives*, 298

38 'Reminiscence of Mrs White of White Mills near Cobourg, Upper Canada. Formerly Miss Catherine Chrysler (Cysdale) of Sydney, near Bell(e)ville. Aged 79,' *Loyalist Narratives*, 353

39 'Reminiscences of the Hon. Henry Ruttan of Cobourg,' *Loyalist Narratives*, 299

40 'Reminiscences of Captain James Dittrick,' *Loyalist Narratives*, 66–8

41 'Testimonial of Roger Bates,' *Loyalist Narratives*, 31

42 'Reminiscences of Captain James Dittrick,' *Loyalist Narratives*, 63

43 'Reminiscence of Mrs White,' *Loyalist Narratives*, 354

44 'Memoirs of Colonel John Clark of Port Dalhousie, C.W.,' *Ontario Historical Society Papers and Records* VII (1906), 162, 164

45 'Reminiscence of Mrs White,' *Loyalist Narratives*, 355

46 'Historical Memoranda of Mrs. Amelia Harris, of Eldon House, London, Ontario, only daughter of the Late Colonel Samuel Ryerse, and sister of the late Rev. Geo. J. Ryerse,' in Ryerson, *Loyalists*, vol. II, 236, 245

47 'Memoirs of Colonel John Clark,' *Ontario Historical Society Papers and Records*, 163

48 NAC, George Coventry Papers, 'Reminiscence of John Kilborn, Esq. born at Brockville, U.C., 1794, whose Grandfather was with General Amherst, and left in charge of Fort Oswego, 1759,' 219

49 'Reminiscences of Captain James Dittrick,' *Loyalist Narratives*, 68

50 'Reminiscences of Capt. Thomas Gummersall Anderson,' *Loyalist Narratives*, 2–3, 14, 8

51 'Reminiscences of the Hon. Henry Ruttan' and 'Testimonial of Roger Bates,' *Loyalist Narratives*, 302, 38

52 Robert N. Butler, 'The Life Review: An Interpretation of Reminiscence in the Aged,' *Psychiatry: Journal for the Study of Interpersonal Processes*, 26 (1963), 66–73

53 Fred Davis, *Yearning for Yesterday: A Sociology of Nostalgia* (New York 1979), 34. Also see Christopher Shaw and Malcolm Chase, eds, *The Imagined Past: History and Nostalgia* (Manchester and New York 1989).

54 Canniff, *Settlement of Upper Canada*, 1

55 William Kirby, *The U.E.: A Tale of Upper Canada. A Poem in XII Cantos*, (Niagara 1859), iii, 56

56 Kirby's great grandmother left Virginia and settled in England at the outbreak of the Revolution. William Kirby, *Reminiscences of a Visit to Quebec, July 1839*, (Niagara 1903).

57 Lorne Pierce, *William Kirby: Portrait of a Tory Loyalist* (Toronto 1929), 2–10

58 The results of Kirby's genealogical research appeared in 1884 in the April and

May issues of the *Canadian Methodist Magazine* under the title 'The United
Empire Loyalists of Canada.' An expanded version of the article appeared in
the transactions of the Niagara Historical Society in 1901.

59 Dennis Duffy, *Gardens, Covenants, and Exiles: Loyalism in the Literature of Upper
Canada / Ontario* (Toronto 1982), 29–32

60 'Susan Burnham Greeley's "Sketches of the Past,"' *Loyalist Narratives*, 107

61 'Testimonial of Mr Roger Bates,' *Loyalist Narratives*, 40

62 'Reminiscence of the Hon. Henry Ruttan,' *Loyalist Narratives*, 302

63 A similar phenomenon developed in the United States. The death of the last
signer of the Declaration of Independence in 1832 symbolically marked the
passing of the revolutionary generation and resulted in a concerted effort to
collect the memoirs and reminiscences of the remaining survivors. Americans
were also repeatedly exhorted to revere the Founding Fathers and protect
their achievements. David Lowenthal maintains that 'such injunctions posed
the sons a terrible dilemma. They could not resemble the Founding Fathers
without endangering their legacy, or preserve it without acknowledging their
subordination. Simply to save the legacy relegated them to everlasting inferi-
ority as sons unable to act on their own'; *The Past Is a Foreign Country*, 117–18.
Also see Kammen, *A Season of Youth*, 50–1.

64 'Egerton Ryerson to Sophia Harris, 11 August 1872; 1 Jan. 1871,' in *My Dearest
Sophie: Letters from Egerton Ryerson To His Daughter*, ed. C.B. Sissons (Toronto
1955) 227, 201

65 'Egerton Ryerson to Sophia Harris, 9 October 1875,' in *My Dearest Sophie*, 283

66 UCA, Ryerson Papers, Box 2, 'Egerton Ryerson to Sophia Harris, 14 April
1880'

67 *Journals of the Legislative Assembly of the Province of Canada*, XXII (15 Sept. 1863)
126, (24 Sept. 1863), 177

68 Killan, *Preserving Ontario's Heritage*, 8

69 J.J. Talman suggests that the library committee's decision to withdraw funding
for the collection of documents was a response to George Coventry's poor
research. Talman notes that 'where it is possible to check his version against
other sources, many discrepancies became apparent.' It is highly unlikely that
committee members bothered to compare Coventry's records with other
sources; *Loyalist Narratives from Upper Canada*, xiii.

70 Ryerson, *Loyalists*, Vol. I, 191

71 See: Hayden White, *The Content and the Form: Narrative Discourse and the Historical Representation* (Baltimore 1987); Dominick LaCapra, *Rethinking Intellectual
History: Texts, Contexts, Language* (Ithaca 1983).

72 On the influence of romance and the writings of Sir Walter Scott on nineteenth-century English Canadian historical writing see Carole Gerson, *A Purer*

Taste: The Writing and Reading of Fiction in English in Nineteenth-Century Canada
(Toronto 1989), chaps 5 and 7.

73 Canniff, *Settlement of Upper Canada*, 50, 45
74 Ryerson, *Loyalists*, Vol. I, 12
75 Ibid., 265; Canniff, *Settlement of Upper Canada*, 54–5
76 Ryerson, *Loyalists*, Vol. I, 408, 507 Also see Canniff, *Settlement of Upper Canada*, 51.
77 Ryerson, *Loyalists*, Vol. II, 189; Canniff, *Settlement of Upper Canada*, 580–1
78 Ryerson, *Loyalists*, Vol. II, 316 Also see Canniff, *Settlement of Upper Canada*, 633–4. This characterization marked the beginning of a transformation in the mythology of the War of 1812. The older militia myth – the assertion that Upper Canada had been saved from the Americans almost entirely through the efforts of the Canadian militia – was by definition more inclusive than the emerging Loyalist tradition. Canniff's and Ryerson's portrayals of the War of 1812 as a vindication of Loyalist principles were the first steps in the full incorporation of the war into the matrix of the Loyalist tradition. Also see William F. Coffin, *1812: The War and Its Moral: A Canadian Chronicle* (Montreal 1864).
79 Janice Potter-Mackinnon, *While the Women Only Wept: Loyalist Refugee Women in Eastern Ontario* (Montreal and Kingston 1993), 158
80 Edward H. Hale, 'Memoir of the Hon. Lorenzo Sabine, A.M.,' *Proceedings of the Massachusetts Historical Society*, xvii (1879–80), 375
81 Gregory Palmer, 'Introduction,' *Biographical Sketches of the Loyalists of the American Revolution* (1864; rpt Westport and London 1984), xxvii
82 Sabine, 'Review of *A History of the Operations of a Partisan Corps called the Queen's Rangers,'* North American Review* (Oct. 1844), 263.
83 Sabine, *Biographical Sketches*, 12, 52–4, 88–91
84 Hale, 'Memoir of the Hon. Lorenzo Sabine, A.M.,' *Proceedings of the Massachusetts Historical Society*, xvii (1879–80), 377
85 Sabine, *Biographical Sketches*, 40
86 Sabine, 'Review of *Queens Rangers*,' 262–3, 278
87 Canniff, *Settlement of Upper Canada*, 41–2; Ryerson, *Loyalists*, Vol. II, 185
88 Alpheus Todd, 'Is Canadian Loyalty a Sentiment or a Principle?' *Canadian Monthly* (Nov. 1881), 5–6, 9
89 W.D. LeSueur, 'The True Idea of Canadian Loyalty,' *Rose-Belford's Canadian Monthly and National Review* (Jan. 1882), 1–4

3: Community Factionalism

1 Berger, *The Sense of Power*, 84
2 Kingston *Daily News*, 25 Feb. 1884.

3 Forneri kept a record of his efforts to honour the Loyalists in a scrapbook containing newspaper clippings, a daily diary of his activities, copies of letters, and the texts of speeches and sermons he gave to promote his plans for the 1884 Loyalist centennial. The scrapbook is a rich source of information on the individuals, events, and interests that shaped the 1884 Adolphustown celebrations. The scrapbook is located at the Anglican Diocese of Ontario Archives.

4 *Daily News*, 20 Nov. 1883, in Forneri Scrapbook, 2

5 Belleville *Intelligencer*, 27 Dec. 1883

6 John King, *McCaul, Croft, Forneri: Personalities of Early University Days* (Toronto 1914), 190–8

7 *Daily News*, 20 Nov. 1883

8 Forneri Scrapbook, 71–2

9 *Intelligencer*, 27 Dec. 1884

10 An examination of the 1881 manuscript census for the townships of Adolphustown and North Fredericksburgh reveals the following breakdown in religious affiliation: Canadian Methodists, 279 (38.1 per cent); Church of England, 233 (31.8 per cent); Episcopal Methodists, 125, (17 per cent); Christian Brethren, 46 (6.2 per cent); Roman Catholics, 23 (3.2 per cent); Primitive Methodists, 9 (1.2 per cent); Quakers, 9 (1.2 per cent); Presbyterians, 6 (0.82 per cent); and Universalists, 1 (0.13 per cent).

11 Napanee *Standard*, 5 Jan. 1884

12 Toronto *Mail*, n.d., in Forneri Scrapbook, 13

13 *Daily News*, n.d., in Forneri Scrapbook, 16

14 Napanee *Beaver*, n.d., in Forneri Scrapbook, 20

15 Toronto *Mail*, n.d., in Forneri Scrapbook, 20. Forneri identifies 'A Loyalist' as J.J. Watson, a member of his congregation.

16 Forneri Scrapbook, 5–6

17 The sponsors of the meeting scheduled for 10 January 1884 were D.W. Allison, J.H. Roblin, J.J. Watson, Parker Allen, Thomas Trumpour, A.C. Davis, Elisha Ruttan, and S.M. Outwater. Only Allison was not a member of Forneri's congregation. Allison's wife, however, was an Anglican and the church organist.

18 *Intelligencer*, 27 Dec. 1883

19 Ibid., 12 Jan. 1884

20 Napanee *Express*, 4 Jan. 1884, Kingston *British Whig*, 5 Jan. 1884

21 The 23 January meeting received extensive comment in Forneri's scrapbook, taking up two full pages. Unfortunately, both pages have been partially removed. Although incomplete, the fragmentary text that remains is highly suggestive.

22 *Express*, 4 Jan. 1884; *British Whig*, 5 Jan. 1884

23 *Intelligencer*, 16 July 1884

24 *British Whig*, 29 Jan. 1884

25 Forneri Scrapbook, 12

26 Frank B. Edwards, *The Smiling Wilderness: An Illustrated History of Lennox and Addington County* (Camden East 1984), 37–41

27 For a fuller discussion of politics in Lennox see: Lorne Brown, 'The Macdonald-Cartwright Struggle in Lennox, November 1873,' *Ontario History*, 61 (1969), 35–50 and James Eadie, 'The Federal Election in Lennox Riding and Its Aftermath, 1883–1883: A Glimpse of Victorian Political Morality,' *Ontario History*, 76 (1984), 354–72.

28 Unidentified clipping, Forneri Scrapbook, 28

29 Watson was president of the Lennox Liberal-Conservative Association (Napanee *Standard*, 16 Feb. 1884).

30 Picton *Gazette*, n.d., in Forneri Scrapbook, 26

31 *Gazette*, 7 March 1884, in Forneri Scrapbook, 30

32 *Intelligencer*, 22 Feb. 1884

33 *Standard*, 23 Feb. 1884

34 *British Whig*, 2 May 1884

35 Ibid.

36 *Standard*, 8 March 1884

37 Ibid., 22 March 1884

38 AO, Macdonald Papers, 'Petition to the Right Honourable Sir John A. Macdonald and the Honourable Members of the Executive Council of the Dominion of Canada in Council,' MS 335, reel 124

39 *Intelligencer*, 22 March 1884

40 *Mail*, n.d., in Forneri Scrapbook, 24

41 *Standard*, 15 March 1884; 24 May 1884

42 *British Whig*, 13 June 1884

43 Belleville *Daily Ontario*, 5 June 1884

44 *Intelligencer*, 27 Dec. 1883; 4 Feb. 1884

45 Ibid., 22 Feb. 1884; 17 May 1884

46 Ibid., 6 May 1884; *Standard*, 10 May 1884

47 LACM, R.S. Forneri to William Canniff, 18 April 1884

48 Forneri Scrapbook, 35

49 *British Whig*, 19 June 1884

50 *Daily Ontario*, 17 June 1884

51 *Intelligencer*, 21 June 1884

52 Ibid., 16 July 1884

53 *Express*, 27 June 1884

54 *The Centennial of the Settlement of Upper Canada by the United Empire Loyalists,*

1774–1884: The Celebrations at Adolphustown, Toronto, and Niagara (Toronto 1885; rpt Boston 1972), 46. This source is hereafter cited as *CSUC.*

55 *Express*, 27 June 1884
56 *Daily Ontario*, 20 June 1884
57 *CSUC*, 24, 25, 12, 29
58 *Globe*, 21 May 1884
59 *CSUC*, 25–9
60 Ibid., 33
61 Ibid., 42–3 Also see the remarks of Captain Grace (40–1) and G.E. Henderson (41–2).
62 *British Whig*, 19 June 1884; *CSUC*, 47
63 *CSUC*, 22
64 Berger, *The Sense of Power*, 105
65 *CSUC*, 11–12
66 *British Whig*, 18 June 1884
67 *Intelligencer*, 19 Dec. 1883; 2 Jan. 1884; 21 Jan. 1884
68 *British Whig*, 12 Jan. 1884
69 *Standard*, 5 Jan. 1884
70 *CSUC*, 32
71 *Standard*, 1 March 1884
72 Berger, *The Sense of Power*, 84
73 T.W.C. Casey, *Adolphustown Ramblings* (Kingston 1896), 8–9

4: The Politics of Commemoration

1 *CSUC*, 84
2 Ibid., 85–6, 62, 60, 57, 109–10, 96, 73
3 Ibid., 62, 59, 91, 101–2
4 Ibid., 70, 68, 96
5 Ibid., iv–v
6 Toronto *Evening Telegram*, 8 June 1876
7 Berger, *The Sense of Power*, 99
8 *CSUC*, iv–v
9 MTRL, 'W.B. McMurrich to the Members of the Citizen's Semi-Centennial Committee, 9 Dec. 1882.' For an overview of the Toronto semi-centennial celebrations see J.M.S. Careless's essay 'The First Hurrah: Toronto's Semi-Centennial of 1884,' in *Forging a Consensus: Historical Essays on Toronto*, ed. Victor L. Russell (Toronto 1984), 141–54.
10 *CSUC*, v
11 AO, Canniff Papers, William Canniff to Sir Alexander Campbell, 15 Dec. 1883

12 The meeting was attended by Dr Canniff, Lieutenant-Colonel George Taylor Denison, William Foster, Dr J.S. King, D.B. Read, C.E. Ryerson, George S. Ryerson, Dr E.W. Spragge, and Rev. Dr William Withrow; *CSUC,* v–vi.

13 Toronto *Daily Mail,* 24 Nov. 1883

14 AO, Canniff Papers, D.B. Read to William Canniff, 1 Dec. 1883

15 *Daily Mail,* 24 Nov. 1883

16 See: Appendix I.

17 Berger, *The Sense of Power,* 79–81

18 *CSUC,* 22

19 William Canniff, *Canadian Nationality: Its Growth and Development* (Toronto, 1875), 7, 14–15, 20

20 AO, Canniff Papers, 'Patriotic Address'

21 Henry James Morgan, *The Canadian Men and Women of the Time. A Handbook of Canadian Biography* (Toronto 1898), 261–3

22 G.M. Rose, ed., *Cyclopedia of Canadian Biography: Being Chiefly Men of the Times* (Toronto 1886), 244–5

23 Rose, *Cyclopedia of Canadian Biography,* 245–6 For a more complete history of the Denison family see David Gagan, *The Denison Family of Toronto, 1792–1925* (Toronto 1973).

24 On Frederick and Septimus Denison see Gagan, *The Denison Family of Toronto.* On A. Maclean Howard see Rose, *Cyclopedia of Canadian Biography,* 300 and *Commemorative and Biographical Record of the County of York, Ontario* (Toronto 1907), 278.

25 Morgan, *Canadian Men and Women,* 422

26 Canniff Haight, *Country Life in Canada Fifty Years Ago: Personal Recollections and Reminiscences of a Sexagenarian* (Toronto 1885), 124, 49, 215, 219

27 On Withrow see Rose, *Cyclopedia of Canadian Biography,* 135; Morgan, *Canadian Men and Women,* 1097–8. On D.B. Read see Morgan, *Canadian Men and Women,* 847.

28 On George Sterling Ryerson see Morgan, *Canadian Men and Women,* 6. On Charles Egerton Ryerson see *History of Toronto and the County of York* (Toronto 1885), 394–5.

29 Toronto *News,* 3 Dec. 1883

30 NAC, Denison Papers, George Taylor Denison to Lord Grey, 25 Feb. 1907

31 AO, William Canniff Papers, Senator G.W. Allan to William Canniff, 18 Dec. 1883

32 AO, William Canniff Papers, G.H. Hale to William Canniff, 1 Dec. 1883

33 MTRL, Henry Scadding Collection, 'U.E. Loyalist Centennial. Circular to Editors, County and Township Municipal Officers, and Others.'

34 *Globe,* 29 Nov. 1883

35 Ibid., 4 Dec. 1883
36 Ibid., 7 Dec. 1883
37 *News*, 5 Jan. 1884
38 *Daily Mail*, 20 Feb. 1884 Among those present from beyond Toronto were Rev. R.S. Forneri from Adolphustown, Rev. A. McNab and Levi Van Camp from Bowmanville, and Alexander Servos, R.N. Ball, and Col. D. McFarland from Niagara.
39 *Daily Mail*, 21 Feb. 1884
40 Ibid., 20 Feb. 1884; *Evening News*, 20 Feb. 1884
41 The following subcommittees were created: Reception at Government House: George Taylor Denison (chair), Lieutenant-Governor John Beverley Robinson, S.J. VanKoughnet; Finance: Fred Denison (chair), J.J. Withrow, C.E. Ryerson; Correspondence: Col. G.T. Denison (chair), D.B. Read, Rev. Dr Withrow, C.E. Ryerson; Religious Services: Rt Rev. Fuller (chair), Rev. Dr Caven, Dr Daniel Wilson, Rev. Hugh Johnston; Museum of Antiquities and Historical Documents: A. Mclean Howard (chair), Rev. Dr Scadding, Dr Canniff, James H. Morris, D.B. Read, Dr Ryerson.
42 *Globe*, 7 April 1884
43 *Daily Mail*, 9 May 1884
44 Niagara-on-the-Lake *Echo of Niagara*, 17 May 1884; *Mail*, 27 June 1884
45 Welland *Tribune*, 4 July 1884
46 Forneri Scrapbook, 12
47 *Tribune*, 4 July 1884
48 *CSUC*, 104–5
49 *Tribune*, 1 Aug. 1884. I.P. Wilson was a member of the general committee responsible for organizing the Niagara celebrations. The letter to the *Tribune* was written at the suggestion of the Secretary of the committee, Daniel Servos; AO, William Kirby Collection, I.P. Wilson to Daniel Servos, 9 July 1884.
50 AO, William Kirby Collection, George Taylor Denison to William Kirby, 22 July 1884
51 *CSUC*, 105
52 AO, William Canniff Papers, William Withrow to William Canniff, 20 Feb. 1884
53 *Daily Mail*, 17 April 1884
54 *News*, 7 May 1884
55 AO, William Canniff Papers, William Canniff to Hon. William McDougall, 28 May 1884
56 AO, William Canniff Papers, Hon. William McDougall to William Canniff, 30 May 1884
57 AO, William Canniff Papers, William Canniff to Hon. William McDougall, 4 June 1884

58 AO, William Canniff Papers, William Canniff to Judge Dean, 5 June 1884
59 *Globe*, 14 June 1884
60 *CSUC*, 54
61 *Globe*, 4 July 1884
62 *Daily Mail*, 5 July 1884
63 Toronto *Week*, 17 July 1884
64 *News*, 16 Aug. 1884
65 Toronto *World*, 5 July 1884
66 *News*, 4 July 1884
67 *World*, 5 July 1884
68 *Globe*, 16 Aug. 1884
69 *CSUC*, 73
70 For a discussion of the impact of industrialization and urbanization on class structure in late nineteenth-century Canada see Gordon Darroch and Lee Soltow, *Property and Inequality in Victorian Ontario: Structural Patterns and Cultural Communities in the 1871 Census* (Toronto 1994) and T.W. Acheson, 'Changing Social Origins of the Canadian Industrial Elite, 1880–1910,' *Business History Review*, 47 (1973), 19–217. For the impact of industrialization on labour see Gregory S. Kealey, *Toronto Workers Respond to Industrial Capitalism, 1867–1892* (Toronto 1980). On the transformation of business see Michael Bliss, *A Living Profit: Studies in the Social History of Canadian Business, 1883–1911* (Toronto 1974).
71 Hobsbawm, 'Mass Producing Traditions,' *The Invention of Tradition*, 291
72 Mosse, 'Caesarism, Circuses and Monuments,' 167–9
73 Haight, *Country Life in Canada*, 38, 104, 49, 116, 218–19
74 On the changing images of Native peoples see Robert Berkhoffer, Jr, *The Whiteman's Indian: Images of the American Indian from Columbus to the Present* (New York 1979); and Daniel Francis, *The Imaginary Indian: The Image of the Indian in Canadian Culture* (Vancouver 1992).
75 *CSUC*, 38, 119
76 Ibid., 89–90
77 On the importance of parades as modes of cultural communication see Susan G. Davis, *Parades and Power: Street Theatre in Nineteenth-Century Philadelphia* (Berkeley 1988).
78 *Globe*, 19 May 1884
79 Born at Grand River in 1841, Martin paid for his own education at the Wesleyan Academy at Wilbraham, Massachusetts. He was introduced to the Prince of Wales during his visit in 1860 and invited to study in England. After three years at Oxford, Martin returned to Canada and completed a medical degree at the University of Toronto.
80 Deseronto *Tribune*, n.d., in Forneri scrapbook, 65

81 *Expositor*, 25 Oct. 1884
82 On the celebrations held to commemorate the centennial of American independence in 1876 see Craven, *The Legend of the Founding Fathers*; James W.
Campbell, *America in her Centennial Year, 1876* (Washington 1980); Dee Hart,
The Year of the Century: 1876 (New York 1966); William Pierce Randall, *Centennial: American Life in 1876* (Philadelphia 1969); Lyn Spillman, 'Centennial Celebrations in 1876 and 1888: Creating Integration and Enacting Dependence
in the United States and Austrialia,' unpublished paper presented to the
Annual Meeting of the American Historical Association, 1992.

5: The Loyalists in Ontario Publications, 1884–1918

1 Henry Scadding, *The Revised Significance of the Initials U.E.* (Toronto 1892), 7
2 *CPUC*, 6–7
3 Rev. E.J. Fessenden, *Upper Canada: A Centenary Study* (Welland 1892), 3, 25–6
4 Goldwin Smith, *Loyalty, Aristocracy and Jingoism: Three Lectures Delivered before the
Young Men's Liberal Club, Toronto* (Toronto 1891), 71, 12, 25
5 Sir John Bourinot, 'The United Empire Loyalists of Canada,' *Acta Victoriana*,
23 (1899), 142–3
6 Burwash, 'Founders of Our Institutions,' 35
7 Nathanael Burwash, 'The Moral Character of the U.E. Loyalists,' UELO,
Transactions 1901–2, 63
8 See: Ruth Miller Elson, *Guardians of Tradition: American Schoolbooks of the
Nineteenth Century* (Lincoln 1964); J.M. Goldstrom, *The Social Content of
Education, 1808–1870: A Study of the Working Class School Reader in England
and Ireland* (Shannon 1972); Houston and Prentice, *Schooling and Scholars*
chap. 8.
9 Cited in Robert M. Stamp, *The Schools of Ontario, 1876–1976* (Toronto 1982),
33.
10 Ibid., chap. 4; Elizabeth Parvin, *Authorization of Textbooks for the Schools of
Ontario, 1876–1950* (Toronto 1965), 58–9
11 G. Mercer Adams and W.J. Robertson, *Public School History of England and
Canada* (Toronto 1886), iii
12 Dennis Duffy looks at the portrayal of the Loyalists in school textbooks in
'Upper Canadian Loyalism: What the Textbooks Tell,' *Journal of Canadian
Studies*, 12 (1977), 17–26. Duffy is more concerned with the textbooks as cultural artefacts than with their social and ideological utility.
13 Charles G.D. Roberts, *A History of Canada* (Toronto 1897), 195
14 David M. Duncan, *The Story of the Canadian People* (Toronto 1907), 219
15 J. Frith Jeffers, *History of Canada* (Toronto 1881), 47

16 Adams and Robertson, *Public School History,* 160
17 Duncan, *Story of the Canadian People,* 213
18 Jeffers, *History of Canada,* 35
19 W.H.P. Clement, *The History of the Dominion of Canada* (Toronto 1897),
   122 Clement's history won a contest in 1893 sponsored by the Dominion
   Educational Association to produce a Canadian history text to be used
   throughout the country. Although the selection committee, which consisted
   of the ministers of education of each province, were impressed by Clement's
   'dignified, erudite and balanced style,' the text did not prove very popular
   outside Ontario; P.J. Read, 'The Dominion History Contest: An Episode
   in the Search for Canadian Unity,' M.A. thesis, University of Toronto,
   1969, 33.
20 On the efforts of educational authorities to create political stability by inculcating deferential political values see Prentice, *The School Promoters.*
21 J. George Hodgins, *A History of Canada and the other British Provinces in North
   America* (Montreal 1866), 145–6. Hodgins's text was still in use in many schools
   during this period.
22 W.L. Grant, *Ontario High School History of Canada* (Toronto 1914), 144–5
23 Clement, *History of the Dominion,* vi, 341
24 For a discussion of these values see Walter E. Houghton, *The Victorian Frame of
   Mind* (New Haven 1957); W.L. Morton, 'Victorian Canada,' *The Shield of Achilles: Aspects of Canada in the Victorian Age* (Toronto 1968); P.F.W. Rutherford,
   'The New Nationality, 1864–1897: A Study of the National Aims and Ideas of
   English Canada in the Late Nineteenth Century,' Ph.D. dissertation, University of Toronto, 1973, chap. IV.
25 Hodgins, *Canada and the Other British Provinces,* 144–8
26 Roberts, *History of Canada,* 207, 205
27 Clement, *History of the Dominion,* 126
28 Jeffers, *History of Canada,* 48
29 Hodgins, *Canada and the Other British Provinces,* 148
30 Roberts, *History of Canada,* 195
31 Grant, *High School History of Canada,* 143
32 W.S. Herrington, *Heroines of Canadian History* (Toronto 1910), 69–74, 66
33 Ibid., 78
34 UELO, *Transactions* (1899), 39
35 Curtis, *Building the Educational State* 370.
36 Killan, *Preserving Ontario's Heritage,* chap. 1; Taylor, *Promoter, Patriots, and Partisans,* 255–8
37 J.A. Macdonnell, *Sketches Illustrating the Early Settlement and History of Glengarry
   in Canada* (Montreal 1893), 5–6

38 W.S. Herrington, *Pioneer Life among the Loyalists in Upper Canada* (Toronto 1915), 12

39 William Canniff, 'Adolphustown, or the township of Adolphus or fourth Town, the First Settlement by U.E. Loyalists,' UELO, *Transactions* (1900), 77, 80–1

40 J. Smyth Carter, *The Story of Dundas; being a History of the County from 1784 to 1904* (Iroquois 1905), 37

41 Macdonnell, *History of Glengarry*, 60. These views were echoed by A.C. Casselman in 'The Highland Scotch U.E. Loyalists,' UELO, *Transactions* 1901–2, and D.W. Clendennan in 'Some Presbyterian U.E. Loyalists,' Ontario Historical Society, *Papers and Records*, vol. 3, 1901.

42 Rev. A.B. Sherk, 'Influence of the U.E. Loyalists on the Development of the Canadian Commonwealth,' UELO, *Transactions* 1903–4, 39–40

43 E.A. Owen, *Pioneer Sketches of Long Point Settlement or Norfolk's Foundation Builders and their Family Genealogies* (Toronto 1898), vi, 74

44 Ibid., 166

45 Ibid., vi

46 Allan Smith, 'The Myth of the Self-Made Man in English Canada, 1850–1914,' *Canadian Historical Review*, 59 (1978), 189–95

47 *Ontarian Genealogist and Family Historian*, 1 (July 1898), 1–2

48 Genealogical and family histories accounted for 48.5 per cent of the papers published in the *Transactions* of the United Empire Loyalist Association of Ontario between 1898 and 1913. Of the remaining papers, general Loyalist history accounted for 24.1 per cent, local history accounted for 15.5 per cent, and polemical works accounted for 12 per cent.

49 UELO, *Transactions* (1901–2), 73–4

50 Ibid., (1903–4), 75–6

51 Ibid., (1900), 38

52 John Ruch and Violet Coderre-Smith, 'Montreal's Loyalist Associations,' in *The Loyalists of Quebec, 1774–1825: A Forgotten History* (Montreal 1989), 460–3. Forsyth claimed to have been born in Montreal. He apparently felt that his American citizenship would prove a liability in his effort to promote his cause in Canada.

53 NPAC, Samuel Rawson Papers, 'Circular, Viscount de Fronsac, 16 December 1903,' MG 55, no. 90.

54 UELO, *Transactions* (1901–2), 72–9

55 Ibid. (1903–4), 77–85

56 Ibid. (1899), 48

57 Ibid. (1898), 24–5

58 Ibid. (1900), 37

59 Canniff Haight, *A Genealogical Narrative of the Daniel Haight Family by His Grandson Canniff Haight* (Toronto 1899), 4

60 Bernard Bailyn, 'The Losers: Notes on the Historiography of Loyalism,' *The Ordeal of Thomas Hutchinson* (Cambridge 1974), 391–3

61 W.E.H. Lecky, *History of England in the Eighteenth Century*, vol. 3 (London: 1878), 414, 443

62 Michael Krauss and Davis D. Joyce, *The Writing of American History* (Norman 1986), 211

63 Bailyn, 'The Losers,' 393–4

64 John Higham, *Strangers in the Land: Patterns of American Nativism, 1860–1925* (New York 1972), chap. 4

65 George E. Ellis, 'The Loyalists and their Fortunes,' in *Narrative and Critical History of America*, ed. Justin Winsor (Boston and New York 1888), 185

66 James K. Hosmer, *Samuel Adams* (Boston and New York 1899), 247–8

67 James K. Hosmer, *A Short History of Anglo-saxon Freedom: The Polity of the English-speaking Race* (New York 1903), 222

68 Moses Coit Tyler, 'The Party of the Loyalists in the American Revolution,' *American Historical Review*, 1 (1896), 27–31

69 Charles Kendall Adams, 'Some Neglected Aspects of the Revolutionary War,' *Atlantic Monthly*, 82 (Aug. 1898), 175

70 Sydney George Fisher, *The True History of the American Revolution* (Philadelphia 1902), 7

71 Adams, 'Some Neglected Aspects of the Revolutionary War,' 180–1, 189

72 Edward Harris, *History and Historiettes: United Empire Loyalists* (Toronto 1897), 1

73 Arthur Johnston, *Myths and Facts of the American Revolution: A Commentary on United States History as it is Written* (Toronto 1908), 12, 15

74 Alexander Clarence Flick, *Loyalism in New York during the American Revolution* (New York 1901), 12, 35–6

75 Claude Van Tyne, *The Loyalists in the American Revolution* (New York 1902), 165

76 Carl Berger, *The Writing of Canadian History: Aspects of English-Canadian Historical Writing since 1900*, 2nd ed. (Toronto 1986), 1–8

77 Taylor, *Promoters, Patriots, and Partisans*, 270

78 Other members of the group included George Wrong, Adam Shortt, and Chester Martin. For Wallace's views on the writing of history see 'Some Vices of Clio,' *Canadian Historical Review*, 7 (1926), 197–203.

79 William Stewart Wallace, *The United Empire Loyalists: A Chronicle of the Great Migration* (Toronto 1914), 2–3

80 Ibid., 15–16, 83, 11–14

81 Robert Craig Brown and Ramsay Cook, *Canada, 1896–1921: A Nation Transformed* (Toronto 1974), chap. 14

6: Loyalist Monuments and the Creation of Usable Pasts

1 Robert Shipley, *To Mark Our Place: A History of Canadian War Memorials* (Toronto 1987) and C.J. Taylor, *Negotiating the Past: The Making of Canada's National Historic Parks and Sites* (Montreal and Kingston 1990) make passing reference to nineteenth-century monuments. Drawing upon the work of Carl Berger, both Shipley and Taylor interpret the rash of monuments commemorating the battles of the War of 1812 that appeared towards the end of the century as a product of the Loyalist tradition.

2 Cited in Killan, *Preserving Ontario's Heritage*, 80. Similar views were expressed by Sarah Curzon in *Canada in Memoriam, 1812–14: Her Duty in the Erection of Monuments in Memory of Her Distinguished Sons and Daughters* (Welland 1891) and by James Coyne in 'Memorial to the U.E. Loyalists' and Janet Carnochan in 'Monuments,' both of which appeared in Niagara Historical Society, *Transactions,* 4 (1898), 1–10 and 24–9, respectively.

3 On the functions of monuments see Marianne Doezema and June Hargrove, *The Public Monument and Its Audience* (Cleveland 1977); Christopher D. Geist, 'Historic Sites and Monuments as Icons,' in *Icons of America,* ed. Ray B. Browne and Marshall Fishwick (Bowling Green 1978), 57–65; K.S. Inglis, 'The Homecoming: The War Memorial Movement in Cambridge, England,' *Journal of Contemporary History,* 27 (1992), 583–605, Barry Schwartz, 'The Social Context of Commemoration: A Study in Collective Memory,' *Social Forces,* 61 (1982), 374–402; Daniel Sherman, 'The Nation: In What Community? The Politics of Commemoration in Postwar France,' in *Ideas and Ideals: Essays on Politics in Honor of Stanley Hoffman,* ed. Linda B. Miller and Michael Joseph Smith (Boulder, Colorado 1993), 277–95.

4 Brantford *Expositor,* 13 Oct. 1886; Brantford *Courier,* 13 Oct. 1886

5 *Expositor,* 14 Oct. 1886

6 *Courier,* 14 Oct. 1886

7 Barbara Graymont, 'Thayendanegea,' *DCB,* vol. 5, 803–11

8 William L. Stone, *Life of Joseph Brant – Thayendanegea,* vol. II (Cooperstown, New York 1845), 523–6

9 Ibid., vol. I, xvii–xxix

10 Ibid., vol. II, 489–98

11 Berkhoffer, *The Whiteman's Indian,* 86–9

12 Kecheahgahemequa, *The Life of Captain Joseph Brant (Thayendanegea): An Account of His Reinterment at Mohawk, 1850, and of the Corner Stone Ceremony in the Erection of the Brant Memorial, 1886* (Brantford n.d.), 29–34

13 Cleghorn was born in Edinburgh, Scotland in 1822. His family emigrated to Montreal in 1832. He served as director of the Buffalo and Lake Huron Rail-

way, chair of the Board of License Commissioners, chair of the Board of Public School Trustees, and president of the St Andrew's Society; *Expositor*, 13 Oct. 1886.

14 The divisions among the Six Nations at Grand River are described by Sally Weaver in 'Six Nations of the Grand River, Ontario,' *Handbook of North American Indians: The North East* (Washington 1978), 528–34.

15 F. Douglas Reville, *History of the County of Brant* (Brantford 1920), 53

16 *Expositor*, 19 April 1876, 27 April 1876

17 Ibid., 13 Aug. 1877

18 Ibid., 4 Sept. 1877

19 Ibid., 5 March 1883

20 On boosterism and urban reform in the late nineteenth-century see: Alan F.J. Artibise, 'Boosterism in the Development of Prairie Cities, 1867–1913,' in *Town and City: Aspects of Western Canadian Urban Development* (Regina 1981), 209–35; Paul-Andre Linteau, *The Promoters City: Building the Industrial Town of Maisonneuve, 1883–1918* (Toronto 1985); Paul Rutherford, 'Tomorrow's Metropolis: The Urban Reform Movement in Canada, 1880–1920,' Canadian Historical Association, *Historical Papers* (1971), 203–24; W. van Nus, 'The Fate of City Beautiful Thought in Canada, 1893–1930,' in *The Canadian City: Essays in Urban History*, ed. Gilbert Stelter and Alan F.J. Artibise (Toronto 1977), 162–85; John C. Weaver, 'Elitism and the Corporate Ideal: Businessmen and Boosters in Canadian Civic Reform, 1890–1920,' in *Cities in the West*, ed. A.R. McCormack and Ian Macpherson (Ottawa 1975), 48–73.

21 *History of the County of Brant* (Toronto 1883), 144; C.M. Johnston, *Brant County: A History, 1784–1945* (Toronto 1967), 100

22 *Expositor*, 5 March 1883

23 Ibid., 13 Oct. 1886

24 On the ambivalent views of Native peoples at the end of the nineteenth-century see Berkhoffer, *The Whiteman's Indian*, and Daniel Francis, *The Imaginary Indian*.

25 *Expositor*, 12 Aug. 1886

26 Johnston, *Brant County*, 100.

27 Chief John Buck, *Expositor*, 12 Aug. 1886

28 Ontario Historical Society, *Annual Report* (Toronto 1911), 44–7

29 UELO, *Transactions* (1904–13), 61 The First World War significantly changed Lofts views. Serving in an Indian unit of the Canadian army, Loft met with Natives from across the country and became acquainted with their problems and grievances. Following the war, Loft emerged as one of the nation's leading advocates for Native rights and was elected the first president of the Indian League of Canada.

30 On the process of racialization see Kay J. Anderson, *Vancouver's Chinatown: Racial Discourse in Canada, 1875–1980* (Montreal and Kingston 1991), chap. 1.

31 See: Carol Lee Bacchi, *Liberation Deferred: The Ideas of the English-Canadian Suffragists, 1877–1918* (Toronto 1983); Veronica Strong-Boag, *The Parliament of Women: The National Council of Women of Canada, 1893–1929* (Ottawa 1976).

32 Mary A. Fitzgibbon, 'A Historic Banner,' Women's Canadian Historical Society of Toronto, *Transaction*, 1 (1896), 3

33 The significance of Laura Secord's warning to Fitzgibbon has been the subject of considerable debate. In *The Story of Laura Secord: A Study in Historical Evidence* (Toronto 1932), William Stewart Wallace concluded that Laura's exploits were largely 'myth' and that her actions 'played no part in determining the issue of the Battle of Beaver Dams' (23). George Ingram concluded that the 'debunking' had gone too far, in 'The Story of Laura Secord Revisited,' *Ontario History*, 57 (1965), 87–97. Ruth Mckenzie went even further in restoring Secord's place in history in *Laura Secord: The Legend and the Lady* (Toronto and Montreal 1971).

34 Both documents are reproduced by Ingram in 'Laura Secord Revisited,' 96–7

35 Ibid., 90–7

36 Toronto, *Church*, 18 April 1845; Mackenzie, *Laura Secord*, 89–90

37 Gilbert Auchinleck, 'History of the War of 1812,' *Anglo-American Magazine*, 5 (Nov. 1853), 467. Auchinleck's serialized treatment of the war was published in 1855 as *A History of the War of 1812 between Great Britain and the United States of America during the Years 1812, 1813, 1814* (Toronto).

38 The *Niagara Mail* recounted the story of Laura Secord's efforts to have her signature included on the address in its editions of 27 March 1861 and 3 April 1861.

39 Coffin, *1812*, 147–9. Among the later writers who drew heavily upon Coffin's account were Sarah Curzon, Ernest Cruikshank, and Emma Currie.

40 Sarah was born near Birmingham, England, in 1833. She married Robert Curzon in 1858 and emigrated with him to Canada in 1862; Morgan, *Canadian Men and Women*, 235–6.

41 Sarah Anne Curzon, *Laura Secord, The Heroine of 1812: A Drama and Other Poems* (Toronto 1887), 23, 8–9. A similar argument on the symbolic force of Laura Secord is presented by Cecilia Morgan in '"Of Slender Frame and Delicate Appearance": The Placing of Laura Secord in the Narratives of Canadian Loyalist History,' *Journal of the Canadian Historical Association*, 5 (1994), 195–212.

42 Curzon, *Heroine of 1812*, 9

43 *Mail*, 26 July 1887; *World*, 26 July 1887

44 Sarah Anne Curzon, *The Story of Laura Secord, 1813* (Toronto 1891), 14

45 Janet Carnochan, 'Laura Secord Monument at Lundy's Lane,' Niagara Historical Society, *Transactions*, (1913), 12

46 *Constitution and By-Laws of the Women's Canadian Historical Society of Toronto* (Toronto: 1896), 2; Sarah Anne Curzon, 'Historical Societies,' Wentworth Historical Society, *Journals and Transactions*, 1 (1892), 106

47 Laura's heroism was celebrated in verse by Agnes Machar in 'Laura Secord.' The poem was included in *Lays of the True North and Other Poems* published in 1887. Mary Fitzgibbon lauded Secord's exploits in *A Veteran of 1812* (Toronto: 1895), a biography of her grandfather, Colonel James Fitzgibbon. Matilda Edgar devoted considerable attention to Laura in *Ten Years of Upper Canada in Peace and War, 1805–1815* (Toronto, 1895).

48 Carnochan, 'Laura Secord Monument at Lundy's Lane,' 12–13

49 Ontario Historical Society, *Annual Report* (1900), 54

50 *Globe*, n.d. in UELATB Scrapbook.

51 Ontario Historical Society, *Annual Report* (1901), 52

52 The line is from a sonnet composed for the occasion by Janet Carnochan, 'Laura Secord Monument at Lundy's Lane,' 14.

53 Ibid., 14–16; *Globe*, 24 June 1901

54 UELATB, Copy of a Resolution of the United Empire Loyalists Association of Ontario re: Laura Secord Monument, Miscellaneous Material, Box 2

55 R.E.A. Land, *A National Monument to Laura Secord: Why It Should Be Erected. An Appeal to the People of Canada from the Laura Secord National Monument Committee* (Toronto 1901)

56 Emma Currie, *The Story of Laura Secord and Canadian Reminiscences* (Toronto 1900), 1

57 *Globe*, 6 July 1911

58 *Christian Guardian*, 4 Aug. 1909

59 Ibid.

60 *Christian Guardian*, 25 May 1859

61 Ibid.

62 The correspondence was reproduced by John Carroll in a lengthy article outlining the history of the controversy which appeared in the *Christian Guardian* of 25 May 1859.

63 Ibid., 13 July 1859

64 Ibid., 2 April 1862

65 Abel Stevens, *The Women of Methodism: Its Three Foundresses, Susanna Wesley, the Countess of Huntingdon, and Barbara Heck; with Sketches of Their Female Associates and Successors in the Early History of the Denomination* (New York 1866), 175–6

66 'Brief Sketch of the American Ladie's Centenary Movement,' in Stevens, *Women of Methodism*, 301

67 Louise Queen, 'The Centennial of American Methodism,' *Methodist History*, 4 (Jan. 1966), 44 Nancy Hardesty effectively demonstrates the close relationship between nineteenth-century feminism in the United States and the evangelical tradition in *Women Called to Witness: Evangelical Feminism in the 19th Century* (Nashville 1984).

68 William Withrow, *Barbara Heck: A Tale of Early Methodism* (Toronto 1895), 59–63

69 A. Brian McKillop, 'Canadian Methodism in 1884,' *Canadian Methodist Historical Society Papers*, 4 (1984), 5–6

70 Egerton Ryerson, 'Loyal Origin of Canadian Methodism,' In *Canadian Methodism: Its Epochs and Characteristics* (Toronto 1882), 1–14

71 UCA, 'Barbara Heck Memorial' (1897), 'To the Women of Methodism' (1897), Barbara Heck Biography File

72 *Christian Guardian*, 4 Aug. 1909

73 Ruth Compton Brouwer, 'The Canadian Methodist Church and Ecclesiastical Suffrage for Women, 1902–1914,' *Canadian Methodist Historical Society Papers*, 2 (1980), 4

74 *Christian Guardian*, 10 Aug. 1904, 26 Feb. 1908

75 'Address to the Lieutenant Governor,' United Empire Loyalist Association of Canada, *Transactions* (1917–26), 164

76 The statue was erected by Mr and Mrs Stanley Mills of Hamilton; Hamilton *Spectator*, 24 May 1929.

7: The United Empire Loyalist Association of Ontario, 1896–1914

1 UELATB, William Hamilton Merritt to George Sterling Ryerson, 12 May 1896, Box 1

2 Wallace Evan Davies, *Patriotism on Parade: The Story of Veterans' and Hereditary Organizations in America, 1783–1900* (Cambridge 1955), chap. 3

3 The United Empire Loyalist Association of Nova Scotia was not formed until 11 May 1897.

4 George Sterling Ryerson, *Looking Backward* (Toronto 1924), 153

5 Toronto *Empire*, 1 Oct. 1894

6 UELATB, Margaret Clarkson to E.M. Chadwick, 18 Jan. 1898, Box 1

7 AO, Administrative and Historical Records of the Governor Simcoe Branch of the United Empire Loyalist Association of Canada, 1897–1980, 'The United Empire Loyalist Association of Ontario, Constitution and By-Laws, 1897'

8 AO, Administrative and Historical Records of the Governor Simcoe Branch of

the United Empire Loyalist Association of Canada, 1897–1980, 'United Empire Loyalists Association of Ontario. Revised Constitution and By-Laws. Adapted April 14th, 1898'

9 UELO, *Transactions* (1901–2), 135

10 Morgan, *Canadian Men and Woman*, 648

11 Ibid., 1013–14

12 UELO, *Transactions* (1903–4), 87–8

13 Ibid., (1900), 20

14 Morgan, Canadian Men and Women, 255

15 UELATB, Margaret Clarkson to E.M. Chadwick, 15 March 1898, Box 1

16 Ibid., n.d.

17 UELATB, George Sterling Ryerson to E.M. Chadwick, 17 Jan. 1898, Box 1.

18 *Globe*, 11 March 1898

19 Ibid.

20 AO, Administrative and Historical Records of the Governor Simcoe Branch of the United Empire Loyalist Association of Canada, 1897–1980, 'The United Empire Loyalists Association of Ontario, Constitution and By-Laws, 1897'

21 'Constitution and By-Laws,' UELO, *Transactions* (1901–02), 13

22 William Hamilton Merritt's great-grandfather Thomas Merritt remained a resident of New York until 1796.

23 UELO, *Transactions* (1898), 5

24 *Globe*, 10 Oct. 1900

25 UELO, *Transactions* (1903–4), 20–1; (1904–13), 28–9

26 Ibid., (1898), 5

27 Ibid., (1901–2), 12–13

28 Ibid.

29 PAC, Denison Papers, Lord Grey to George Taylor Denison, 22 Feb. 1907; George Taylor Denison to Lord Grey, 25 Feb. 1907

30 UELATB, R.E.A. Land to George Taylor Denison, 14 March 1898, Box 1

31 UELO, *Transactions* (1901–2), 28–9

32 HPL, United Empire Loyalist Association of Ontario, Head-of-the-Lake Branch, *Transactions* (1901–2), (1903–4)

33 UELATB, W.E. Tisdale to Margaret Clarkson, 27 April 1907, Box 1

34 *Globe*, 9 March 1900

35 UELO, *Transactions* (1899), 17

36 Edward Marion Chadwick, *The People of the Longhouse* (Toronto 1897), 148–52

37 See, for example, W. Napier Keefer, 'Some Incidents in the Life of an Early Settler in the Niagara Frontier,' UELO, *Transactions* (1899), 40–59; D.B. Read, 'A Glance at the Early Canadians,' ibid. (1901–2), 47–57.

38 Ibid. (1900), 46–7
39 UELATB, Scrapbook, unidentified newspaper clipping
40 UELO, *Transactions* (1899), 40–1
41 Colin Snider, 'The Past and Present of the Six Nations Iroquois,' ibid. (1903–4), 27–33
42 UELATB, Frank Keefer to George Sterling Ryerson, 30 June 1914; Frank Keefer to Helen Merrill, 30 June 1914, Box 1
43 UELO, *Transactions*, (1900), 52
44 See, for example, Mary Dunn, 'A Sketch of Some of the Secords from 1775 until 1866,' ibid., (1899), 97–103; Sophia Rowe, 'Memoir of Captain Samual Anderson,' ibid., 85–8; Mrs Morden, *U.E. Loyalist Women: An Address delivered before the General Brock Lodge Daughters of the Empire, by Mrs. Morden, Brockville, October 21st, 1902* (Brockville 1902); Mary A. Fitzgibbon, 'A Historic Banner,' 1–5
45 See: Appendix V.
46 See: Appendices III and IV.
47 Richard Hofstadter, *The Age of Reform: From Bryan to FDR* (New York 1955), chap. 4
48 Berger, *The Sense of Power*, 85–6
49 *Globe*, 21 Nov. 1896
50 Gidney and Millar, *Professional Gentlemen*, 203–4. On the changing role and definition of the middle class in the nineteenth-century also see Stuart Blumin, *The Emergence of the Middle Class: Social Experience in the American City, 1760–1910* (Cambridge 1989); John Gilkeson, *Middle Class Providence: 1820–1940* (Princeton 1986); Mary Ryan, *Cradle of the Middle Class: The Family in Oneida County, New York, 1790–1865* (Cambridge 1981) and Robert H. Weibe, *The Search for Order, 1877–1920* (New York 1967).
51 Harold Perkin, *The Rise of Professional Society: England since 1880* (London and New York: Routledge, 1989), 4–6
52 Bliss, *A Living Profit*, 116–17
53 Gidney and Millar, *Professional Gentlemen*, 281–7
54 Perkins, *Rise of Professional Society*, 27–9
55 UELATB, 'Petition to the Queen's Most Excellent Majesty,' Box 2
56 Ryerson, *Looking Backward*, 154
57 PAC, Laurier Papers, David Erskine to Wilfrid Laurier, 22 Nov. 1897, vol. 57, 18159–60
58 Ryerson, *Looking Backward*, 155
59 *Globe*, 10 Oct. 1900
60 UELO, *Transactions* (1901–2), 19
61 Ibid., 22–9

62 *Globe*, 10 Nov. 1898; UELO, *Transactions* (1899), 18

63 *Mail*, Oct. 1898, in UELATB Scrapbook

64 *Globe*, 4 May 1901

65 Quebec *Daily Mercury*, 18 May 1901, in UELATB Scrapbook

66 UELATB, E.F. Clarke to E.M. Chadwick, 19 Feb. 1902; E.M. Chadwick to E.F. Clarke, 25 Feb. 1902; E.F. Clarke to E.M. Chadwick, 17 March 1902; E.M. Chadwick to E.F. Clarke, 2 May 1902; Box 1. House of Commons *Debates*, 2nd session, 9th Parliament, vol. xxxv, 138–9

67 UELO, *Transactions* (1903–4), 22

68 UELATB, E.M. Chadwick to A.E. Kemp, 22 Jan. 1906, Box 1. See also H.H. Robertson to E.M. Chadwick, 7 Dec. 1905, E.M. Chadwick to H.H. Robertson, 8 Dec. 1905

69 UELATB, 'The Petition of the United Empire Loyalists' Association of Ontario to the Right Honorable, the Earl Grey, G.C.M.G., the Governor General of Canada,' Box 1

70 UELO, *Transactions* (1904–13), 24

71 UELATB, William Hearst to Helen Merrill, 2 Nov. 1912, Box 1

72 Killan, *Preserving Ontario's Heritage*, 77–81

73 John Stewart Carstairs, 'The Late Loyalist of Upper Canada,' UELO, *Transactions* (1901–2), 110, 112–13, 122

74 UELATB, E.M. Chadwick to R.E.A. Land, 3 Dec. 1901; R.E.A. Land to E.M. Chadwick, 5 Jan. 1902; E.M. Chadwick to R.E.A. Land, 6 Feb. 1902; Box 1

75 *Globe*, 12 March 1897

76 UELO, *Transactions* (1899), 20–2

77 *Mail*, 19 May 1900, in UELATB Scrapbook

78 Ibid., 18 Feb. 1905

79 UELO, *Transactions* (1901–2), 26–9

80 William Kirby, *Annals of Niagara* (Toronto 1927), 119

81 UELATB, George A. Bull to E.M. Chadwick, 18 May 1900, Box 1

82 UELATB, Janet Carnochan to E.M. Chadwick, 21 May 1900, Box 1

83 UELATB, J.G. Currie to E.M. Chadwick, 16 May 1900, Box 1

84 UELATB, E.M. Chadwick to R.E.A. Land, 25 May 1900, Box 1

85 UELATB, 'To the Honourable the Minister of Militia the Memorial of the United Empire Loyalists' Association of Ontario,' Box 1

86 UELATB, E.M. Chadwick to R.E.A. Land, 5 Dec. 1901, Box 1; 'An Act for the preservation of Butler's Burying Ground at Niagara-on-the-Lake,' (1901), Box 2

87 UELATB, E.M. Chadwick to the Hon. J.O. Reaume, 20 March 1907, Box 1

88 UELATB, E.M. Chadwick to J.W. Langmuir, 22 May 1907, Box 1

89 Ibid., 16 June 1909, Box 1

90 Alexander Fraser, ed., *Brock Centenary, 1812–1912. Account of the Celebration at Queenston Heights, Ontario, on the 12th October, 1912* (Toronto 1913), 21

91 Fraser, *Brock Centenary*, 25–7

92 Ibid., 45–8

Conclusion

1 On the eclipse of imperial and anti-American sentiment following the First World War see Brown and Cook, *Canada 1896–1921*, chap. 14

2 J.M. Bumsted, *Understanding the Loyalists* (Sackville 1986), 17

3 Kammen, *Mystic Chords of Memory*, 285

4 Burt, *The Old Province of Quebec*, vol. II, chap. 15; George Wrong, *Canada and the American Revolution* (New York 1935), 476–8 and 'The Background of the Loyalist Movement, 1763–1783,' Ontario Historical Society, *Papers and Records*, 30 (1934), 171–80

5 R.O. MacFarlane, 'The Loyalist Migrations: A Social and Economic Movement,' in *Manitoba Essays. Written in Commemoration of the Sixtieth Anniversary of the University of Manitoba*, ed. R.C. Lodge (Toronto 1937), 106–7

6 On the rise of mass culture see Maria Tippet, *Making Culture: English-Canadian Institutions and the Arts before the Massey Commission* (Toronto 1990). On tourism see Patricia Jasen, *Wild Things: Nature, Culture, and Tourism in Ontario, 1790–1914* (Toronto 1995); John A. Jakle, *The Tourist: Travel in Twentieth-Century North America* (Lincoln 1985); Ian McKay, 'Among the Fisherfolk: J.F.B. Livesay and the Invention of Peggy's Cove,' *Journal of Canadian Studies*, 23 (1988), 23–45, and 'Tartansim Triumphant: The Construction of Scottishness in Nova Scotia, 1933–1954,' *Acadiensis*, 21 (1992), 5–47.

7 The scrapbooks of the Governor Simcoe Branch of the United Empire Loyalist Association at the Archives of Ontario contain a thorough collection of newspaper articles that detail the association's ongoing activities.

8 Kammen, *Mystic Chords of Memory*, chap. 10

9 AO, Scrapbook, Governor Simcoe Branch United Empire Loyalist Association

10 On the impact of the Massey report see Taylor, *Negotiating the Past*, 131–41

11 Toronto, *Globe and Mail*, 12 June 1984, 23 June 1984

12 *Globe and Mail*, 6 Oct. 1983, 12 Jan. 1984; Toronto *Star*, 8 Jan. 1984

13 Wilson, *As She Began*, 10. Also see Phyliss R. Blakely and John N. Grant, eds, *Eleven Exiles: Accounts of Loyalists of the American Revolution* (Toronto 1982); Wallace Brown and Hereward Senior, *Victorious in Defeat: The Loyalists in Canada* (Toronto 1984); Joan Magee, ed., *Loyalist Mosaic: A Multi-Ethnic Heritage* (Toronto 1984).

Select Bibliography

I. PRIMARY SOURCES

Government Documents

Canada, Assembly, *Journals and Proceedings*, 1841–67
– Assembly, *Report on a System of Public Elementary Instruction for Upper Canada*, 1846
– House of Commons, *Debates*, 1884–1918
– *Manuscript Census*, 1881. District 117, Lennox, b township of Adolphustown and e township of North Fredericksburgh
Lennox and Addington, County Council, *Minutes*, 1884
Toronto, City Council, *Minutes*, 1882–4
Upper Canada, Assembly, *Journals and Proceedings*, 1791–1840
Lincoln, County Council, *Minutes*, 1884

Manuscript Collections

Archives of Ontario
A.C. Belcher Papers
William Canniff Papers
Edgar Family Papers
Fessenden Family Papers
W.A. Foster Papers
A. Maclean Howard Papers
William Kirby Collection
John A. Macdonald Papers
Lundy's Lane Historical Society Records
Merritt Family Papers

Niagara Historical Society Collection
Pamphlet Collection
T.C. Patteson Papers
Tweedsmuir Histories, Adolphustown
Roaf Family Papers
Administrative and Historical Records of the Governor Simcoe Branch of the
    United Empire Loyalist Association of Canada, 1897–1980

Diocese of Ontario Archives
Adolphustown Vestry, *Minute Book*, 1863–1959
Bay of Quinte Clerical Union, *Minute Book*, 1863–1959
Rev. R.S. Forneri, Scrapbook, 1883–92
Canon A.S. Spenser, *Letterbook*, 1884–5

Hamilton Public Library
Hamilton Branch, United Empire Loyalist Association of Canada, Archives,
    Inventories, Calendars
Wentworth Historical Society Records

Lennox and Addington County Museum
T.W. Casey Papers
Lennox and Addington Historical Society Collection

Loyalist Museum, Adolphustown
Bay of Quinte Branch, United Empire Loyalist Association of Canada, Papers and
    Records

Metropolitan Toronto Reference Library
Broadside Collection
Denison Family Papers
Henry Scadding Papers
Toronto Public Library Scrapbooks

National Archives of Canada
Wilfrid Campbell Papers
George Coventry Papers
E.A. Cruikshank Papers
Colonel George Taylor Denison Papers
Edward Farrer Papers
Grey of Howick Papers

Wilfrid Laurier Papers
J.P. Merritt Papers
Henry Morgan Papers
George Parkin Papers
Samuel Rawson Papers

Ontario Institute for Studies in Education
Textbook Collection

Queen's University Archives
H.C. Burleigh Papers
Cartwright Family Papers
Fairfield Family Papers
United Empire Loyalist Park Scrapbook

Regional Room, University of Western Ontario
J.H. Coyne Papers

United Church of Canada Archives
Paul and Barbara Heck Files
Egerton Ryerson Papers

United Empire Loyalist Association of Canada Archives
Administrative Records

United Empire Loyalist Association, Toronto Branch Archives
Correspondence, 1896–1934
Minutes, 1896–1934
Miscellaneous Papers, 1896–1934
Scrapbook, 1896–1931

Printed Works

Adams, Charles Kendall. 'Some Neglected Aspects of the Revolutionary War.'
    Atlantic Monthly, 82 (Aug. 1898), 174–89.
Adam, G. Mercer, and W.J. Robertson. *Public School History of England and Canada*.
    Toronto: Copp Clark, 1886.
Auchinleck, Gilbert. *A History of the War between Great Britain and the United States of
    America during the Years 1812, 1813, 1814*. Toronto: Maclean, 1855.

Bangs, Nathan. *A History of the Methodist Episcopal Church*. 3rd ed. New York: Carlton and Phillips, 1853.

Barker, John S. 'A Brief History of David Barker, A United Empire Loyalist.' Ontario Historical Society, *Papers and Records*, 3 (1901), 169–70.

Bourinot, Sir John. 'United Empire Loyalists of Canada,' *Acta Victoriana*, 23 (1899), 127–43.

Brant-Sero, J. 'The Six Nations Indians in the Province of Ontario, Canada.' Wentworth Historical Society, *Journals and Transactions*, 2 (1899), 62–73.

– 'Some Descendants of Joseph Brant.' Ontario Historical Society, *Papers and Records*, 1 (1899), 113–17.

The Canadian Biographical Dictionary and Portrait Gallery of Eminent and Self-made Men. Toronto: H.C. Cooper, Jr, 1880.

Canniff, William. *History of the Settlement of Upper Canada with special reference to the Bay of Quinté*. Toronto: Dudley and Burns, 1869.

– *Canadian Nationality: Its Growth and Development*. Toronto: Hart and Rawlinson, 1875.

Carnochan, Janet. 'Monuments.' Niagara Historical Society, *Transactions*, 4 (1898), 24–9.

– 'Laura Secord Monument at Lundy's Lane.' Niagara Historical Society, *Transactions*, 25 (1913), 12–3.

– *History of Niagara*. Toronto: William Briggs, 1914.

Carter, J. Smyth. *The Story of Dundas; being a History of the County from 1784 to 1904*. Iroquois: St Lawrence News, 1905.

Casey, T.W.C. *Adolphustown Ramblings*. Kingston: British Whig, 1896.

– 'The Adolphustown U.E.L. Burying Ground.' Lennox and Addington Historical Society, *Papers and Records*, 3 (1911), 44–9.

Casselman, Alexander Clark. *The United Empire Loyalists of Dundas, Ontario*. Toronto: privately printed, 1901.

Centennial of the Province of Upper Canada, 1792–1892: Proceedings at the Gathering held at Niagara-on-the-Lake, July 16, 1892 and also the Proceedings at the Meeting held in front of the New Parliament Buildings, Toronto, September 17, 1892. Toronto: Arbuthnot and Adamson, 1893.

The Centennial of the Settlement of Upper Canada by the United Empire Loyalists, 1774–1884: The Celebrations at Adolphustown, Toronto, and Niagara. Toronto: Rose, 1885; Rpt Boston: 1972.

Chadwick, Edward Marion. *Ontarian Families: Genealogies of United Empire Loyalist and Other Pioneer Families of Upper Canada*. Toronto: Rolph and Smith, 1894.

– *The People of the Longhouse*. Toronto: Church of England Publishing, 1897.

Charlesworth, Hector. *A Cyclopedia of Canadian Biography.* Toronto: Hunter-Rose, 1919.

Clement, W.H.P. *The History of the Dominion of Canada.* Toronto: William Briggs, 1897.

Clendennan, D.W. 'Some Presbyterian U.E. Loyalists.' Ontario Historical Society, *Papers and Records,* 3 (1901).

Cochrane, W. *The Canadian Album. Men of Canada; or Success by Example in Religion, Patriotism, Business, Law, Medicine, Education and Agriculture.* Brantford: Bradley-Garretson, 1891.

Coffin, William F. *1812: The War and Its Moral. A Canadian Chronicle.* Montreal: John Lovell, 1864.

Commemorative and Biographical Record of the County of York, Ontario. Toronto: Beers, 1907.

Coyne, James. 'Memorial to the U.E. Loyalists.' Niagara Historical Society, *Transactions,* 4 (1898), 1–10.

Croil, James. *Dundas or A Sketch of Canadian History ...* Montreal: B. Dawson and Sons, 1861.

Cruikshank, Ernest, ed. *The Settlement of the United Empire Loyalists on the Upper St. Lawrence and Bay of Quinte in 1784.* Toronto: Ontario Historical Society, 1934.

Cumberland, Robert W. *The United Empire Loyalist Settlements between Kingston and Adolphustown.* Kingston: Jackson Press, 1923.

Currie, Emma A. *The Story of Laura Secord and Canadian Reminiscences.* Toronto: William Briggs, 1900.

Curzon, Sarah Anne. *Laura Secord, the Heroine of 1812: A Drama and Other Poems.* Toronto: C. Blankett Robinson, 1887.

– *Canada in Memoriam, 1812–14: Her Duty in the Erection of Monuments in Memory of Her Distinguished Sons and Daughters.* Welland: Telegraph, 1891.

– *The Story of Laura Secord, 1813.* Toronto: Williamson, 1891.

– 'Historical Societies,' Wentworth Historical Society, *Journals and Transactions,* 1 (1892), 106–14.

Davidson, John. 'The Loyalist Tradition in Canada.' *Macmillan's Magazine* (Sept. 1904), 390–400.

Davis, A.R. *The Old Loyalist: A Story of United Empire Loyalist Descendants in Canada.* Toronto: William Briggs, 1908.

Denison, George Taylor. 'The United Empire Loyalists and Their Influence Upon the History of this Continent.' Royal Society of Canada, *Proceedings and Transactions,* 31 (1905).

– *The Struggle for Imperial Unity: Recollections and Experiences.* Toronto: Macmillan, 1909.

Dent, J.C. *The Canadian Portrait Gallery.* 4 vols. Toronto: J.B. Magurn, 1880.

Duncan, David M. *The Story of the Canadian People.* Toronto: George N. Morang, 1907.

Ellis, George E. 'The Loyalists and Their Fortunes.' In *Narrative and Critical History of America,* vol. VII, ed. Justin Winsor. Boston and New York: Houghton, Mifflin, 1888.

Evans, W. Sanford. 'Empire Day: A Detailed History of Its Origin and Inception.' *Canadian Magazine,* 13 (1899).

Fessenden, Clementina. *The Genesis of Empire Day.* Hamilton: George B. Midgley, 1910.

Fessenden, Rev. E.J. *Upper Canada: A Centenary Study. A Paper Read before the Lundy's Lane Historical Society.* Welland, Ontario: Tribune, 1892.

– 'The United Empire Loyalists of the 18th Century and Imperialist Federation.' Wentworth Historical Society, *Journals and Transactions,* 1 (1892), 85–105.

Fisher, Sydney George. 'The Legendary and Myth-making Process in Histories of the American Revolution.' *Proceedings of the American Philosophical Society,* 51 (April–June 1912), 53–75.

– *The True History of the American Revolution.* Philadelphia: J.B.Lippincott, 1902.

Flick, Alexander Clarence. *Loyalism in New York during the American Revolution.* New York: Columbia University Press, 1901.

Forneri, Rev. R.S. *The United Empire Loyalists of Canada. A Sermon by the Reverend R.S. Forneri, B.D., rector of Adolphustown, preached at St. George's Cathedral, Kingston, Ontario, Sunday May 18th, 1884.* Kingston: Daily News, 1884.

– *The United Empire Loyalists and the Memorial Church, Adolphustown, Ontario. A Sketch by the Rev. R.S. Forneri.* Belleville: Intelligencer, 1888.

Forsyth, Frederic Gregory. *Memorial of the De Forsyths de Fronsac.* Boston: Rockwell and Churchill, 1897.

– *Rise of the United Empire Loyalists: A Sketch of American History.* Kingston: British Whig, 1906.

Foster, William. *Canada First, or Our New Nationality: An Address by the late W.A. Foster, Esq., Q.C.* Toronto: William Briggs, 1888.

Fraser, Alexander. *Second Report of the Bureau of Archives for the Province of Ontario, 1904.* Toronto: King's Printer, 1905.

– *A History of Ontario: Its Resources and Development.* Toronto: Canada History, 1907.

– ed. *Brock Centenary, 1812–1912. Account of the Celebration at Queenston Heights, Ontario on the 12th October 1912.* Toronto: William Briggs, 1913.

Grant, W.L. *Ontario High School History of Canada.* Toronto: T. Eaton, 1914.

Griffen, George D. 'The U.E. Loyalists in 1837.' Wentworth Historical Society, *Journals and Transactions,* 3 (1920), 13–18.

Griffen, Justus A. *The United Empire Loyalists.* Hamilton: n.p., 1865.

Haight, Canniff. *Country Life in Canada Fifty Years Ago: Personal Recollections and Reminiscences of a Sexagenarian.* Toronto: Hunter, Rose, 1885.

– *A United Empire Loyalist in Great Britain: Here and There in the Home Land.* Toronto: William Briggs, 1895.

– *Before the Coming of the Loyalists.* Toronto: Haight, 1897.

– *Coming of the Loyalists.* Toronto: Haight, 1899.

– *A Genealogical Narrative of the Daniel Haight Family by his Grandson Canniff Haight.* Toronto: Rowsell and Hutchinson, 1899.

Harris, Edward. *History and Historiettes: United Empire Loyalists.* Toronto: William Briggs, 1897.

Hayden, Andrew. *Pioneer Sketches of the District of Bathurst.* Toronto: Ryerson Press, 1925.

Herrington, W.S. *Heroines of Canadian History.* Toronto: William Briggs, 1910.

– *History of the County of Lennox and Addington.* Toronto: Macmillan, 1913.

– *Pioneer Life among the Loyalists in Upper Canada.* Toronto: Macmillan, 1915.

History of the County of Brant, Ontario. Toronto: Beers, 1883.

History of the County of Welland, Ontario. Its Past and Present. Welland: Tribune, 1887.

History of Toronto and the County of York. Toronto: Beers, 1885.

Hodgins, J. George. *The Geography and History of British America and of the Other Colonies of the Empire.* Toronto: Maclear, 1857.

– *A History of Canada and of the Other British Provinces in North America.* Montreal: John Lovell, 1866.

Hopkins, J. Castell, ed. *Canada: An Encyclopedia of the Country.* Toronto: Linscott, 1898.

Hosmer, James K. *Samuel Adams.* Boston and New York: Houghton, Mifflin, 1899.

– *A Short History of Anglo-saxon Freedom: The Polity of the English-speaking Race.* New York: Charles Scribner and Sons, 1903.

Illustrated Historical Atlas of Frontenac, Lennox and Addington Counties, Ontario. Toronto: J.H. Meacham, 1878.

Jeffers, J. Frith. *History of Canada.* Toronto: Canada Publishing, 1881.

Johnston, Arthur. *Myths and Facts of the American Revolution: A Commentary on United States History as it is Written.* Toronto: William Briggs, 1908.

Kecheahgahmequa. *The Life of Captain Joseph Brant (Thayendanegea): An Account of His Reinterment at Mohawk, 1850, and of the Corner Stone Ceremony in the Erection of the Brant Memorial, 1886.* Brantford: B.H. Rothwell, n.d.

– *Sketch of the Life of Captain Joseph Brant, Thayendanegea.* Montreal: John Douglas and Son, 1872.

Kirby, William. *The U.E.: A Tale of Upper Canada. A Poem in XII Cantos.* Niagara-on-the-Lake: privately printed, 1859.

- 'United Empire Loyalists of Canada.' *Canadian Methodist Magazine,* 19, 20 (April, May 1884), 350–9, 426–33.
- *Annals of Niagara.* 1896; rpt Toronto: Macmillan, 1927.
- 'Memoirs of the Whitmore Family of Niagara.' Niagara Historical Society, *Papers and Records,* 8 (1901).
- *Reminiscences of a Visit to Quebec, July 1839.* Niagara-on-the-Lake: n.p., 1903.
Land, R.E.A. *A National Monument to Laura Secord: Why It Should Be Erected. An Appeal to the People of Canada from the Laura Secord National Monument Committee.* Toronto: Imrie, Graham and Co., 1901.
Macdonald, H.S. 'The U.E. Loyalists of the Old Johnstown District.' Ontario Historical Society, *Papers and Records,* 12 (1914), 13–31.
Macdonnell, J.A. *Sketches Illustrating the Early Settlement and History of Glengarry in Canada.* Montreal: Wm Foster, Brown, 1893.
McCollom, W.A. 'Family Memoirs of the McCollom Family, U.E. Loyalists.' Royal Society of Canada, *Proceedings and Transactions,* 8 (1902), 121–6.
McLeod, Donald. *A Brief Review of the Settlement of Upper Canada by the UE Loyalists.* Cleveland: F.B. Penneman, 1841.
McMullen, John Mercier. *The History of Canada from its Discovery to the Present Time.* Brockville, Ontario: McMullen, 1855.
Memoir of the Distinguished Mohawk Indian Chief, Sachem and Warrior, Capt. Joseph Brant ... Brantford: C.E. Stevens, 1872.
Merritt, Catherine Nina. *When George the III was King: An Historical Drama in III Acts.* Toronto: Rowsell and Hutchison, 1897.
Merritt, J.P. *Biography of the Hon. W.H. Merritt, M.P., of Lincoln District of Niagara, including an Account of the Origin, Progress and Completion of some of the Most Important Public Works in Canada.* St Catharines: M.S. Leavenworth, 1875.
Mickel, Sara. 'Some United Empire Loyalist Epitaphs.' Women's Canadian Historical Society of Toronto, *Transactions,* 5 (1905), 23–32.
Middleton, J.E. *The Municipality of Toronto: A History.* Toronto: Dominion, 1923.
Mikel, W.C. *Some Bay of Quinte Reminiscences: An Address Delivered before the United Empire Loyalist Association of Toronto, April 27, 1922.* Toronto: n.p., 1922.
Moodie, J.W. *Scenes and Adventures as a Soldier and Settler during half a century.* Montreal: John Lovell, 1866.
Morden, Mrs. *U.E. Loyalist Women: An Address delivered before the General Brock Lodge Daughters of the Empire, by Mrs. Morden, Brockville, October 21st, 1902.* Brockville, Ontario: H.S. Seaman, 1902.
Morgan, Henry James. *The Canadian Men and Women of the Time: A Handbook of Canadian Biography.* Toronto: William Briggs, 1898.
- *Types of Canadian Women and of Women who have been connected with Canada.* Toronto: William Briggs, 1903.

Mulvany, C. Pelham. *Toronto: Past and Present. A Handbook.* Toronto: W.E. Caigere,
1884.

Owen, E.A. *Pioneer Sketches of Long Point Settlement, or Norfolk's Foundation Builders
and their Family Genealogies.* Toronto: William Briggs, 1898.

Playter, George F. *The History of Methodism in Canada.* Toronto: Wesleyan Printing,
1862.

Powell, William Dummer. *Story of a Refugee.* York: Patriot, n.d.

Pringle, J.F. *Lunenburgh or the Old Eastern District.* 1890; rpt Belleville: Mika, 1972.

Read, D.B. *The Lieutenant Governors of Upper Canada and Ontario, 1792–1899.*
Toronto: William Briggs, 1900.

Roberts, Charles G.D. *A History of Canada.* Toronto: George N. Morang, 1897.

Robinson, C.W. *Life of Sir John Beverley Robinson Bart., C.B. D.C.L.: Chief Justice of
Upper Canada.* London: William Blackwood and Sons, 1904.

Robinson, John Beverley. *Canada and the Canada Bill: Being an
Examination of the Proposed Measure for the Future Government of Canada; with an
Introductory Chapter, Containing Some General Views Respecting the British Provinces
in North America.* London: Hatchard and Sons, 1840.

Rose, G.M., ed. *Cyclopedia of Canadian Biography: Being Chiefly Men of the Times.*
Toronto: Rose, 1886.

Ryerson, Egerton. *The Loyalists of America and Their Times from 1620–1816.* 2 vols.
Toronto: George N. Morang, 1880.

– *Canadian Methodism: Its Epochs and Characteristics.* Toronto: William Briggs,
1882.

– *The Story of My life; being Reminiscences of Sixty Years Public Service in Canada.*
Toronto: William Briggs, 1883.

Ryerson, George Sterling. *Looking Backward.* Toronto: Ryerson Press, 1924.

– *United Empire Loyalists: The Aftermath of Revolution.* Toronto: William Briggs,
1896.

Sabine, Lorenzo. 'Review of *A History of the Operations of a Partisan Corps Called the
Queen's Rangers, commanded by Lieut. Col. J.G. Simcoe, during the War of the American
Revolution,* by J.G. Simcoe.' *North American Review* (Oct. 1844), 261–302.

– 'British Colonial Politics.' *North American Review,* 126 (Jan. 1845), 85–126.

– 'British Colonial Politics.' *North American Review,* 140 (July 1848), 1–26.

– *Biographical Sketches of the Loyalists of the American Revolution.* 1864; rpt Westport
and London: Meckler, 1976.

Scadding, Henry. *Toronto: Past and Present, Historical and Descriptive A Memorial Volume for the Semi-centennial of 1884.* Toronto: Hunter and Rose, 1884.

– *Centennial of Upper Canada, Now the Province of Ontario: The Hundredth Anniversary
of the Establishment of the Representative System, July 16, 1792.* Toronto: The Week,
1892.

– *The Revived Significance of the Initials U.E.* Toronto: Copp Clark, 1892.

Scherck, Michael Gonder. *Pen Pictures of Early Life in Upper Canada.* Toronto: William Briggs, 1905.

Siebert, Wilbur. 'The Loyalists and Six Nations Indians in the Niagara Peninsula.' Royal Society of Canada, *Proceedings and Transactions*, 9 (1915), 79–128.

Sissons, C.B., ed. *My Dearest Sophie: Letters from Egerton Ryerson to his Daughter.* Toronto: Ryerson Press, 1955.

Smith, Goldwin. *Loyalty, Aristocracy and Jingoism: Three Lectures Delivered before the Young Men's Liberal Club, Toronto.* Toronto: Hunter, Rose, 1891.

– 'The Schism in the Anglo-saxon Race.' *Canadian Leaves: A Series of Papers read before the Canadian Club of New York.* ed. G.M. Fairchild, Jr, and Thomas Willing. New York: Napoleon Thompson, n.d.

Smith, W.L. *Pioneers of Old Ontario.* Toronto: George N. Morang, 1923.

Stark, James H. *The Loyalists of Massachusetts and the Other Side of the American Revolution.* Boston: W.B. Clarke, 1910.

Stevens, Abel. *The Women of Methodism: Its Three Foundresses, Susanna Wesley, the Countess of Huntingdon, and Barbara Heck; with Sketches of Their Female Associates and Successors in the Early History of the Denomination.* New York: Carlton and Porter, 1866.

Stone, William L. *Life of Joseph Brant – Thayendanegea.* 2 vols. Cooperstown, New York: H.E. Phinney, 1845.

Talman, J.J. *Loyalist Narratives from Upper Canada.* Toronto: Champlain Society, 1946.

Tasker, Lawrence Hemion. *The United Empire Loyalist Settlement at Long Point, Lake Erie.* Toronto: William Briggs, 1900.

Thomas, Charles. 'The Revolutionary War.' Brant Historical Society, *Papers and Records* (1908–11), 79–82.

Tippet, H. 'Story of a United Empire Loyalist.' Women's Canadian Historical Society of Toronto, *Transactions*, 4 (1912), 24–31.

Todd, Alpheus. 'Is Canadian Loyalty a Sentiment or a Principle?' *Canadian Monthly* (Nov. 1881), 523–30.

Tyler, Moses Coit. 'The Party of the Loyalists in the American Revolution.' *American Historical Review*, 1 (1895–6), 89–103.

– *The Literary History of the American Revolution, 1763–1783.* 2 vols. New York: 1897

Van Tyne, Claude. *The Loyalists in the American Revolution.* New York: Macmillan, 1902.

– *England and America: Rivals in the American Revolution.* Cambridge: Cambridge University Press, 1927.

United Empire Loyalist Association of Canada, *Annual Transactions*, 1914–27.

United Empire Loyalist Association of Ontario, *Annual Transactions*, 1897–1914.

Van Wart, Horace Hume. *A Brief Outline of the United Empire Loyalist Movement.* Toronto: United Empire Loyalist Association Press, 1914.

Wakeley, J.B. *Lost Chapters Recovered from the Early History of American Methodism.* New York: Carlton and Porter, 1858.

Wallace, William Stewart. *The United Empire Loyalists: A Chronicle of the Great Migration.* Toronto: Glasgow, Brook and Co., 1914.

Waterbury, W.B. 'Sketch of Peter Teeple, Loyalist and Pioneer, 1762–1847.' Ontario Historical Society, *Papers and Records,* 1 (1899), 123–31.

Withrow, William. *A History of Canada for the Use of Schools and General Readers.* Toronto: William Briggs, 1876.

– *Worthies of Early Methodism.* Toronto: Samuel Rose, 1878.

– 'The United Empire Loyalists.' *Pleasant Hours,* 4 (June 1884), 90–5.

– *Barbara Heck: A Tale of Early Methodism.* Toronto: William Briggs, 1895.

– *Makers of Methodism.* Toronto: William Briggs, 1898.

II. SECONDARY SOURCES

Articles

Abbott, Frank. 'Cold Cash and Ice Palaces: The Quebec Winter Carnival of 1894.' *Canadian Historical Review,* 69 (1988), 167–202.

Acheson, T.W. 'The Changing Social Origins of the Canadian Industrial Elite, 1880–1910.' *Business History Review,* 47 (1973), 189–217.

Artibise, Alan F.J. 'Boosterism in the Development of Prairie Cities, 1867–1913.' In *Town and City: Aspects of Western Canadian Urban Development.* Regina: Canadian Plains Research Centre, 1981.

Barkley, Murray. 'The Loyalist Tradition in New Brunswick: The Growth and Evolution of an Historical Myth, 1825–1914.' *Acadiensis,* 4 (Spring 1975), 3–45

– 'Prelude to Tradition: The Loyalist Revival in the Canadas, 1849–1867.' In *'None was ever better': The Loyalist Settlement of Ontario.* Proceedings of the Annual Meeting of the Ontario Historical Society, Cornwall, June 1984. Cornwall: Stormont, Dundas, and Glengarry Historical Society, 1984.

Bell, David V.J. 'The Loyalist Tradition in Canada.' *Journal of Canadian Studies,* 5 (1970), 22–33

Bowden, Bruce. 'The Bicentennial Legacy: A Second Loyalist Revival.' *Ontario History,* 77 (1985), 65–74

Brouwer, Ruth Compton. 'The Canadian Methodist Church and Ecclesiastical Suffrage for Women, 1902–1914.' *Canadian Historical Society Papers,* 2 (1980), 1–27

Brown, Lorne A. 'The Macdonald-Cartwright Struggle in Lennox, November 1783.' *Ontario History*, 61 (1969), 33–50

Bumsted, J.M. 'Loyalists and Nationalists: An Essay on the Problem of Definitions.' *Canadian Review of Studies in Nationalism*, 6 (1979), 218–32

Butler, Robert N. 'The Life Review: An Interpretation of Reminiscence in the Aged.' *Psychiatry: Journal for the Study of Interpersonal Processes*, 26 (1963), 65–76

Cannadine, David. 'The Transformation of Civic Ritual in Modern Britain: The Colchester Oyster Feast.' *Past and Present*, 94 (1982), 107–30.

Careless, J.M.S. 'The First Hurrah: Toronto's Semi-Centennial of 1884.' In *Forging a Consensus: Historical Essays on Toronto*, ed. Victor L. Russell. Toronto: University of Toronto Press, 1984.

Cheal, David J. 'Ontario Loyalism: A Socio-Religious Ideology in Decline.' *Canadian Ethnic Studies*, 13 (1981), 40–51

Cole, Douglas L. 'Canada's 'Nationalistic' Imperialists.' *Journal of Canadian Studies*, 5 (Aug. 1970), 44–9

Condon, Ann Gorman. 'Marching to a Different Drummer: The Political Philosophy of the American Loyalists.' In *Red, White, and True Blue: The Loyalists in the Revolution*, ed. Esmund Wright. New York: AMS Press, 1976.

Dick, Lyle. 'The Seven Oaks Incident and the Construction of a Historical Tradition, 1816 to 1970.' *Journal of the Canadian Historical Association*, 2 (1991), 91–113.

Duffy, Dennis. 'Upper Canadian Loyalism: What the Textbooks Tell.' *Journal of Canadian Studies*, 12 (1977), 17–26

Eadie, James A. 'The Federal Election in Lennox Riding and Its Aftermath, 1882–83: A Glimpse of Victorian Political Morality.' *Ontario History*, 76 (1984), 354–72

Eisenstadt, S.N. 'Some Observations on the Dynamics of Tradition.' *Comparative Studies in Society and History*, 11 (1969), 451–75

– 'Post-Traditional Societies and the Continuity and Reconstruction of Tradition.' *Daedelus*, 102 (Winter, 1973), 1–27

Fallis, Lawrence S., Jr. 'The Idea of Progress in the Province of Canada: A Study in the History of Ideas.' In *The Shield of Achilles: Aspects of Canada in the Victorian Age*, ed. W.L. Morton. Toronto: McClelland and Stewart, 1968.

Fellows, Jo-Ann. 'The Loyalist Myth in Canada.' Canadian Historical Association, *Historical Papers* (1971), 94–111

Goheen, Peter G. 'Symbols in the Streets: Parades in Victorian Urban-Canada.' *Urban History Review*, 18 (1990), 237–43

Hammerton, Elizabeth, and David Cannadine. 'Conflict and Consensus on a Ceremonial Occasion: The Diamond Jubilee in Cambridge in 1897.' *Historical Journal*, 24 (1981), 111–46.

Handler, Richard, and Jocelyn Linnekin. 'Tradition: Genuine and Spurious.' *Journal of American Folklore*, 97 (1984), 273–90.

Horowitz, Gad. 'Conservatism, Liberalism and Socialism in Canada: An Interpretation.' *Canadian Journal of Economics and Political Science*, 32 (1966), 147–71.

Howell, Colin. 'Reform and the Monopolistic Impulse: The Professionalization of Medicine in the Maritimes.' *Acadiensis*, 11 (Autumn 1981), 3–22.

Hus, W. van. 'The Fate of City Beautiful Thought in Canada, 1893–1930.' In *The Canadian City: Essays in Urban History*. Toronto: McClelland and Stewart, 1977.

Inglis, K.S. 'The Homecoming: The War Memorial Movement in Cambridge, England.' *Journal of Contemporary History*, 27 (1992), 583–605.

Ingram, George. 'The Story of Laura Secord Revisited.' *Ontario History*, 57 (1965), 85–97.

Jennings, Francis. 'Tribal Loyalty and Tribal Independence.' In *Red, White and True Blue: The Loyalists in the Revolution*, ed. Esmund Wright. New York: AMS Press, 1976.

Knowles, Norman. '"Shall we not raise there again but higher some pyramid piercing the skies": The Loyalist Tradition and the Adolphustown Centennial Celebrations of 1884.' *Ontario History*, 80 (1988), 5–30.

Labaree, Leonard Woods. 'The Nature of American Loyalism.' American Antiquarian Society, *Proceedings*, 54 (1944), 15–58.

MacFarlane, R.O. 'The Loyalist Migrations: A Social and Economic Movement.' In *Manitoba Essays: Written in Commemoration of the Sixtieth Anniversary of the University of Manitoba*. ed. R.C. Lodge. Toronto: Macmillan, 1937.

MacKirdy, K.A. 'The Loyalty Issue in the 1891 Federal Election Campaign and an Ironic Footnote.' *Ontario History*, 53 (1966) 143–54.

Mathews, Robin. 'Susanna Moodie, Pink Toryism and Nineteenth Century Ideas of Canadian Identity.' *Journal of Canadian Studies*, 10 (Aug. 1975), 3–15.

McCann, Phillip. 'Culture, State Formation and the Invention of Tradition: Newfoundland, 1832–1855.' *Journal of Canadian Studies*, 23 (Spring/Summer 1988), 87–103.

McRae, K.D. 'The Structure of Canadian History.' *The Founding of New Societies*, ed. Louis Hartz. New York: Harcourt, Brace, 1964.

McKay, Ian. 'Among the Fisher Folk: J.F.B. Livesay and the Invention of Peggy's Cove.' *Journal of Canadian Studies*, 23 (Spring 1988), 23–45.

– 'Tartanism Triumphant: The Construction of Scottishness in Nova Scotia, 1933–1954,' *Acadiensis*, 21 (Spring 1992), 5–47.

– 'History and the Tourist Gaze: The Politics of Commemoration in Nova Scotia, 1935–1964.' *Acadiensis*, 22 (Spring 1993), 102–38.

McKillop, A. Brian. 'Canadian Methodism in 1884.' *Canadian Methodist Historical Society Papers*, 4 (1984) 1–31.

Morgan, Cecilia. '"Of Slender Frame and Delicate Appearance": The Placing of Laura Secord in the Narratives of Canadian Loyalist History.' *Journal of the Canadian Historical Association*, 5 (1994), 195–212.

Morton, W.L. 'Victorian Canada.' In *The Shield of Achilles: Aspects of Canada in the Victorian Age.* Toronto: McClelland and Stewart, 1968.

Mosse, George L. 'Caesarism, Circuses and Monuments.' *Journal of Contemporary History*, 6:2 (1971), 167–83.

Nelles, H.V. 'Loyalism and Local Power: The District of Niagara, 1792–1837.' *Ontario History*, 58 (1966), 99–114.

Norris, Darrel A. 'Household and Transiency in a Loyalist Township: The People of Adolphustown, 1784–1822.' *Histoire Sociale – Social History*, 13 (1980), 399–415.

Potter, Janice. 'Patriarchy and Paternalism: The Case of the Eastern Ontario Loyalist Women.' *Ontario History*, 81 (1989), 3–24.

Queen, Louise. 'The Centennial of American Methodism.' *Methodist History*, 4 (Jan. 1966), 41–9.

Rasporich, A.W. 'Imperial Sentiment in the Province of Canada during the Crimean War, 1854–1856.' In *The Shield of Achilles: Aspects of Canada in the Victorian Age*, ed. W.L. Morton. Toronto: McClelland and Stewart, 1968.

Rearick, Charles. 'Festivals and Politics: The Michelet Centennial of 1898.' *Historians in Politics*, ed. Walter Laquer and George L. Mosse. London: Sage, 1974.

– 'Festivals in Modern France: The Experience of the Third Republic.' *Journal of Contemporary History*, 12 (1977), 435–60.

Rutherford, Paul. 'Tomorrow's Metropolis: The Urban Reform Movement in Canada, 1880–1920.' Canadian Historical Association, *Historical Papers* (1971), 203–24.

Schmidt, Leigh Eric. 'The Commercialization of the Calendar: American Holidays and the Culture of Consumption, 1870–1930.' *Journal of American History*, 21 (1991), 887–916.

Schwartz, Barry. 'The Social Context of Commemoration: A Study in Collective Memory.' *Social Forces*, 61 (1982), 374–402.

Sherman, Daniel. 'The Nation: In What Community? The Politics of Commemoration in Postwar France.' In *Ideas and Ideals: Essays in Politics in Honor of Stanley Hoffman*, ed. Linda B. Miller and Michael Joseph Smith. Boulder, Colorado: Westview Press, 1993.

Shils, Edward. 'Tradition.' *Comparative Studies in Society and History*, 8 (April 1971), 122–59.

Smith, Allan. 'American Culture and the English Canadian Mind at the End of the Nineteenth Century.' *Journal of Popular Culture*, 4 (1971), 1045–51.

- 'Old Ontario and the Emergence of a National Frame of Mind.' In *Aspects of Nineteenth-Century Ontario*, ed. F.H. Armstrong, H.A. Stevenson, and J.D. Wilson. Toronto: University of Toronto Press, 1974
- 'The Myth of the Self-Made Man in English Canada, 1850–1914.' *Canadian Historical Review*, 59 (1978), 189–95.
Smith, David Horton. 'The Importance of Formal Voluntary Organizations for Society.' *Sociology and Social Research*, 50 (1965–6), 483–92.
Spragge, George W. 'The Great Seals and the Arms of Ontario.' *Ontario History*, 51 (1959), 33–7.
Stanley, G.F.G. 'The Significance of the Six Nations' Participation in the War of 1812.' *Ontario History*, 55 (1963), 85–97.
Stouck, David. 'The Wardell Family and the Origins of Loyalism.' *Canadian Historical Review*, 68 (1987), pp. 63–82.
Talman, J.J. 'The United Empire Loyalists.' In *Profiles of a Province: Studies in the History of Ontario*, ed. Judith Frith. Toronto: Ontario Historical Society, 1967.
Weaver, John C. 'Elitism and the Corporate Ideal: Businessmen and Boosters in Canadian Civic Reform, 1890–1920.' In *Cities in the West*, ed. A.R. McCormack and Ian Macpherson. Ottawa: National Museum of Man, 1975.
Weaver, Sally. 'Six Nations of the Grand River, Ontario.' In *Handbook of North American Indians: The North East*. Washington, D.C.: Smithsonian Institution, 1978.
Wood, Gordon S. 'Rhetoric and Reality in the American Revolution.' *William and Mary Quarterly*, 23 (1966), 3–24.
Wrong, George. 'The Background of the Loyalist Movement, 1763–1783.' Ontario Historical Society, *Papers and Records*, 30 (1934), 171–80.

Books

Akenson, Donald. *The Irish in Ontario: A Study in Rural History*. Kingston and Montreal: McGill-Queen's University Press, 1984.
Allan, Robert, ed. *The Loyal Americans: The Military Role of the Loyalist Provincial Corps and Their Settlement in British North America*. Ottawa: National Museum of Man, 1983.
Anderson, Benedict. *Imagined Communities: Reflections on the Origins and Spread of Nationalism*. London and New York: New Left Books, 1983.
Anderson, Kay J. *Vancouver's Chinatown: Racial Discourse in Canada, 1875–1980*. Montreal and Kingston: McGill-Queen's University Press, 1991.
Armstrong, Christopher, and H.V. Nelles. *The Revenge of the Methodist Bicycle Company: Sunday Streetcars and Municipal Reform in Toronto, 1888–1897*. Toronto: Peter Martin, 1977.

Atlick, Richard D. *Victorian People and Ideas.* New York: W.W. Norton, 1973.

Augulhon, M. *Marianne into Battle: Republican Imagery and Symbolism in France, 1789–1880.* Cambridge: Cambridge University Press, 1983.

Aykroyd, Peter H. *The Anniversary Compulsion: Canada's Centennial Celebrations, A Model Mega-Anniversary.* Toronto: Dundurn, 1992.

Axelrod, Paul. *Making a Middle Class: Student Life in English Canada during the Thirties.* Montreal and Kingston: McGill-Queen's University Press, 1990.

Bacchi, Carol Lee. *Liberation Deferred: The Ideas of the English-Canadian Suffragists, 1877–1918.* Toronto: University of Toronto Press, 1983.

Bailyn, Bernard. *The Ordeal of Thomas Hutchinson.* Cambridge: Harvard University Press, 1974.

Bell, David, and Lorne Tepperman. *The Roots of Disunity: A Look at Canadian Political Culture.* Toronto: McClelland and Stewart, 1979.

Bell, D.G. *Early Loyalist Saint John: The Origin of New Brunswick Politics, 1783–1786.* Fredericton: New Ireland Press, 1983.

Benton, William Allan. *Whig Loyalism: An Aspect of Ideology in the American Revolutionary Era.* Rutherford, New Jersey: Associated University Presses, 1969.

Berger, Carl. *The Sense of Power: Studies in the Ideas of Canadian Imperialism, 1867–1914.* Toronto: University of Toronto Press, 1970.

– *The Writing of Canadian History: Aspects of English-Canadian Historical Writing since 1900.* 2nd ed. Toronto: University of Toronto Press, 1986.

Berkhoffer, Robert F., Jr. *The Whiteman's Indian: Images of the American Indian from Columbus to the Present.* New York: Random House, 1979.

Bliss, Michael. *A Living Profit: Studies in the Social History of Canadian Business, 1883–1911.* Toronto: University of Toronto Press, 1974.

Blumin, Stuart. *The Emergence of the Middle Class: Social Experience in the American City, 1760–1900.* Cambridge: Cambridge University Press, 1989.

Bodnor, John. *Remaking America: Public Memory, Commemoration and Patriotism in the Twentieth Century.* Princeton: Princeton University Press, 1992.

Brown, Dee. *The Year of the Century: 1876.* New York: Scribners, 1966.

Brown, Robert Craig, and Ramsay Cook. *Canada, 1896–1921: A Nation Transformed.* Toronto: McClelland and Stewart, 1974.

Brown, Wallace. *The King's Friends: The Composition and Motives of the American Loyalist Claimants.* Providence, Rhode Island: Brown University Press, 1965.

– *The Good Americans: The Loyalists in the American Revolution.* New York: William Morrow, 1969.

Brown, Wallace, and Hereward Senior. *Victorious in Defeat: The Loyalists in Canada.* Toronto: Methuen, 1984.

Bumsted, J.M. *Understanding the Loyalists.* Sackville, New Brunswick: Mount Allison University Press, 1986.

Burt, A.L. *The Old Province of Quebec.* 2 vols. 1933; rpt Toronto: McClelland and Stewart, 1968

Calhoon, Robert McClure. *The Loyalists in Revolutionary America, 1760–1781.* New York: Harcourt, Brace, Jovanovich, 1973.

Campbell, James W. *America in Her Centennial Year, 1876.* Washington, D.C.: University Press of America, 1980.

Careless, J.M.S. *Canada: A Story of Challenge.* 1953; rpt. Toronto: Macmillan, 1974.

– *Toronto to 1918: An Illustrative History.* Toronto: James Lorimer, 1984.

Chancellor, Valerie. *History for Their Masters: Opinion in the English History Textbook, 1800–1914.* New York: Augustus M. Kelley, 1970.

Commager, H.S. *The Search for a Usable Past.* New York: Alfred A. Knopf, 1967.

Craig, Gerald M. *Upper Canada: The Formative Years, 1784–1841.* Toronto: McClelland and Stewart, 1963.

Craven, Wesley Frank. *The Legend of the Founding Fathers.* Ithaca: Cornell University Press, 1965.

Curtis, Bruce. *Building the Educational State: Canada West, 1836–1871.* London, Ontario: Althouse, 1988.

Davies, Wallace Evan. *Patriotism on Parade: The Story of Veterans' and Hereditary Organizations in America, 1783–1900.* Cambridge: Harvard University Press, 1955.

Davis, Fred. *Yearning for Yesterday: A Sociology of Nostalgia.* New York: Macmillan, 1979.

Davis, Susan G. *Parades and Power: Street Theatre in Nineteenth-Century Philadelphia.* Berkeley: University of California Press, 1988.

Doezema, Marianne, and June Hargrove. *The Public Monument and Its Audience.* Cleveland: Cleveland Museum of Art, 1977.

Duffy, Dennis. *Gardens, Covenants, and Exiles: Loyalism in the Literature of Upper Canada / Ontario.* Toronto: University of Toronto Press, 1982.

Edwards, Frank B. *The Smiling Wilderness: An Illustrated History of Lennox and Addington County.* Camden East, Ontario: Camden, 1984.

Elson, Ruth Miller. *Guardians of Tradition: American Schoolbooks of the Nineteenth Century.* Lincoln: University of Nebraska Press, 1964.

Errington, Jane. *The Lion, the Eagle and Upper Canada: A Developing Colonial Ideology.* Montreal and Kingston: McGill-Queen's University Press, 1987.

Ferling, John E. *The Loyalist Mind and the American Revolution.* University Park and London: Pennsylvania State University Press, 1977.

Fryer, Mary Beacock, and Charles J. Humber, eds. *Loyal She Remains: A Pictorial History of Ontario.* Toronto: United Empire Loyalist Association of Canada, 1984.

Francis, Daniel. *The Imaginary Indian: The Image of the Indian in Canadian Culture.* Vancouver: Arsenal Pulp Press, 1992.

Gagan, David. *The Denison Family of Toronto, 1792–1925.* Toronto: University of Toronto Press, 1973.

Gates, Lillian F. *Land Policies of Upper Canada.* Toronto: University of Toronto Press, 1968.

Gerson, Carole. *A Purer Taste: The Writing and Reading of Fiction in English in Nineteenth-Century Canada.* Toronto: University of Toronto Press, 1989.

Gidney, R.D., and W.P.J. Millar. *Professional Gentlemen: The Professions in Nineteenth-Century Ontario.* Toronto: University of Toronto Press, 1994.

Graham, W.A. *Greenbank: Country Matters in Nineteenth Century Ontario.* Peterborough, Ontario: Broadview, 1988.

Grant, George. *Lament for a Nation: The Defeat of Canadian Nationalism.* 1965; rpt Ottawa: Carleton University Press, 1982.

Graymount, Barbara. *The Iroquois in the American Revolution.* Syracuse: Syracuse University Press, 1972.

Greer, Allan, and Ian Radforth, eds. *Colonial Leviathan: State Formation in Mid-Nineteenth-Century Canada.* Toronto: University of Toronto Press, 1992.

Hardesty, Nancy. *Women Called to Witness: Evangelical Feminism in the 19th Century.* Nashville: Abingdon Press, 1984.

Hartz, Louis, ed. *The Founding of New Societies.* New York: Harcourt, Brace, 1964.

Hausknecht, Murray. *The Joiners: A Sociological Description of Voluntary Association Membership in the United States.* New York: Bedminster Press, 1962.

Higham, John. *Strangers in the Land: Patterns of American Nativism, 1860–1925.* New York: Atheneum, 1972.

Hobsbawm, Eric, and Terence Ranger, eds. *The Invention of Tradition.* Cambridge: Cambridge University Press, 1983.

Hodgetts, J.E. *Pioneer Public Service: An Administrative History of the United Canadas.* Toronto: University of Toronto Press, 1955.

Hofstadter, Richard. *The Age of Reform: From Bryan to FDR.* New York: Knopf, 1955.

Houston, Susan E., and Alison Prentice. *Schooling and Scholars in Nineteenth-Century Ontario.* Toronto: University of Toronto Press, 1988.

Jasen, Patricia. *Wild Things: Nature, Culture, and Tourism in Ontario, 1790–1914.* Toronto: University of Toronto Press, 1995.

Johnson, J.K. *Becoming Prominent: Regional Leadership in Upper Canada, 1791–1841.* Montreal and Kingston: McGill-Queen's University Press, 1989.

Johnston, C.M. *Brant County: A History, 1784–1945.* Toronto: Oxford University Press, 1967.

Kammen, Michael. *A Season of Youth: The American Revolution and the Historical Imagination.* New York: Knopf, 1978.

– *Mystic Chords of Memory: The Transformation of Tradition in American Culture.* New York: Knopf, 1991.

Kealey, Gregory S. *Toronto Workers Respond to Industrial Capitalism, 1867–1892*. Toronto: University of Toronto Press, 1980.

Killan, Gerald. *Preserving Ontario's Heritage: A History of the Ontario Historical Society*. Ottawa: Love, 1976.

– *David Boyle: From Artisan to Archaeologist*. Toronto: University of Toronto Press, 1983.

King, John. *McCaul, Croft, Forneri: Personalities of Early University Days*. Toronto: Macmillan, 1914.

LaCapra, Dominick. *Rethinking Intellectual History: Texts, Contexts, Language*. Ithaca: Cornell, 1983.

Lapp, Eula C. *To Their Heirs Forever*. Belleville, Ontario: Mika, 1977.

Lears, T.J. Jackson. *No Place of Grace: Anti-Modernism and the Transformation of American Culture, 1880–1920*. New York: Pantheon, 1981.

Linteau, Paul-Andre. *The Promoters' City: Building the Industrial Town of Maisonneuve, 1883–1918*. Toronto: Lorimer, 1985.

Lipset, Seymour Martin. *The First New Nation*. New York: Basic Books, 1963.

Lowenthal, David. *The Past Is a Foreign Country*. Cambridge: Cambridge University Press, 1985.

Lower, Arthur R.M. *Colony to Nation: A History of Canada*. 5th ed. Toronto: McClelland and Stewart, 1977.

MacKinnon, Neil. *This Unfriendly Soil: The Loyalist Experience in Nova Scotia, 1783–1791*. Montreal and Kingston: McGill-Queen's University Press, 1986.

Macpherson, Ian. *Matters of Loyalty: The Buells of Brockville, 1830–1850*. Belleville, Ontario: Mika, 1981.

Magee, Joan, ed. *Loyalist Mosaic: A Multi-Ethnic Heritage*. Toronto: Dundurn, 1984.

McKenzie, Ruth. *Laura Secord: The Legend and the Lady*. Toronto and Montreal: McClelland and Stewart, 1971.

Mika, Nick. *The United Empire Loyalist Pioneers of Upper Canada*. Belleville, Ontario: Mika, 1976.

Millard, J. Rodney. *The Master Spirit of the Age: Canadian Engineers and the Politics of Professionalism*. Toronto: University of Toronto Press, 1988.

Miller, J.R. *Equal Rights: The Jesuits' Estates Act Controversy*. Montreal and Kingston: McGill-Queen's University Press, 1979.

Mills, David. *The Idea of Loyalty in Upper Canada, 1784–1850*. Montreal and Kingston: McGill-Queen's University Press, 1988.

Moore, Christopher. *The Loyalists: Revolution, Exile, Settlement*. Toronto: Macmillan, 1984.

Moore, Sally F., and Barbara G. Myerhoff, eds. *Secular Ritual*. Amsterdam: Van Gorcum, Assen, 1977.

Morton, W.L. *The Union of British North America, 1857–1873: The Critical Years.* Toronto: McClelland and Stewart, 1968.

Moyles, R.G., and Doug Owram. *Imperial Dreams and Colonial Realities: British Views of Canada, 1880–1914.* Toronto: University of Toronto Press, 1988.

Nelson, William. *The American Tory.* Boston: Beacon Press, 1964.

Noel, S.J.R. *Patrons, Clients, Brokers: Ontario Society and Politics, 1791–1896.* Toronto: University of Toronto Press, 1990.

Owram, Doug. *Promise of Eden: The Canadian Expansionist Movement and the Idea of the West, 1856–1900.* Toronto: University of Toronto Press, 1980.

Perkin, Harold. *The Rise of Professional Society: England since 1880.* London and New York: Routledge, 1989.

Pierce, Lorne. *William Kirby: Portrait of a Tory Loyalist.* Toronto: Macmillan, 1929.

Porter, Roy, ed. *The Myths of the English.* Cambridge: Polity Press, 1992.

Potter, Janice. *The Liberty We Seek: Loyalist Ideology in Colonial New York and Massachusetts.* Cambridge: Harvard University Press, 1983.

Potter-MacKinnon, Janice. *While the Women Only Wept: Loyalist Refugee Women in Eastern Ontario.* Montreal and Kingston: McGill-Queen's University Press, 1993.

Prentice, Alison. *The School Promoters: Education and Social Class in Mid-Nineteenth Century Upper Canada.* Toronto: McClelland and Stewart, 1977.

Randall, William Pierce. *Centennial: American Life in 1876.* Philadelphia: Chilton, 1969.

Reville, F. Douglas. *History of the County of Brant.* Brantford: Hurley, 1920.

Rogers, Edward S., and Donald Smith, eds. *Aboriginal Ontario: Historical Perspectives on the First Nations.* Toronto: Dundurn, 1994.

Rutherford, Paul. *A Victorian Authority: The Daily Press in Late Nineteenth-Century Canada.* Toronto: University of Toronto Press, 1982.

Samuel, Ralph, ed. *Patriotism: The Making and Unmaking of British National Identity.* 3 vols. London and New York:Routledge, 1989.

Shaffer, Arthur H. *The Politics of History: Writing the History of the American Revolution, 1783–1815.* Chicago: Precedent Publishing, 1986.

Shaw, Christopher, and Malcolm Chase, eds. *The Imagined Past: History and Nostalgia.* Manchester and New York: Manchester University Press, 1989.

Sheppard, George. *Plunder, Profit and Paroles: A Social History of the War of 1812 in Upper Canada.* Montreal and Kingston: McGill-Queen's University Press, 1994.

Shils, Edward. *Tradition.* Chicago: University of Chicago Press, 1981.

Shipley, Robert. *To Mark Our Place: A History of Canadian War Memorials.* Toronto: NC Press, 1987.

Stamp, Robert M. *The Schools of Ontario, 1876–1976.* Toronto: University of Toronto Press, 1982.

Strong-Boag, Veronica. *The Parliament of Women: The National Council of Women of Canada, 1893–1929*. Ottawa: National Museum of Man, 1976.

Taylor, C.J. *Negotiating the Past: The Making of Canada's National Historic Parks and Sites*. Montreal and Kingston: McGill-Queen's University Press, 1990.

Taylor, M. Brook. *Promoters, Patriots, and Partisans: Historiography in Nineteenth-Century English Canada*. Toronto: University of Toronto Press, 1989.

Titley, E. Brian. *A Narrow Vision: Duncan Campbell Scott and the Administration of Indian Affairs in Canada*. Vancouver: University of British Columbia Press, 1986.

Turner, Larry. *Voyage of a Different Kind: The Associated Loyalists of Kingston and Adolphustown*. Belleville, Ontario: Mika, 1984.

Upton, L.F.S., ed. *The United Empire Loyalists: Men and Myths*. Toronto: Copp Clark, 1967.

Waite, Peter B. *The Life and Times of Confederation, 1864–1867: Politics, Newspapers, and the Union of British North America*. Toronto: University of Toronto Press, 1962.

– *Arduous Destiny: Canada, 1874–1896*. Toronto: McClelland and Stewart, 1971.

Wallace, William Stewart. *The Story of Laura Secord: A Study in Historical Evidence*. Toronto: 1932.

Warner, William Lloyd. *The Living and the Dead: A Study of the Symbolic Life of Americans*. New Haven: Yale University Press, 1959.

Weibe, Robert H. *The Search for Order, 1877–1920*. New York: Hill and Wang, 1967.

White, Hayden. *The Content of the Form: Narrative Discourse and Historical Representation*. Baltimore: Johns Hopkins University Press, 1987.

Wilson, Bruce. *As She Began: An Illustrated Introduction to Loyalist Ontario*. Toronto: Dundurn, 1981.

Wise, S.F. *God's Peculiar Peoples: Essays on Political Culture in Nineteenth Century Canada*. ed. A.B. McKillop and Paul Romney. Ottawa: Carleton University Press, 1993.

Wise, S.F., and R.C. Brown. *Canada Views the United States: Nineteenth Century Political Attitudes*. Seattle: University of Washington Press, 1967.

Unpublished Manuscripts and Theses

Barkley, Murray. 'The Loyalist Tradition in New Brunswick: A Study in the Evolution of an Historical Myth, 1825–1914.' M.A. thesis, Queen's University, 1971.

Bell, David V.J. 'The United Empire Loyalists and Native Peoples in Upper Canada.' Unpublished manuscript, York University, 1980.

Bowler, R.A. 'Propaganda in Upper Canada.' M.A. thesis, Queen's University, 1964.

Graham, W.R. 'Sir Richard Cartwright and the Liberal Party.' Ph.D. dissertation, University of Toronto, 1950.

Heald, Carolyn. 'Barbara Heck: The Mother of North American Methodism in Symbol and Myth.' Graduate paper, Queen's University, 1987.

MacIntyre, Eldred Alexander. 'Nova Scotian Perceptions of the Loyalists, 1820–1911.' M.A. thesis, Queen's University, 1989.

McKenna, Katherine M.J. 'Treading the Hard Road: Some Loyalist Women and the American Revolution.' M.A. thesis, Queen's University, 1979.

Owens, Gary. 'Remembering '98: The Centenary Movement of 1898 and the Invention of Tradition in Ireland.' Unpublished manuscript, Huron College, 1989.

Read, P.J. 'The Dominion History Contest: An Episode in the Search for Canadian Unity.' M.A. thesis, University of Toronto, 1969.

Rutherford, P.F.W. 'The New Nationality, 1864–1897: A Study of the National Aims and Ideas of English Canada in the Late Nineteenth Century.' Ph.D. dissertation, University of Toronto, 1973.

Sachanska, Anita Margaret. '"Sink Deeply into the Heart": The Dramatic Works of Eliza Lanesford Cushing and Sarah Anne Curzon.' M.A. thesis, York University, 1984.

Sheppard, George C.B. 'Enemies at Home: Upper Canada and the War of 1812.' Ph.D. dissertation, McMaster University, 1989.

Smith, Allan. 'The Imported Image: American Publications and American Ideas in the Evolution of the English Canadian Mind.' Ph.D. dissertation, University of Toronto, 1971.

Walden, Keith. 'Isaac Brock: Man and Myth. A Study of the Militia Myth of the War of 1812 in Upper Canada, 1812–1912.' M.A. thesis, Queen's University, 1971.

Picture Credits

Archives of Ontario: William Hamilton Merritt, S657; William Kirby, S1471; Egerton Ryerson, S623; William Canniff, S409; sketch of R.S. Forneri's planned memorial church, from Rev. R.S. Forneri, *The United Empire Loyalists and the Memorial Church, Adolphustown Ontario: A Sketch* (Belleville: Intelligencer, 1888), Pamphlet Collection, 1888 #22; Col. George Taylor Denison III, S564; Laura Secord monument, Queenston Heights, 1657; George Sterling Ryerson, S639; United Empire Loyalist Association tree planting at Queen's Park, 1902, ACC 16431 S18206

Author's collection: cover of R.E.A. Land's *A National Monument to Laura Secord* (Toronto: Imrie, Graham and Co., 1901)

Hamilton Public Library: United Empire Loyalist monument, Hamilton

Hastings County Historical Society: United Empire Loyalist monument, Belleville. Photo by Kenny Chambers. Mika Collection

Lennox and Addington County Museum: unveiling of Loyalist monument, Adolphustown, N-1

Metropolitan Toronto Reference Library: broadside, Niagara Loyalist centennial celebration, 14 August 1884, 884 U2; broadside, Mohawk centennial celebration, Tyendinaga, 4 September 1884, 884 C2

National Archives of Canada: Joseph Brant monument, Brantford: John Boyd Collection, NA-071296; Laura Secord monument, Lundy's Lane: William Topley Collection, NA-009854; Barbara Heck monument, Prescott, NA-112569

Index